Garfield Eats Crow

BY JIM DAVIS

Ballantine Books • New York

A Ballantine Book
Published by The Random House Publishing Group

www.ballantinebooks.com

Library of Congress Control Number: 2001119049

ISBN 0-345-45201-1

Manufactured in the United States of America

First Edition: January 2003

10 9 8 7 6 5 4 3

GARFIELD'S favorite games to play with Odie

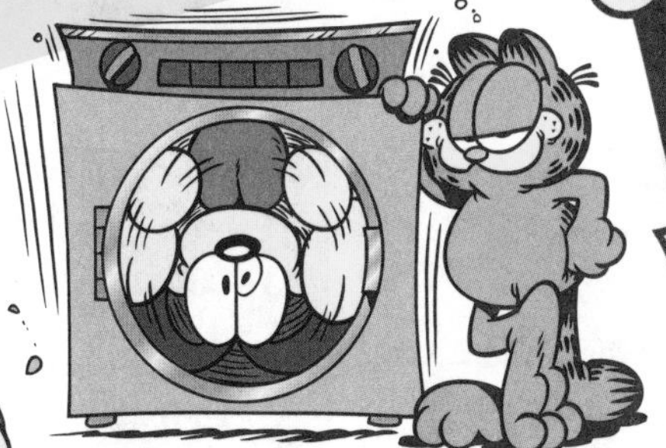

Spin the Beagle

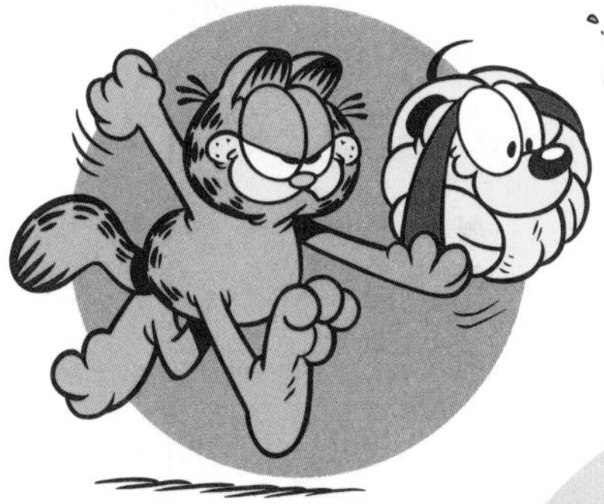

Volley Dog

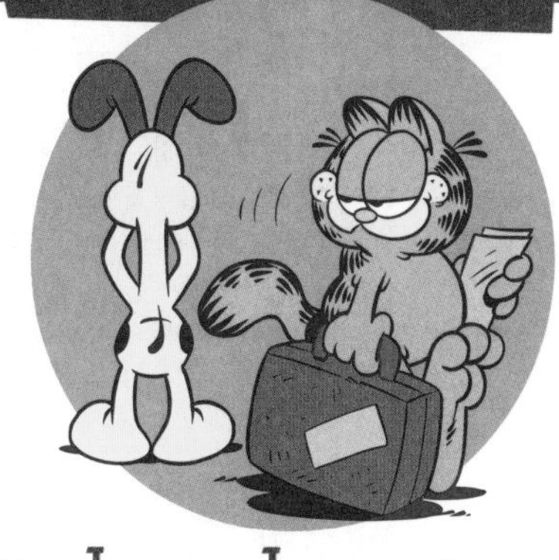

Hide-and-Go-Away

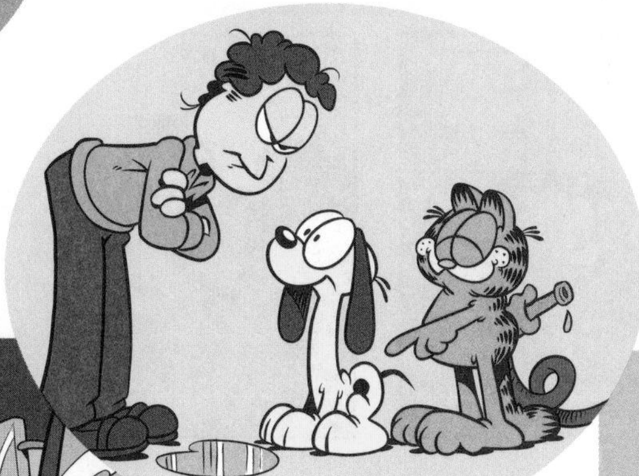

Pin the Blame on the Puppy

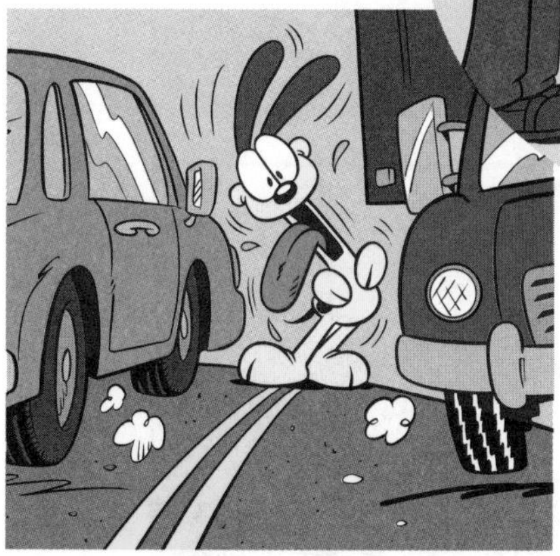

Traffic Twister

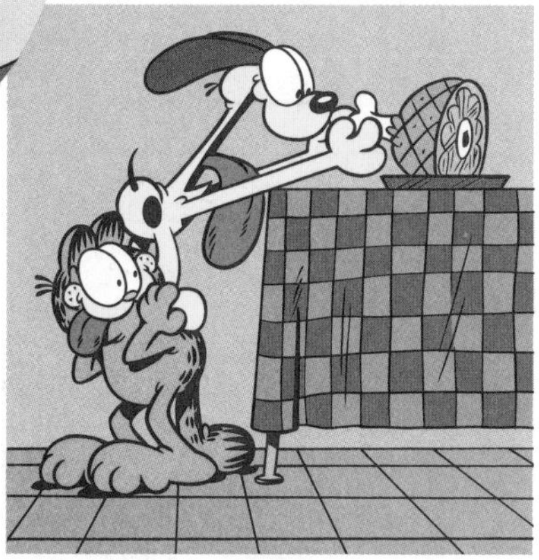

Fetch the Ham

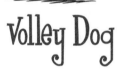

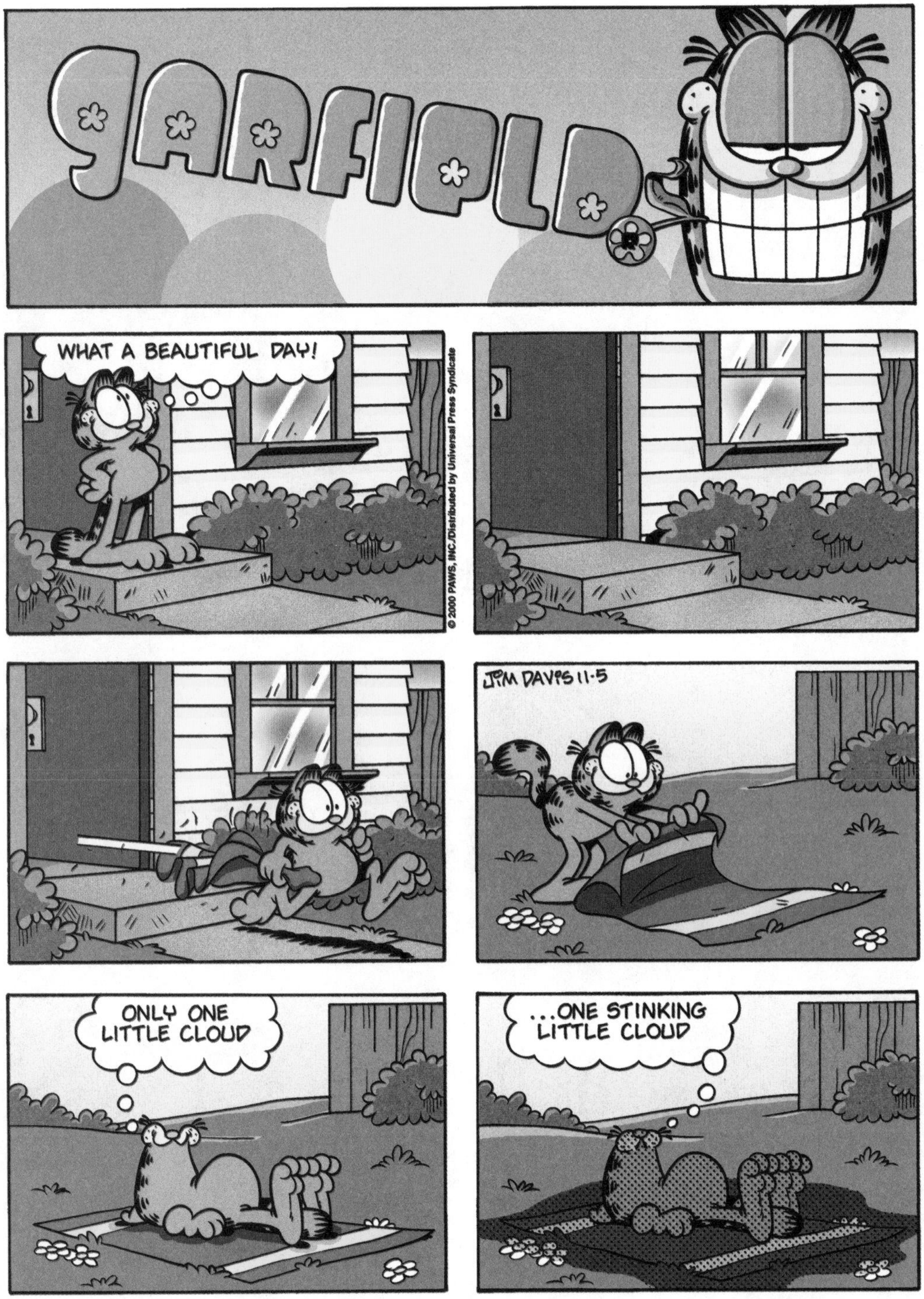
GARFIELD
WHAT A BEAUTIFUL DAY!
© 2000 PAWS, INC./Distributed by Universal Press Syndicate
JIM DAVIS 11-5
ONLY ONE LITTLE CLOUD
...ONE STINKING LITTLE CLOUD

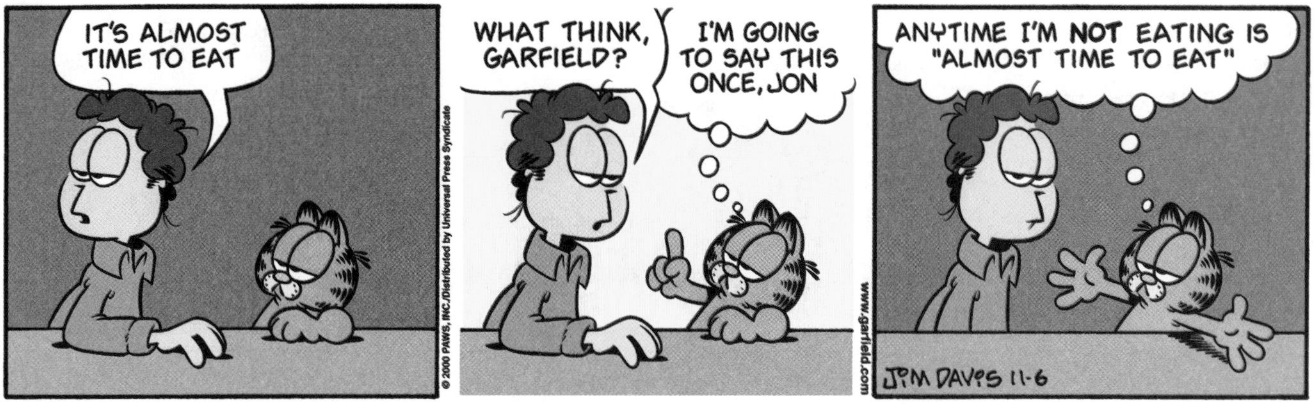
IT'S ALMOST TIME TO EAT
WHAT THINK, GARFIELD?
I'M GOING TO SAY THIS ONCE, JON
ANYTIME I'M NOT EATING IS "ALMOST TIME TO EAT"
© 2000 PAWS, INC./Distributed by Universal Press Syndicate
www.garfield.com
JIM DAVIS 11-6

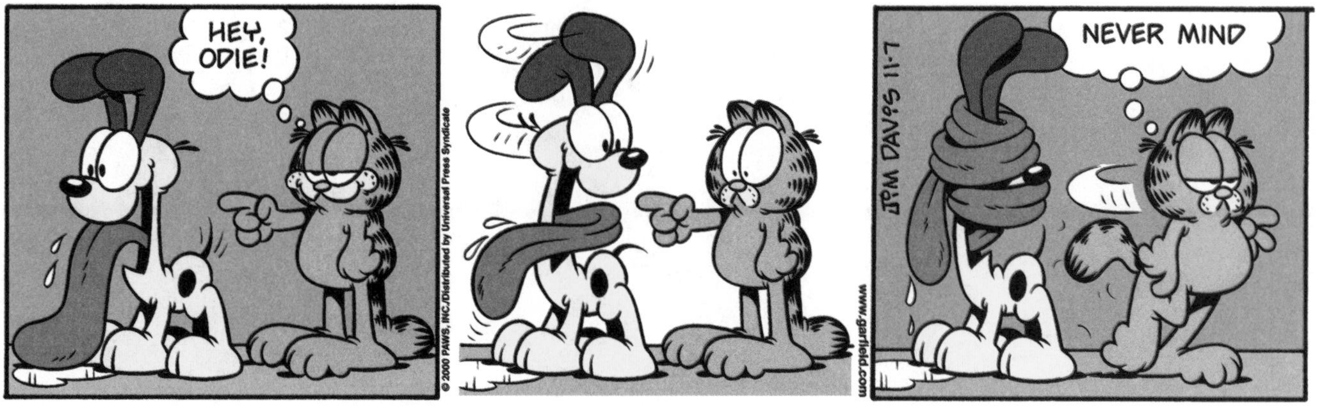
HEY, ODIE!
NEVER MIND
© 2000 PAWS, INC./Distributed by Universal Press Syndicate
www.garfield.com
JIM DAVIS 11-7

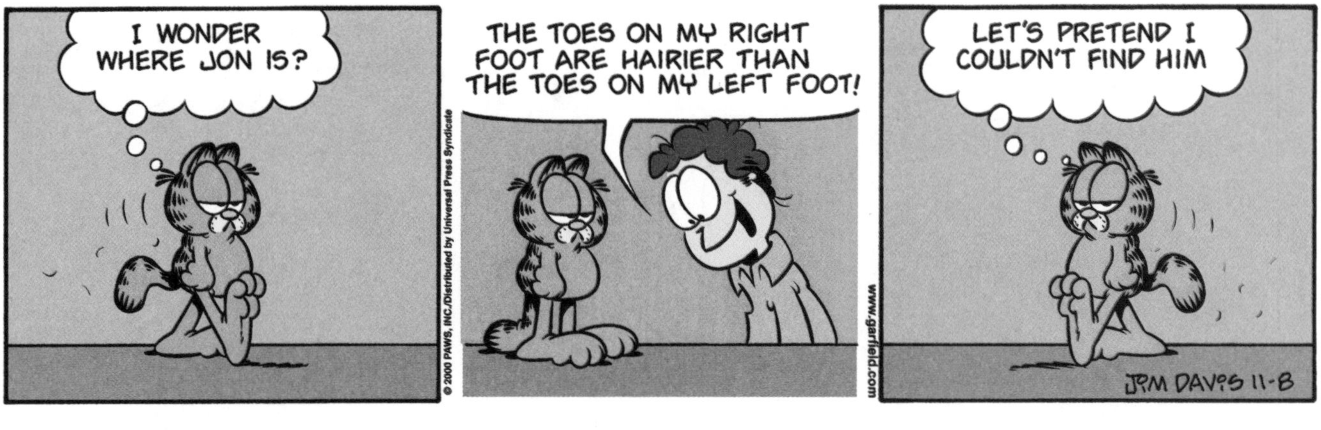
I WONDER WHERE JON IS?
THE TOES ON MY RIGHT FOOT ARE HAIRIER THAN THE TOES ON MY LEFT FOOT!
LET'S PRETEND I COULDN'T FIND HIM
© 2000 PAWS, INC./Distributed by Universal Press Syndicate
www.garfield.com
JIM DAVIS 11-8

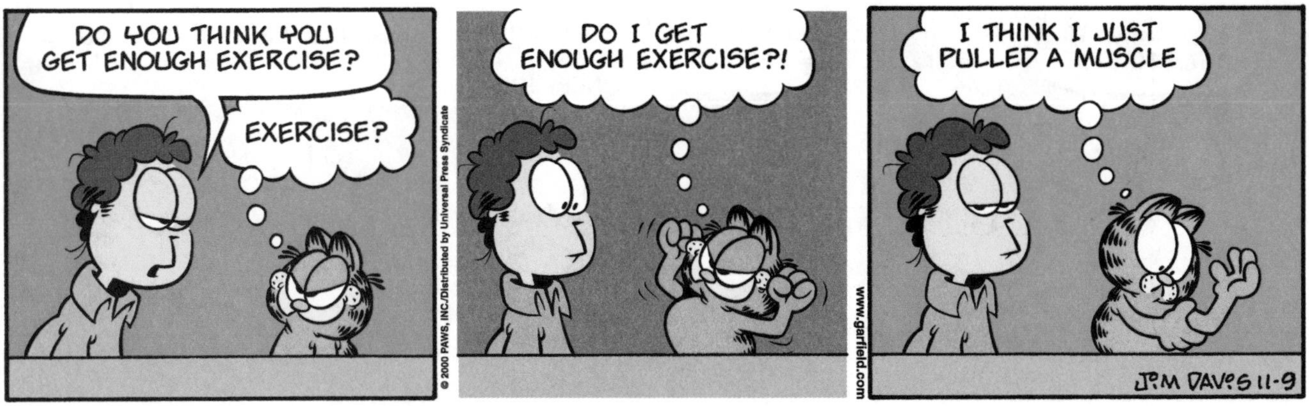
DO YOU THINK YOU GET ENOUGH EXERCISE?
EXERCISE?
DO I GET ENOUGH EXERCISE?!
I THINK I JUST PULLED A MUSCLE
© 2000 PAWS, INC./Distributed by Universal Press Syndicate
www.garfield.com
JIM DAVIS 11-9

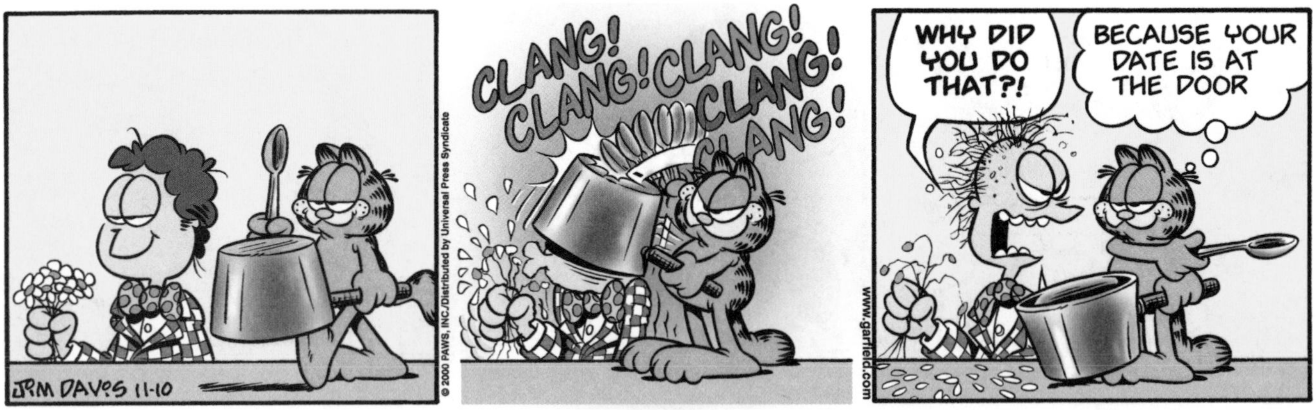
JIM DAVIS 11-10
CLANG! CLANG! CLANG! CLANG! CLANG! CLANG!
WHY DID YOU DO THAT?!
BECAUSE YOUR DATE IS AT THE DOOR
© 2000 PAWS, INC./Distributed by Universal Press Syndicate
www.garfield.com

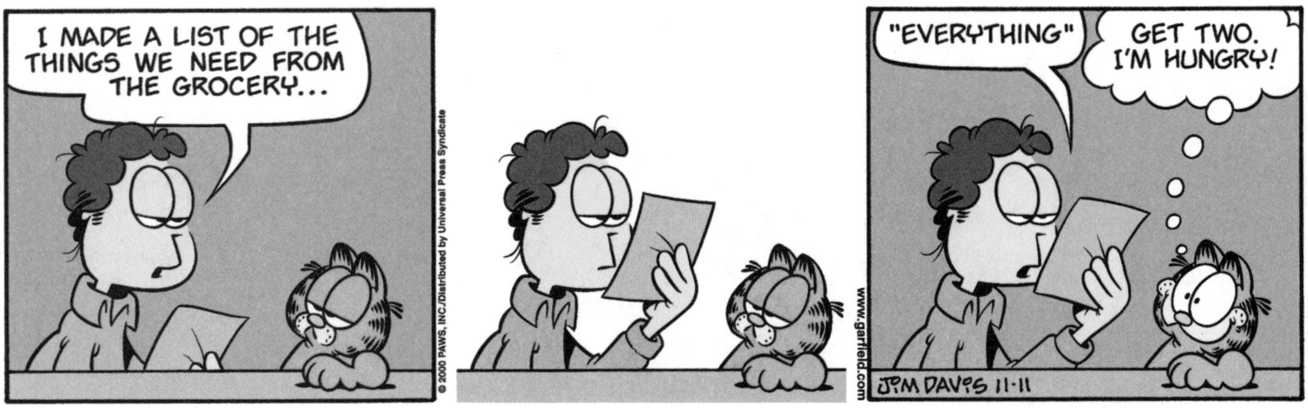
I MADE A LIST OF THE THINGS WE NEED FROM THE GROCERY...
"EVERYTHING"
GET TWO. I'M HUNGRY!
© 2000 PAWS, INC./Distributed by Universal Press Syndicate
www.garfield.com
JIM DAVIS 11-11

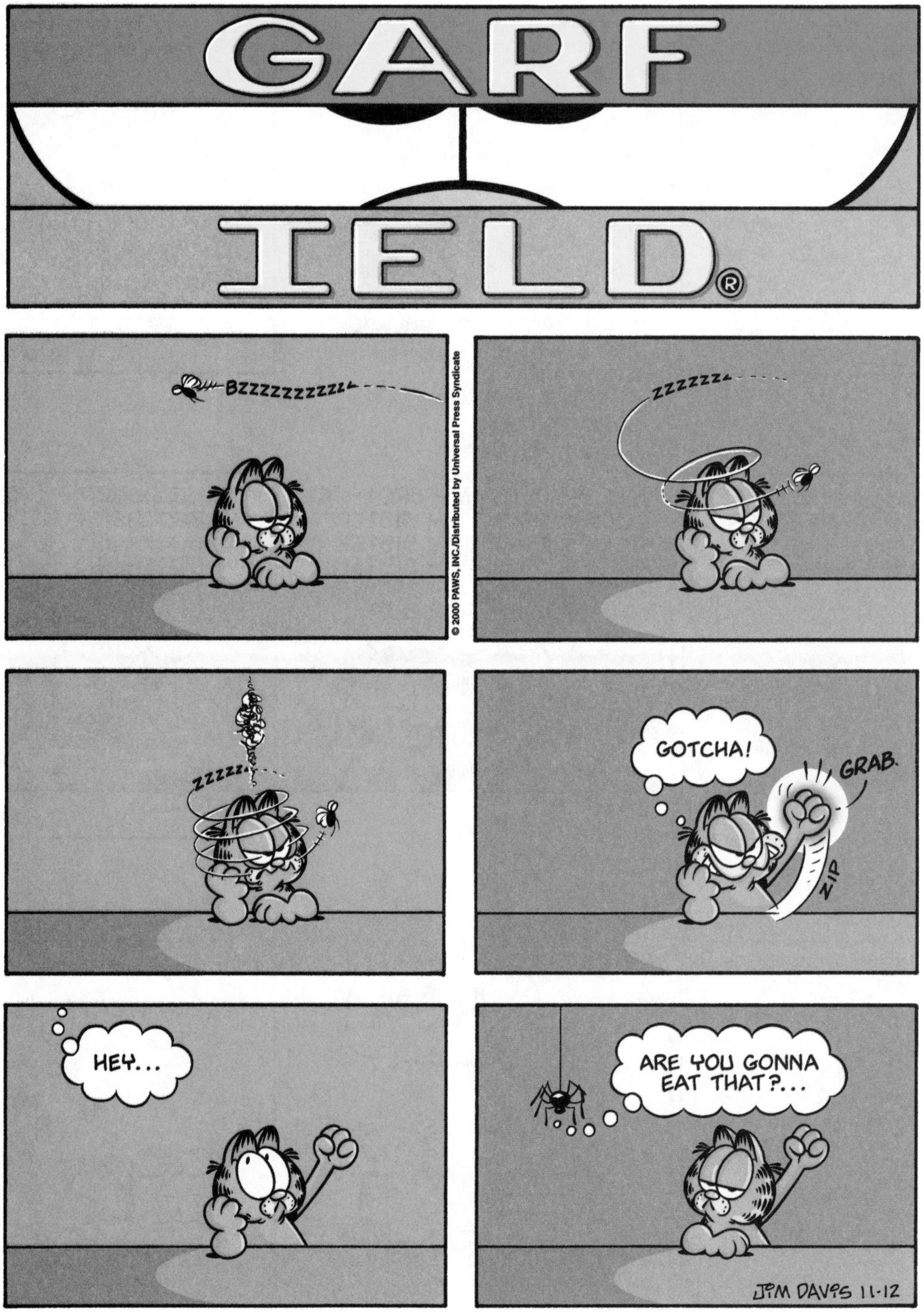
GARFIELD®
© 2000 PAWS, INC./Distributed by Universal Press Syndicate
BZZZZZZZZZZZ
ZZZZZZ
ZZZZZ
GOTCHA!
GRAB.
ZIP
HEY...
ARE YOU GONNA EAT THAT?...
JIM DAVIS 11-12

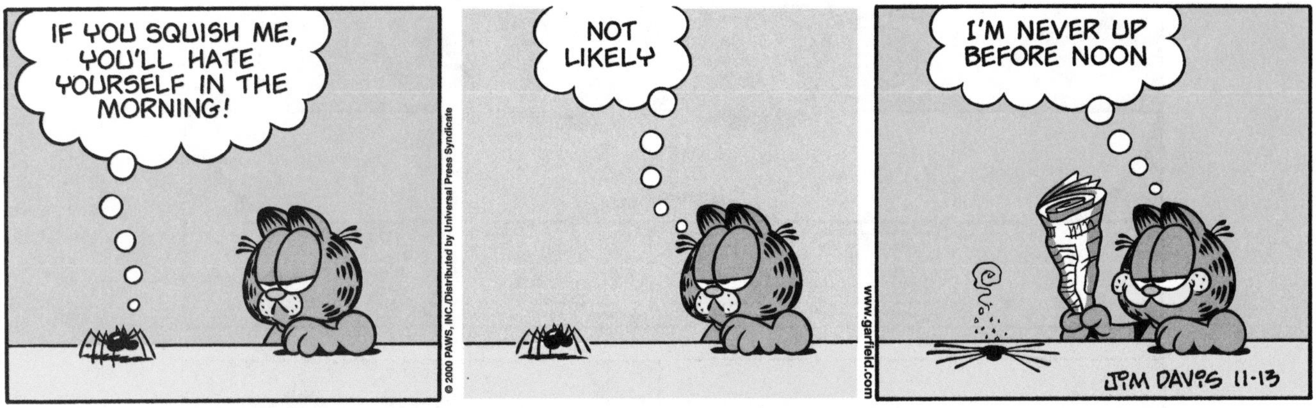
IF YOU SQUISH ME, YOU'LL HATE YOURSELF IN THE MORNING!
NOT LIKELY
I'M NEVER UP BEFORE NOON
© 2000 PAWS, INC./Distributed by Universal Press Syndicate
www.garfield.com
JIM DAVIS 11-13

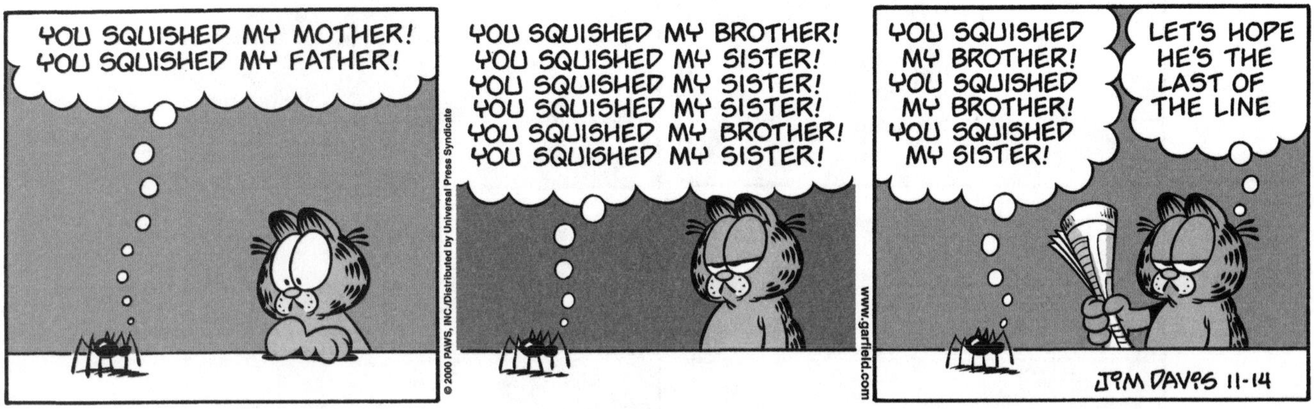
YOU SQUISHED MY MOTHER! YOU SQUISHED MY FATHER!
YOU SQUISHED MY BROTHER! YOU SQUISHED MY SISTER! YOU SQUISHED MY SISTER! YOU SQUISHED MY SISTER! YOU SQUISHED MY BROTHER! YOU SQUISHED MY SISTER!
YOU SQUISHED MY BROTHER! YOU SQUISHED MY BROTHER! YOU SQUISHED MY SISTER!
LET'S HOPE HE'S THE LAST OF THE LINE
© 2000 PAWS, INC./Distributed by Universal Press Syndicate
www.garfield.com
JIM DAVIS 11-14

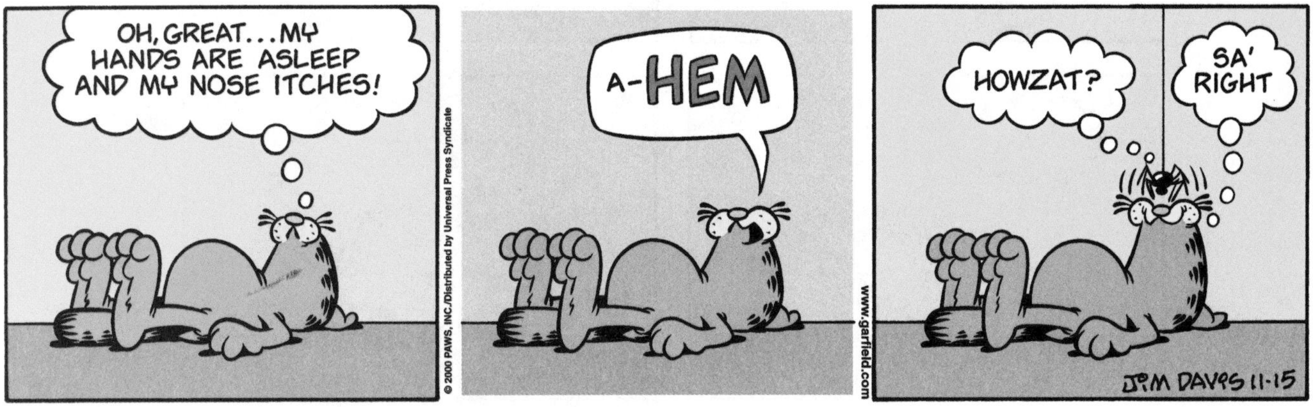
OH, GREAT... MY HANDS ARE ASLEEP AND MY NOSE ITCHES!
A-HEM
HOWZAT?
SA' RIGHT
© 2000 PAWS, INC./Distributed by Universal Press Syndicate
www.garfield.com
JIM DAVIS 11-15

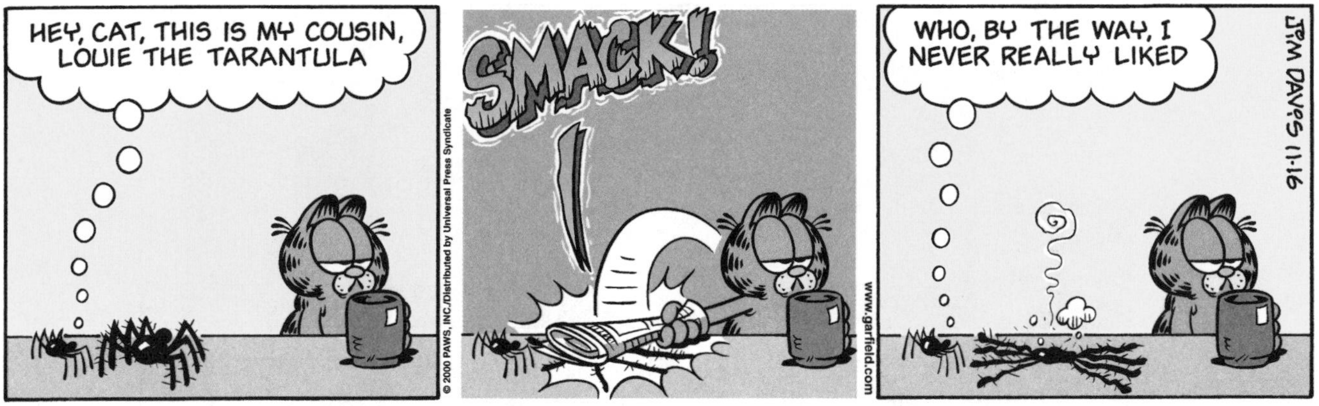
HEY, CAT, THIS IS MY COUSIN, LOUIE THE TARANTULA
SMACK!
WHO, BY THE WAY, I NEVER REALLY LIKED
© 2000 PAWS, INC./Distributed by Universal Press Syndicate
www.garfield.com
JIM DAVIS 11-16

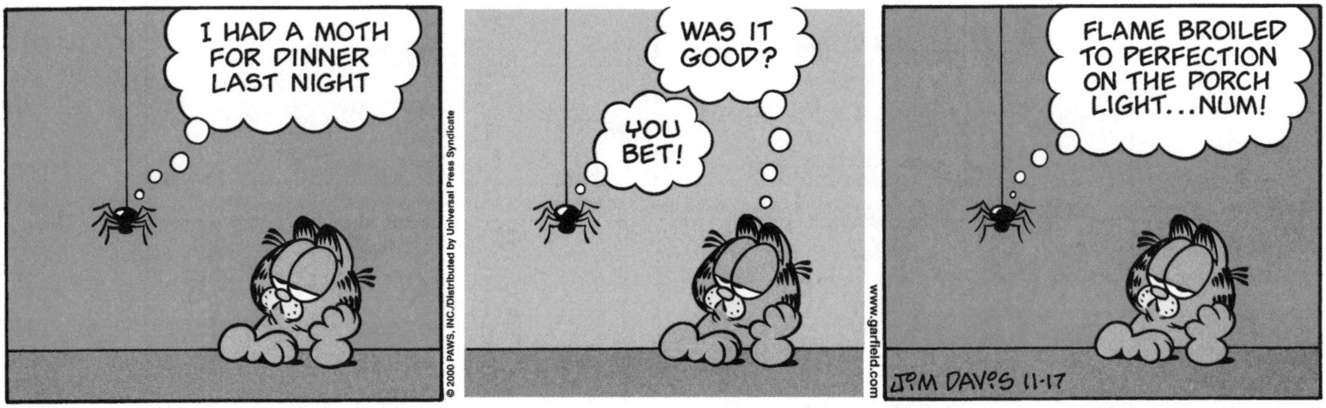
I HAD A MOTH FOR DINNER LAST NIGHT
WAS IT GOOD?
YOU BET!
FLAME BROILED TO PERFECTION ON THE PORCH LIGHT...NUM!
© 2000 PAWS, INC./Distributed by Universal Press Syndicate
www.garfield.com
JIM DAVIS 11-17

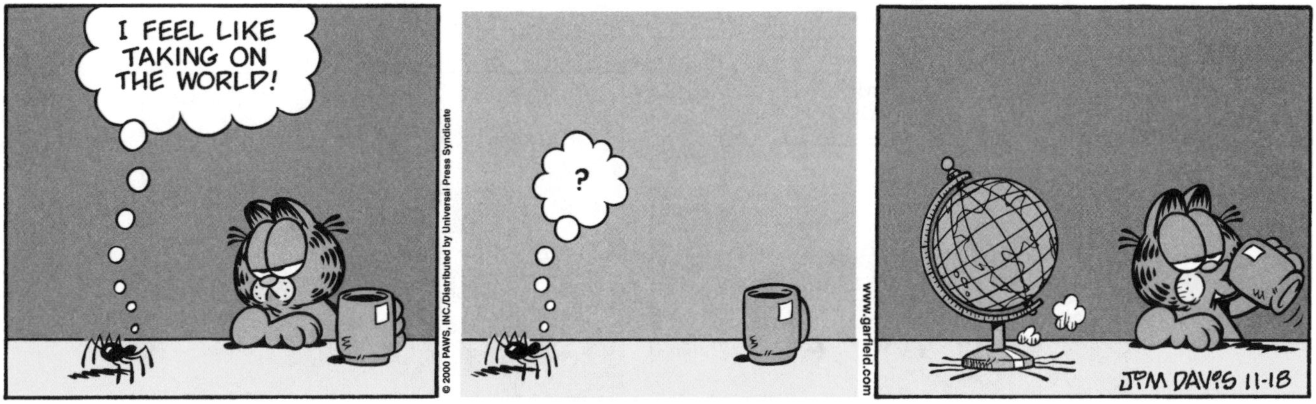
I FEEL LIKE TAKING ON THE WORLD!
?
© 2000 PAWS, INC./Distributed by Universal Press Syndicate
www.garfield.com
JIM DAVIS 11-18

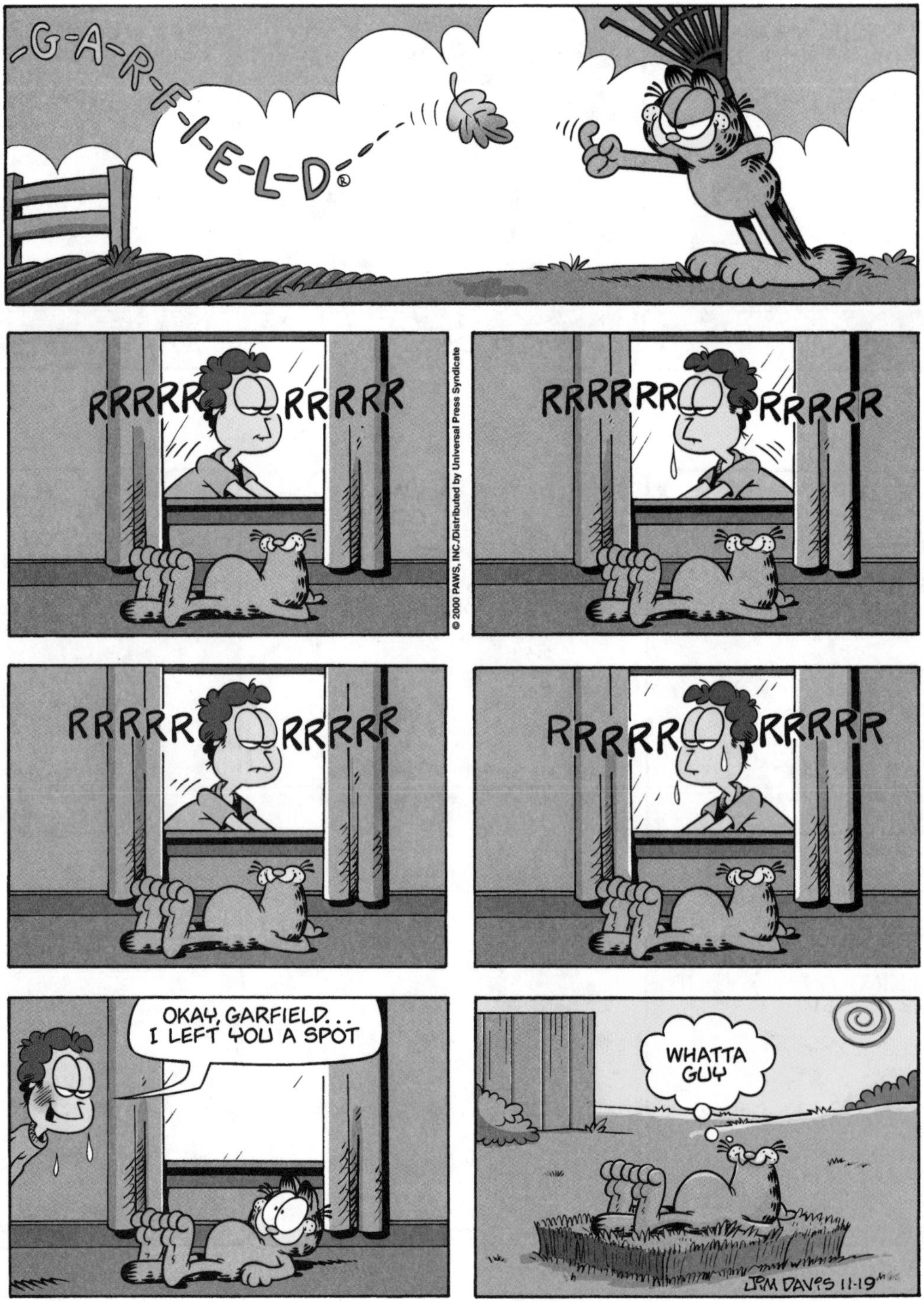
G-A-R-F-I-E-L-D®
© 2000 PAWS, INC./Distributed by Universal Press Syndicate
RRRRR RRRRR
RRRRRR RRRRR
RRRRR RRRRR
RRRRR RRRRR
OKAY, GARFIELD... I LEFT YOU A SPOT
WHATTA GUY
JIM DAVIS 11-19

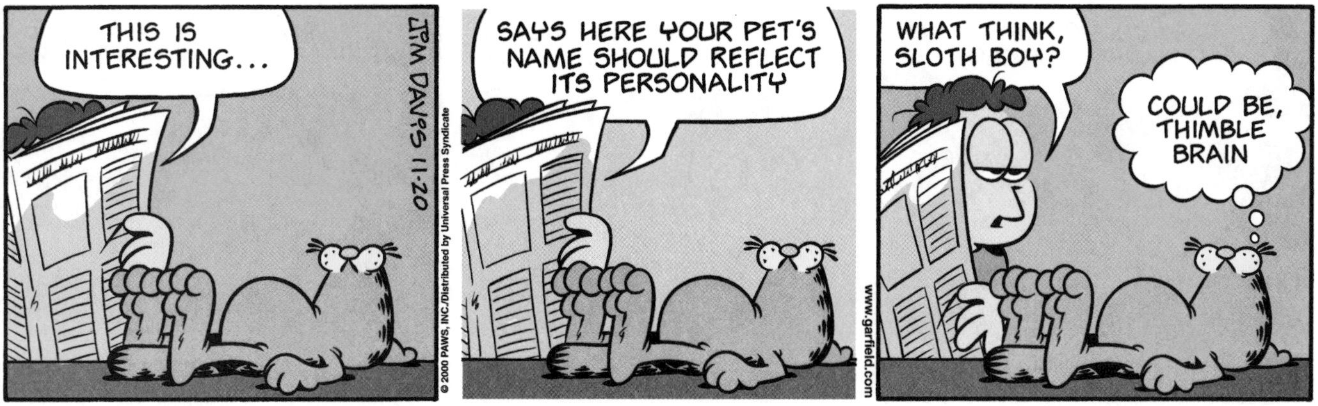
THIS IS INTERESTING...
JIM DAVIS 11-20
© 2000 PAWS, INC./Distributed by Universal Press Syndicate
SAYS HERE YOUR PET'S NAME SHOULD REFLECT ITS PERSONALITY
www.garfield.com
WHAT THINK, SLOTH BOY?
COULD BE, THIMBLE BRAIN

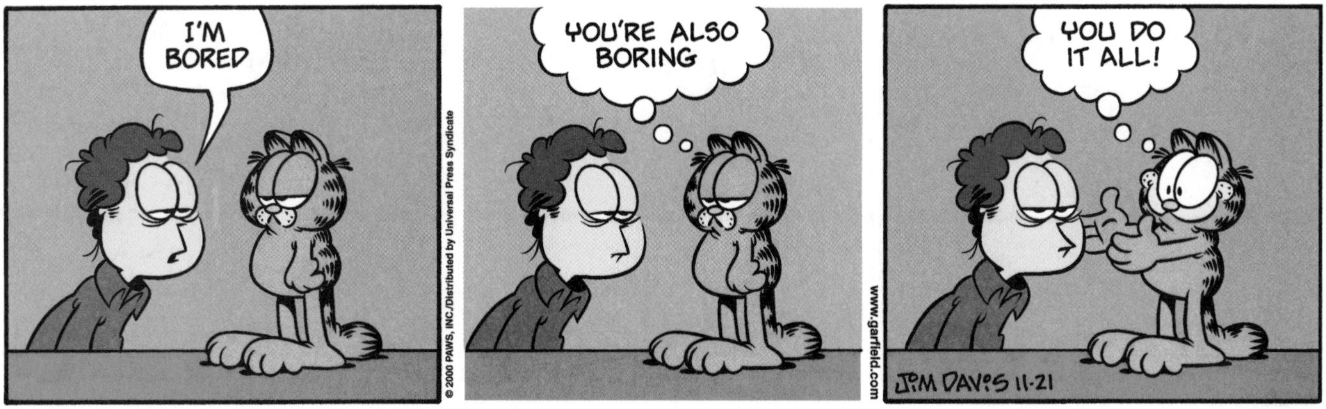
I'M BORED
© 2000 PAWS, INC./Distributed by Universal Press Syndicate
YOU'RE ALSO BORING
www.garfield.com
YOU DO IT ALL!
JIM DAVIS 11-21

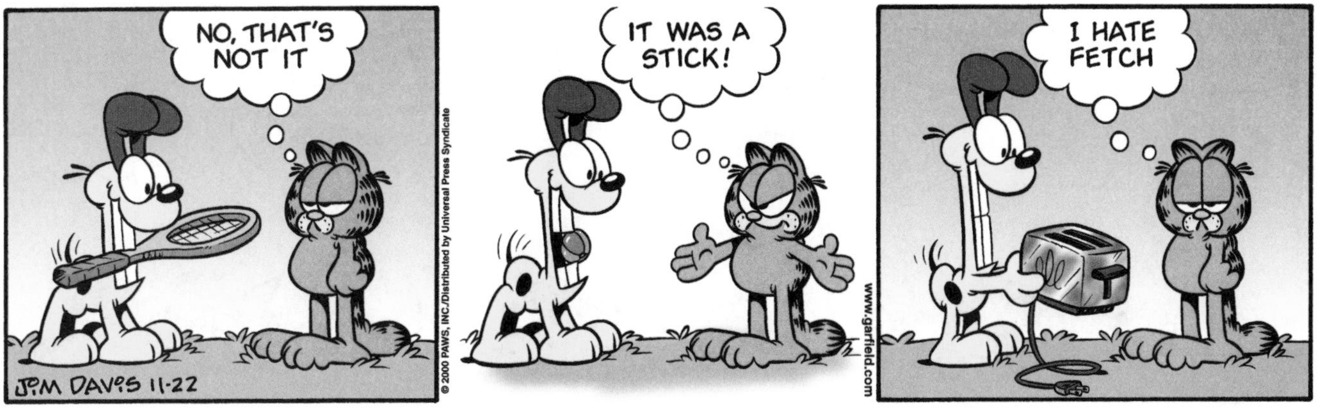
NO, THAT'S NOT IT
JIM DAVIS 11-22
© 2000 PAWS, INC./Distributed by Universal Press Syndicate
IT WAS A STICK!
www.garfield.com
I HATE FETCH

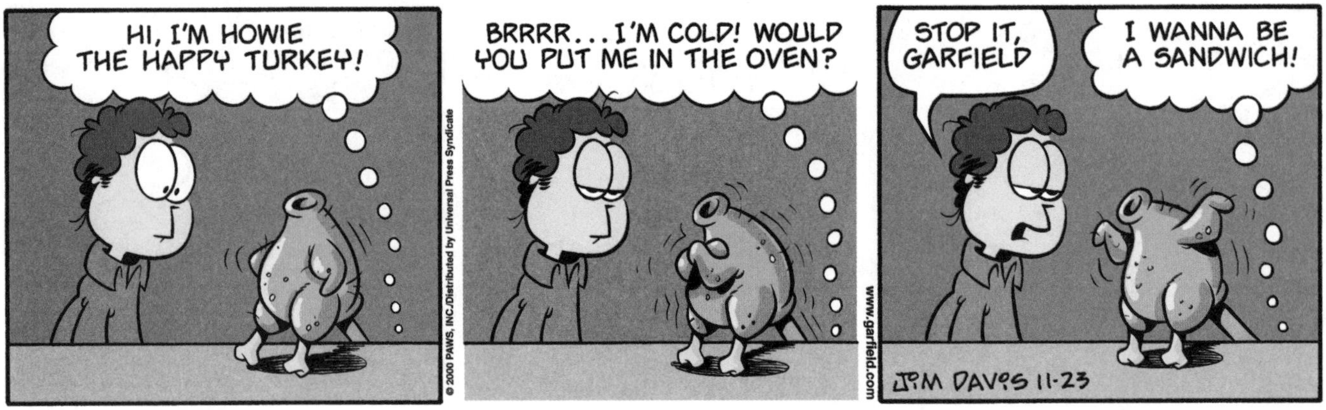
HI, I'M HOWIE THE HAPPY TURKEY!
BRRRR... I'M COLD! WOULD YOU PUT ME IN THE OVEN?
STOP IT, GARFIELD
I WANNA BE A SANDWICH!
JIM DAVIS 11-23
© 2000 PAWS, INC./Distributed by Universal Press Syndicate
www.garfield.com

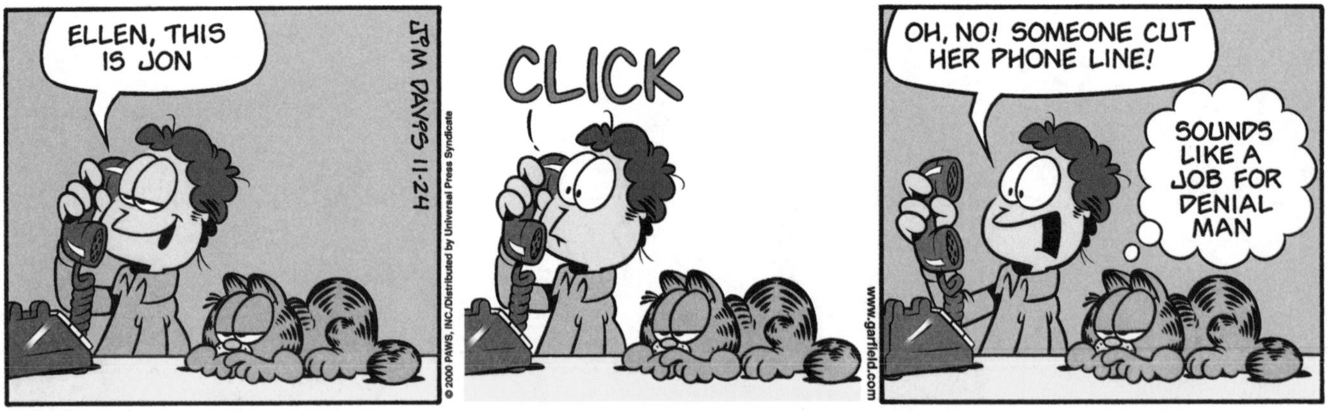
ELLEN, THIS IS JON
JIM DAVIS 11-24
CLICK
OH, NO! SOMEONE CUT HER PHONE LINE!
SOUNDS LIKE A JOB FOR DENIAL MAN
© 2000 PAWS, INC./Distributed by Universal Press Syndicate
www.garfield.com

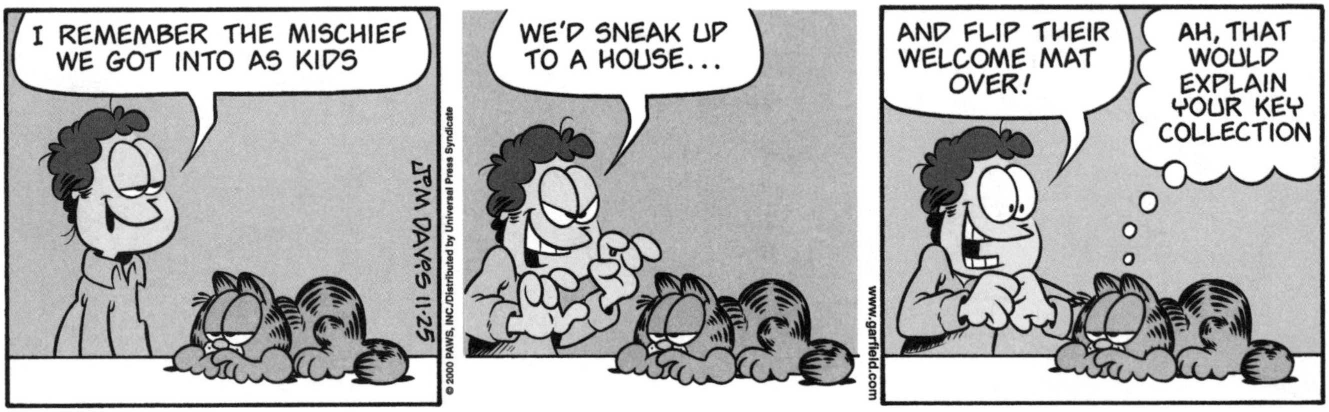
I REMEMBER THE MISCHIEF WE GOT INTO AS KIDS
JIM DAVIS 11-25
WE'D SNEAK UP TO A HOUSE...
AND FLIP THEIR WELCOME MAT OVER!
AH, THAT WOULD EXPLAIN YOUR KEY COLLECTION
© 2000 PAWS, INC./Distributed by Universal Press Syndicate
www.garfield.com

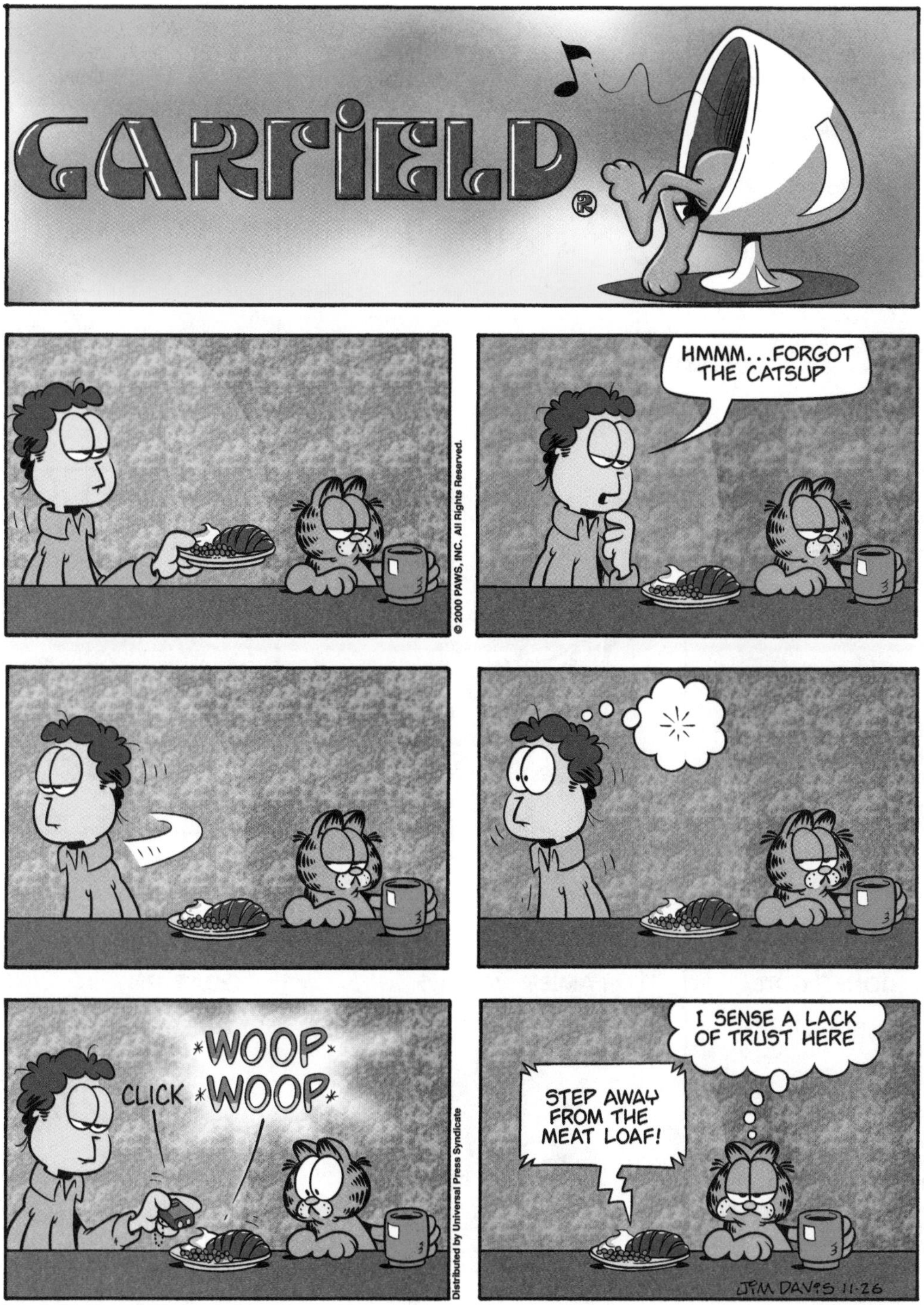
GARFIELD®
HMMM...FORGOT THE CATSUP
© 2000 PAWS, INC. All Rights Reserved.
CLICK
WOOP WOOP
Distributed by Universal Press Syndicate
STEP AWAY FROM THE MEAT LOAF!
I SENSE A LACK OF TRUST HERE
JIM DAVIS 11-26

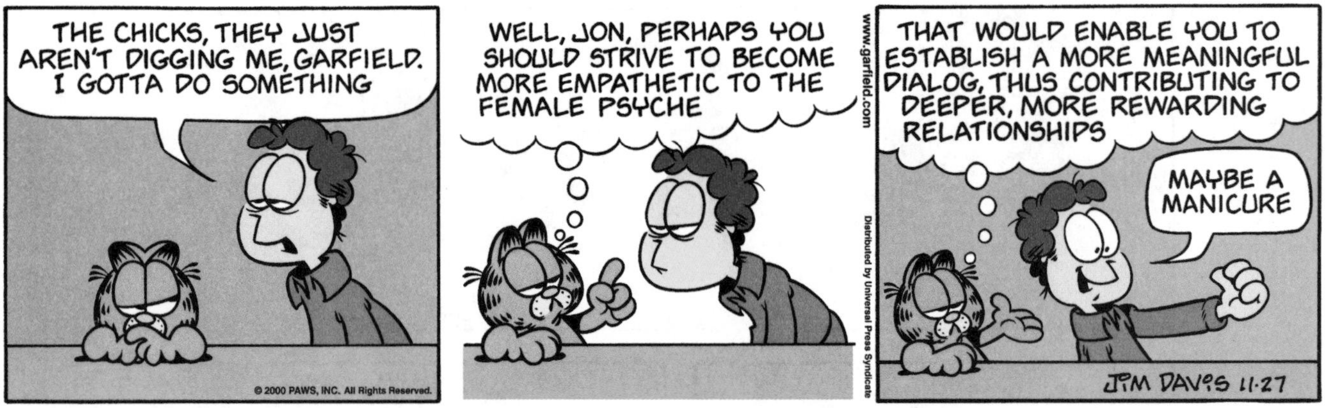
THE CHICKS, THEY JUST AREN'T DIGGING ME, GARFIELD. I GOTTA DO SOMETHING
© 2000 PAWS, INC. All Rights Reserved.
WELL, JON, PERHAPS YOU SHOULD STRIVE TO BECOME MORE EMPATHETIC TO THE FEMALE PSYCHE
www.garfield.com
Distributed by Universal Press Syndicate
THAT WOULD ENABLE YOU TO ESTABLISH A MORE MEANINGFUL DIALOG, THUS CONTRIBUTING TO DEEPER, MORE REWARDING RELATIONSHIPS
MAYBE A MANICURE
JIM DAVIS 11·27

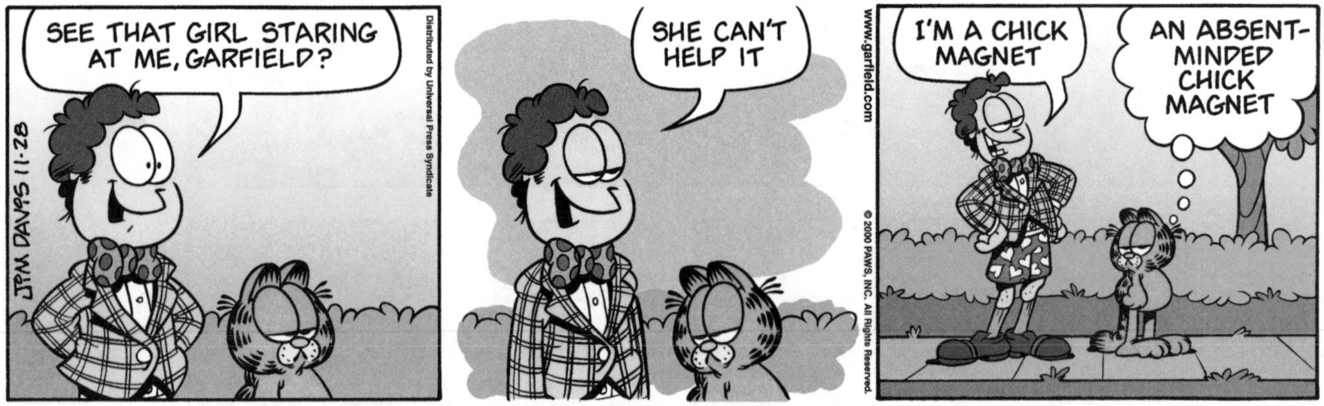
SEE THAT GIRL STARING AT ME, GARFIELD?
JIM DAVIS 11·28
Distributed by Universal Press Syndicate
SHE CAN'T HELP IT
www.garfield.com
© 2000 PAWS, INC. All Rights Reserved.
I'M A CHICK MAGNET
AN ABSENT-MINDED CHICK MAGNET

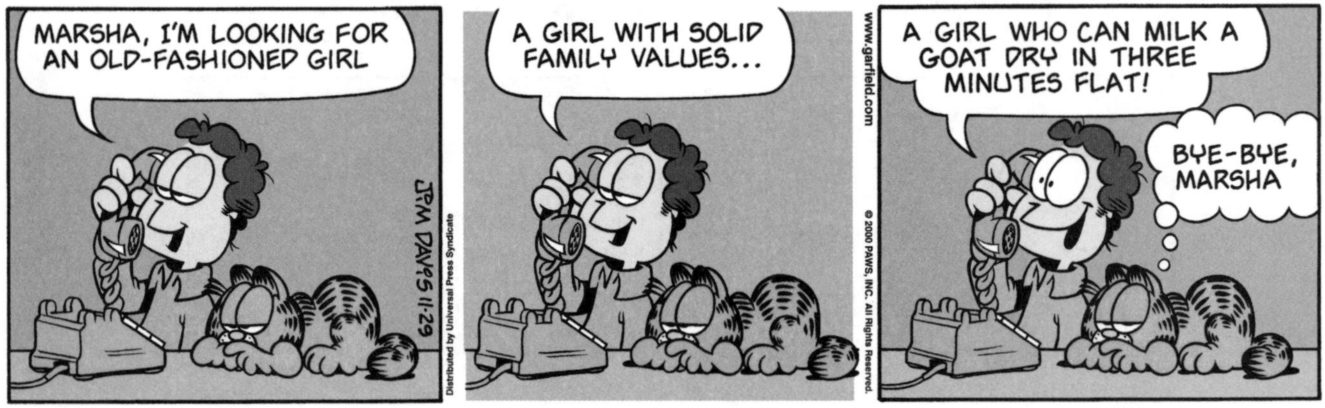
MARSHA, I'M LOOKING FOR AN OLD-FASHIONED GIRL
JIM DAVIS 11·29
Distributed by Universal Press Syndicate
A GIRL WITH SOLID FAMILY VALUES...
www.garfield.com
© 2000 PAWS, INC. All Rights Reserved.
A GIRL WHO CAN MILK A GOAT DRY IN THREE MINUTES FLAT!
BYE-BYE, MARSHA

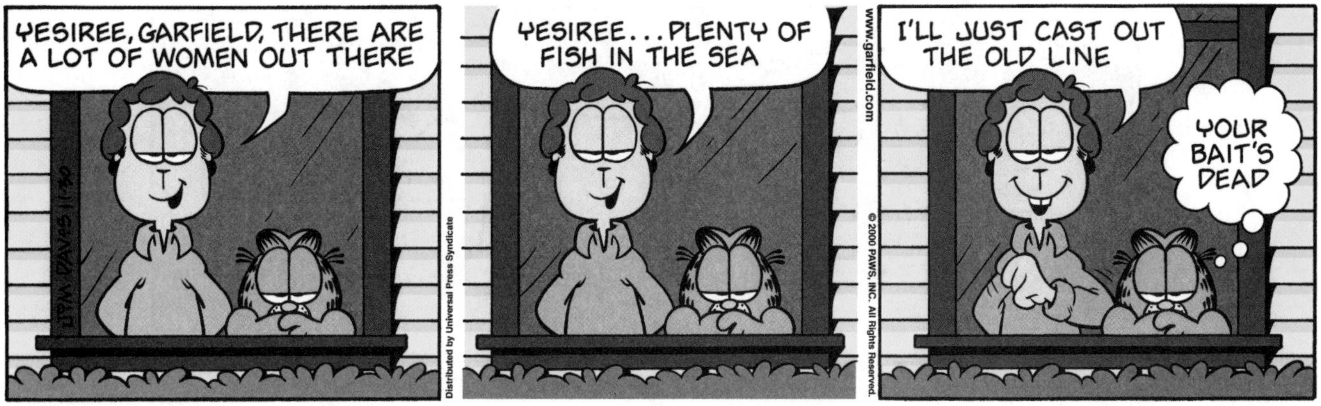
YESIREE, GARFIELD, THERE ARE A LOT OF WOMEN OUT THERE
JIM DAVIS 11-30
Distributed by Universal Press Syndicate
YESIREE . . . PLENTY OF FISH IN THE SEA
www.garfield.com
© 2000 PAWS, INC. All Rights Reserved.
I'LL JUST CAST OUT THE OLD LINE
YOUR BAIT'S DEAD

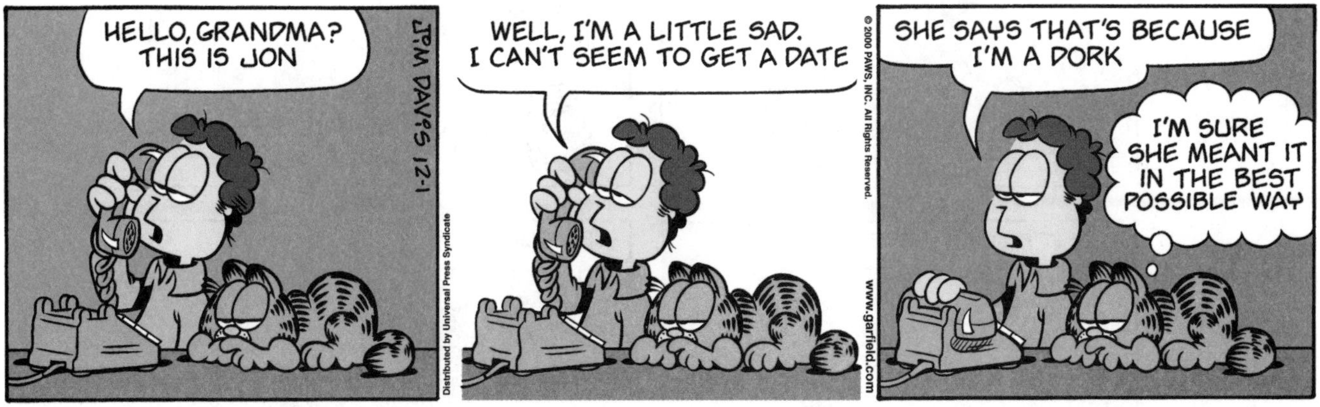
HELLO, GRANDMA? THIS IS JON
JIM DAVIS 12-1
Distributed by Universal Press Syndicate
WELL, I'M A LITTLE SAD. I CAN'T SEEM TO GET A DATE
© 2000 PAWS, INC. All Rights Reserved.
www.garfield.com
SHE SAYS THAT'S BECAUSE I'M A DORK
I'M SURE SHE MEANT IT IN THE BEST POSSIBLE WAY

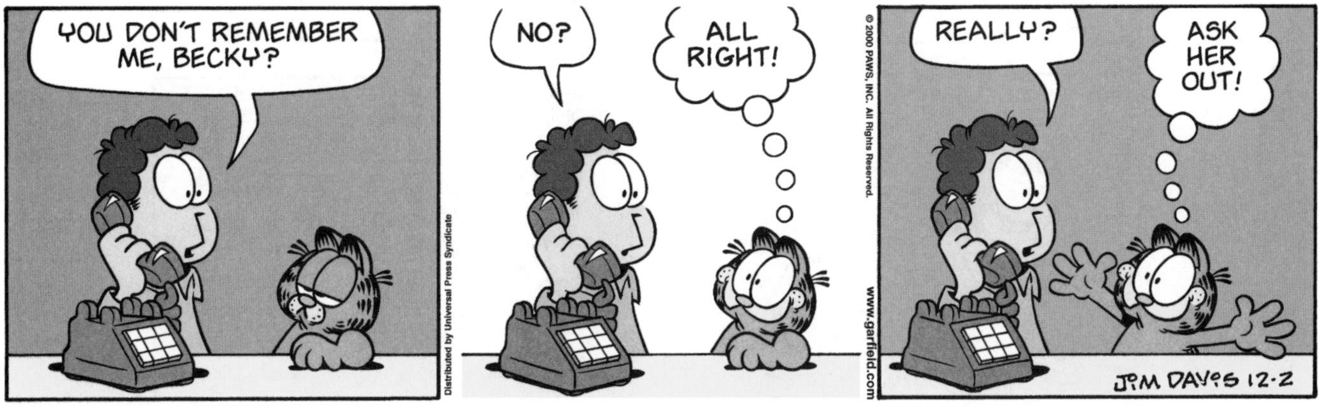
YOU DON'T REMEMBER ME, BECKY?
Distributed by Universal Press Syndicate
NO?
ALL RIGHT!
© 2000 PAWS, INC. All Rights Reserved.
www.garfield.com
REALLY?
ASK HER OUT!
JIM DAVIS 12-2

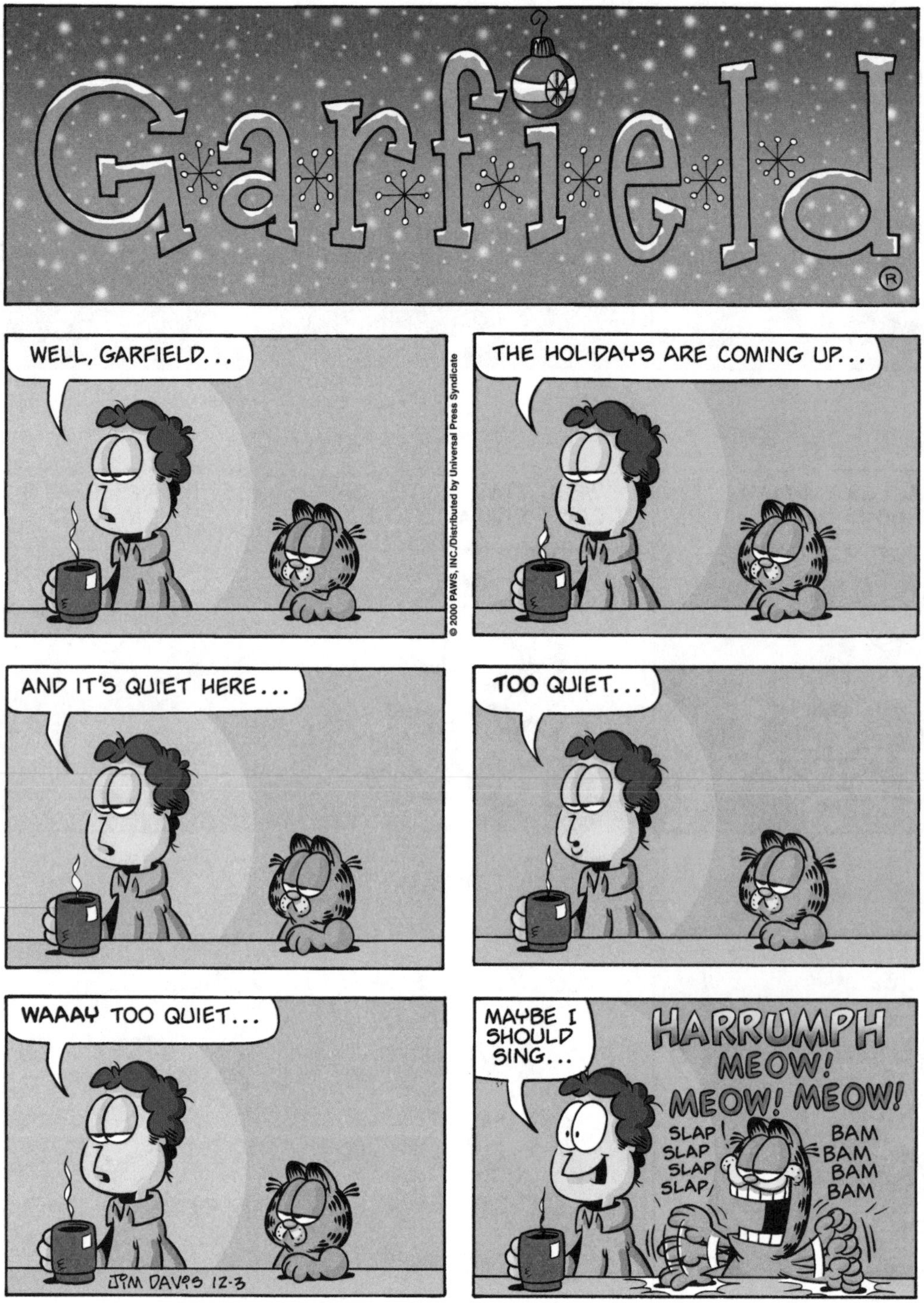
Garfield
WELL, GARFIELD...
© 2000 PAWS, INC./Distributed by Universal Press Syndicate
THE HOLIDAYS ARE COMING UP...
AND IT'S QUIET HERE...
TOO QUIET...
WAAAY TOO QUIET...
JIM DAVIS 12-3
MAYBE I SHOULD SING...
HARRUMPH
MEOW!
MEOW! MEOW!
SLAP! SLAP SLAP SLAP
BAM BAM BAM BAM

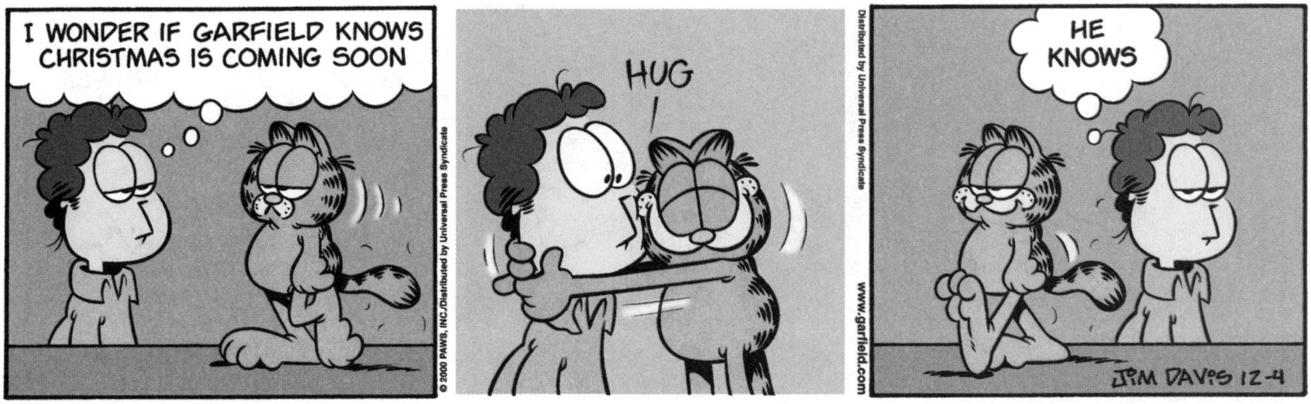
I WONDER IF GARFIELD KNOWS CHRISTMAS IS COMING SOON
HUG
HE KNOWS
JIM DAVIS 12-4
© 2000 PAWS, INC./Distributed by Universal Press Syndicate
Distributed by Universal Press Syndicate
www.garfield.com

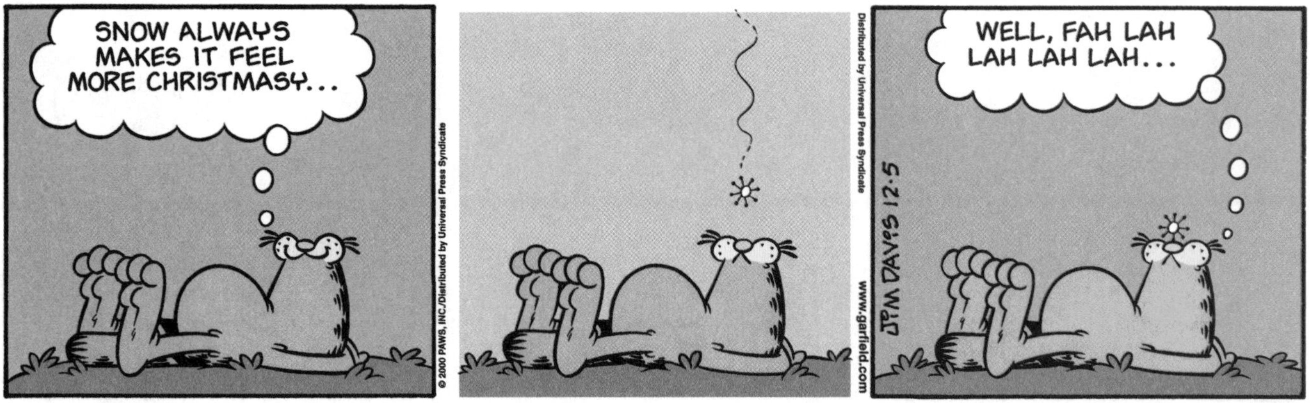
SNOW ALWAYS MAKES IT FEEL MORE CHRISTMASY...
WELL, FAH LAH LAH LAH LAH...
JIM DAVIS 12-5
© 2000 PAWS, INC./Distributed by Universal Press Syndicate
Distributed by Universal Press Syndicate
www.garfield.com

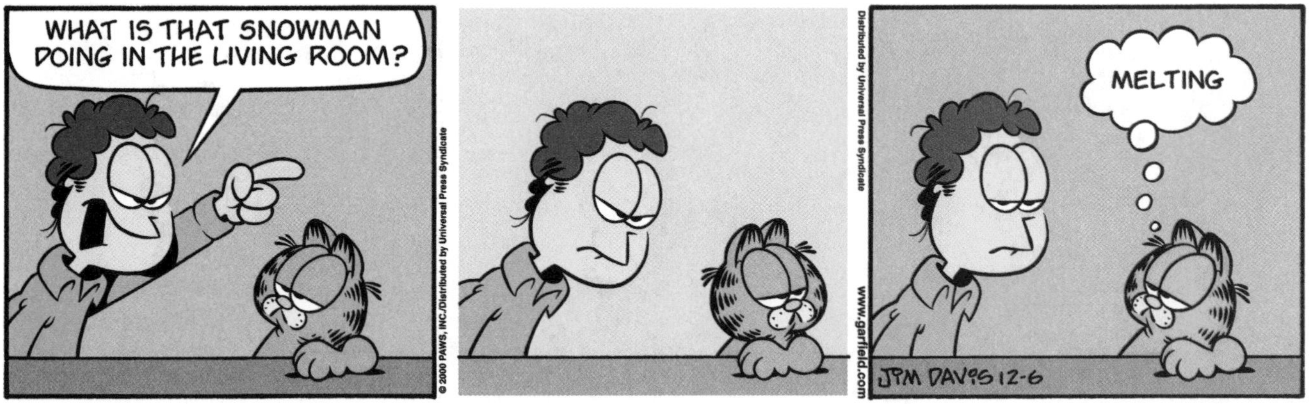
WHAT IS THAT SNOWMAN DOING IN THE LIVING ROOM?
MELTING
JIM DAVIS 12-6
© 2000 PAWS, INC./Distributed by Universal Press Syndicate
Distributed by Universal Press Syndicate
www.garfield.com

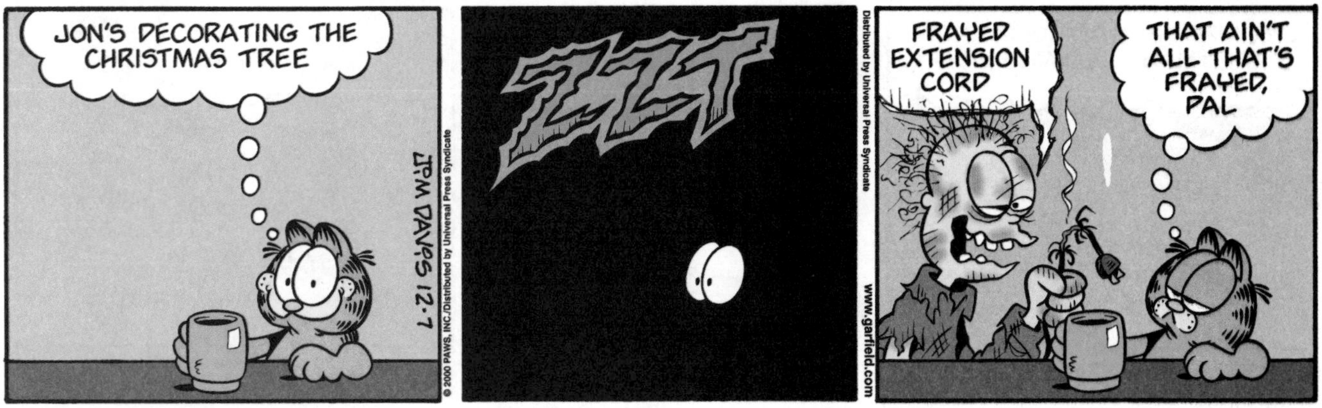
JON'S DECORATING THE CHRISTMAS TREE
JIM DAVIS 12-7
© 2000 PAWS, INC./Distributed by Universal Press Syndicate
ZZZT
Distributed by Universal Press Syndicate
FRAYED EXTENSION CORD
THAT AIN'T ALL THAT'S FRAYED, PAL
www.garfield.com

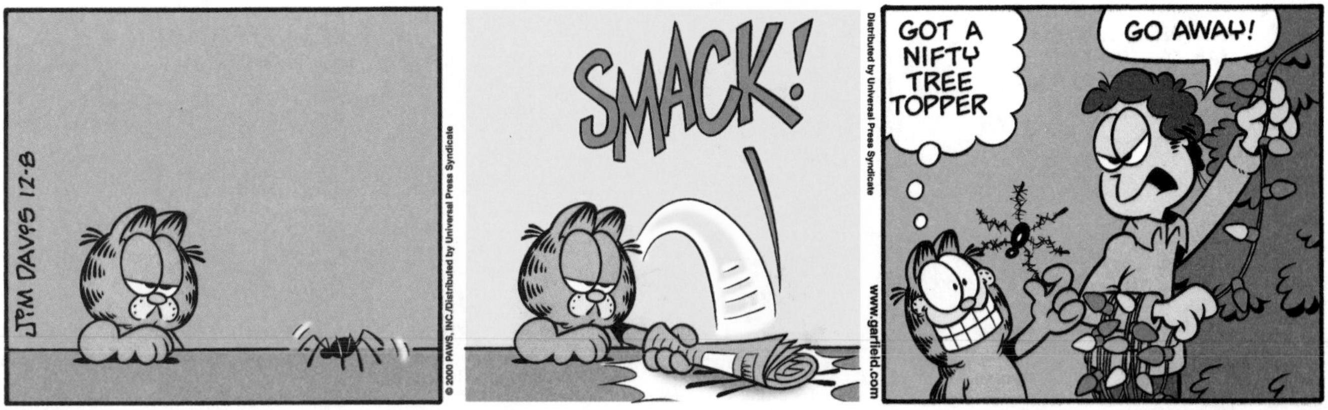
JIM DAVIS 12-8
© 2000 PAWS, INC./Distributed by Universal Press Syndicate
SMACK!
Distributed by Universal Press Syndicate
GOT A NIFTY TREE TOPPER
GO AWAY!
www.garfield.com

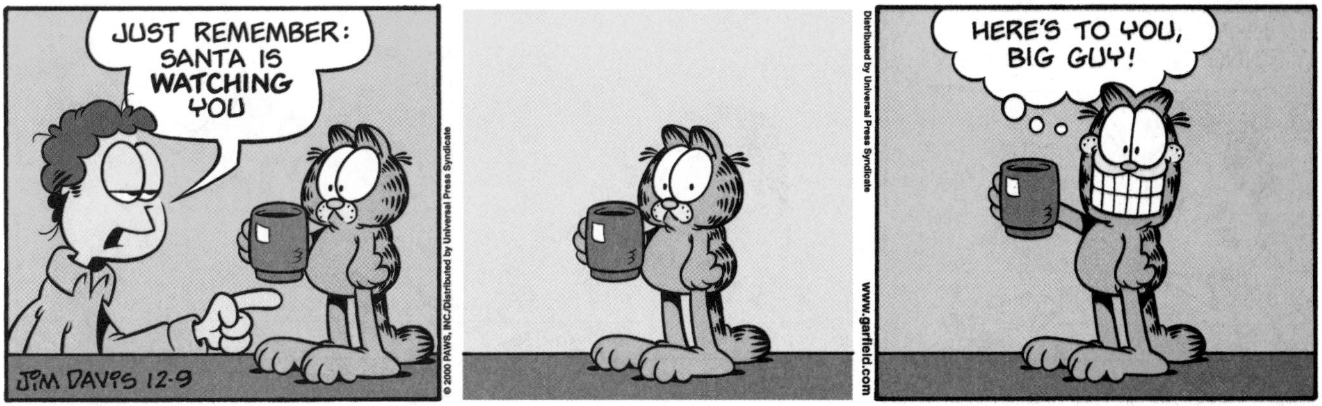
JUST REMEMBER: SANTA IS WATCHING YOU
JIM DAVIS 12-9
© 2000 PAWS, INC./Distributed by Universal Press Syndicate
Distributed by Universal Press Syndicate
HERE'S TO YOU, BIG GUY!
www.garfield.com

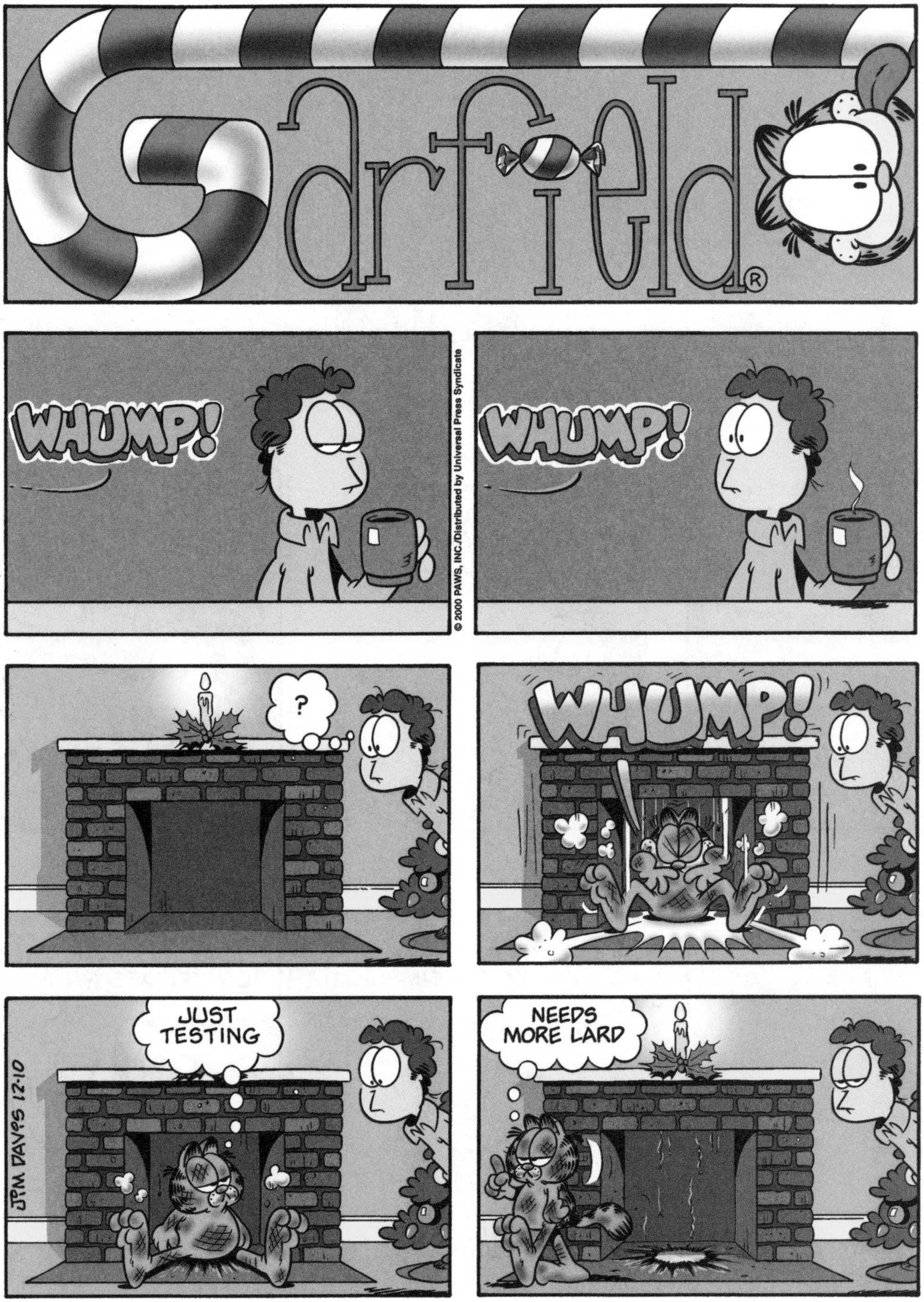
Garfield®
© 2000 PAWS, INC./Distributed by Universal Press Syndicate
WHUMP!
WHUMP!
?
WHUMP!
JIM DAVIS 12-10
JUST TESTING
NEEDS MORE LARD

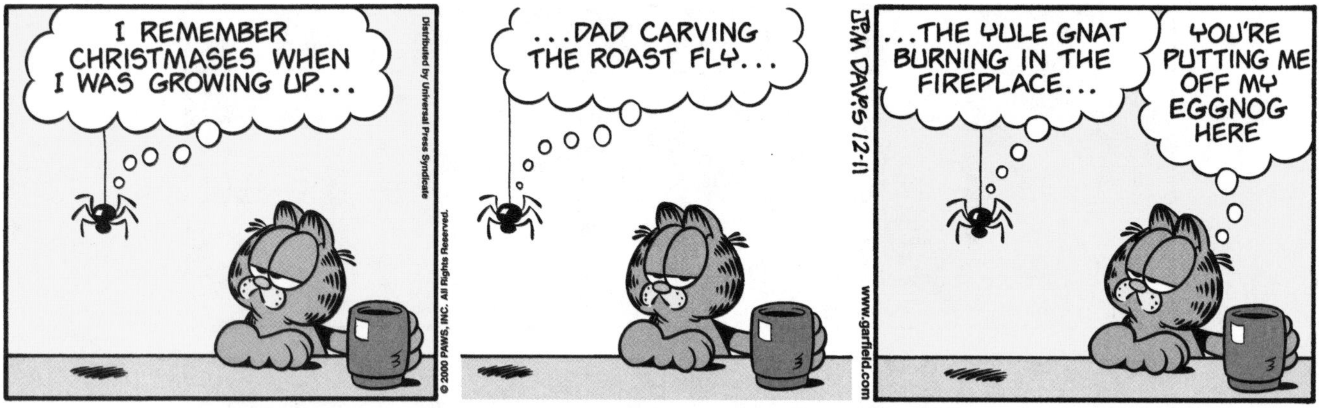
I REMEMBER CHRISTMASES WHEN I WAS GROWING UP...
...DAD CARVING THE ROAST FLY...
...THE YULE GNAT BURNING IN THE FIREPLACE...
YOU'RE PUTTING ME OFF MY EGGNOG HERE
JIM DAVIS 12-11
© 2000 PAWS, INC. All Rights Reserved.
Distributed by Universal Press Syndicate
www.garfield.com

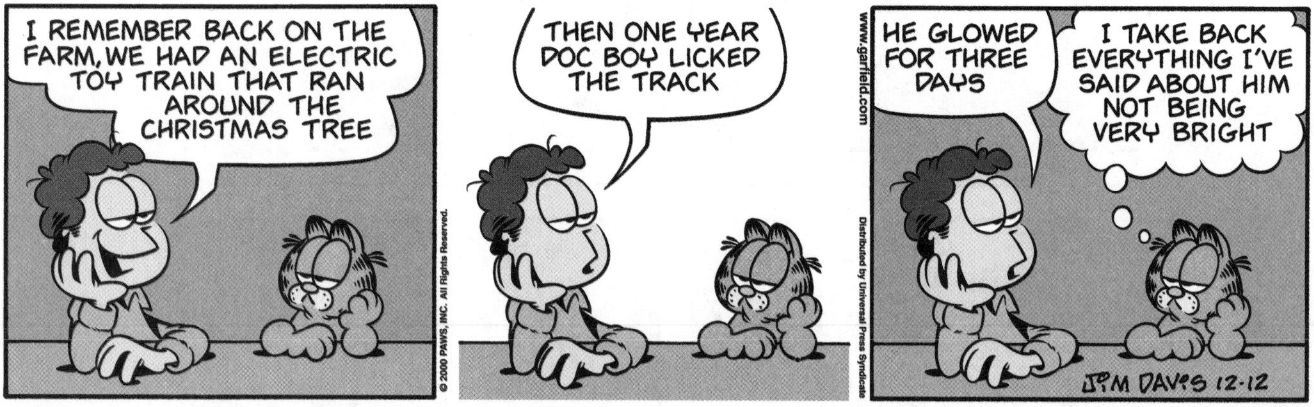
I REMEMBER BACK ON THE FARM, WE HAD AN ELECTRIC TOY TRAIN THAT RAN AROUND THE CHRISTMAS TREE
THEN ONE YEAR DOC BOY LICKED THE TRACK
HE GLOWED FOR THREE DAYS
I TAKE BACK EVERYTHING I'VE SAID ABOUT HIM NOT BEING VERY BRIGHT
JIM DAVIS 12-12
© 2000 PAWS, INC. All Rights Reserved.
Distributed by Universal Press Syndicate
www.garfield.com

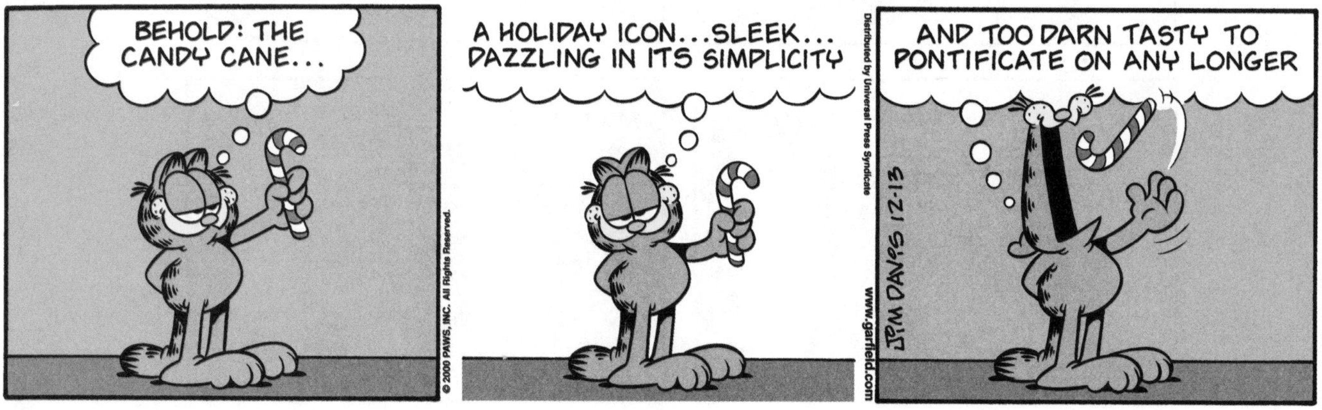
BEHOLD: THE CANDY CANE...
A HOLIDAY ICON...SLEEK... DAZZLING IN ITS SIMPLICITY
AND TOO DARN TASTY TO PONTIFICATE ON ANY LONGER
JIM DAVIS 12-13
© 2000 PAWS, INC. All Rights Reserved.
Distributed by Universal Press Syndicate
www.garfield.com

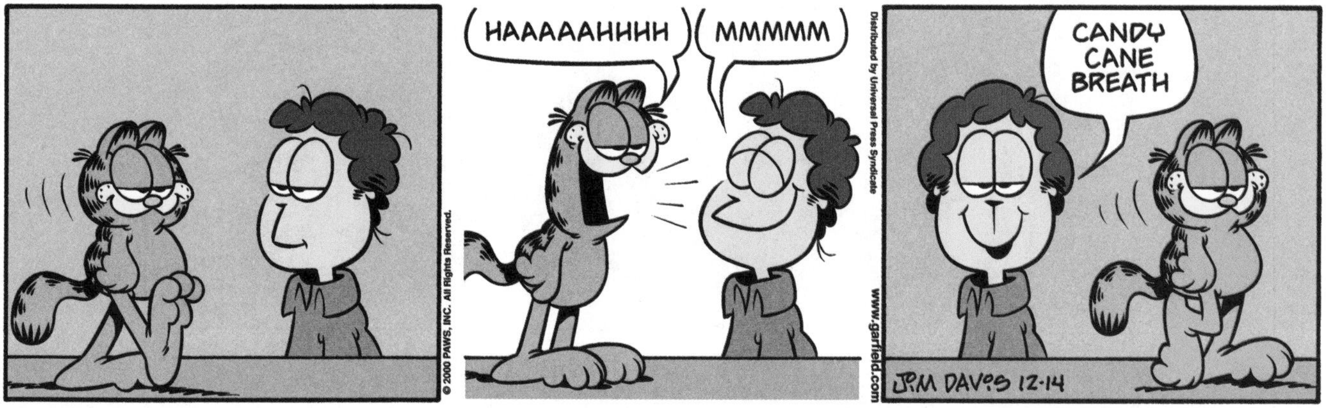
HAAAAAHHHH
MMMMM
CANDY CANE BREATH
© 2000 PAWS, INC. All Rights Reserved.
Distributed by Universal Press Syndicate
www.garfield.com
JIM DAVIS 12-14

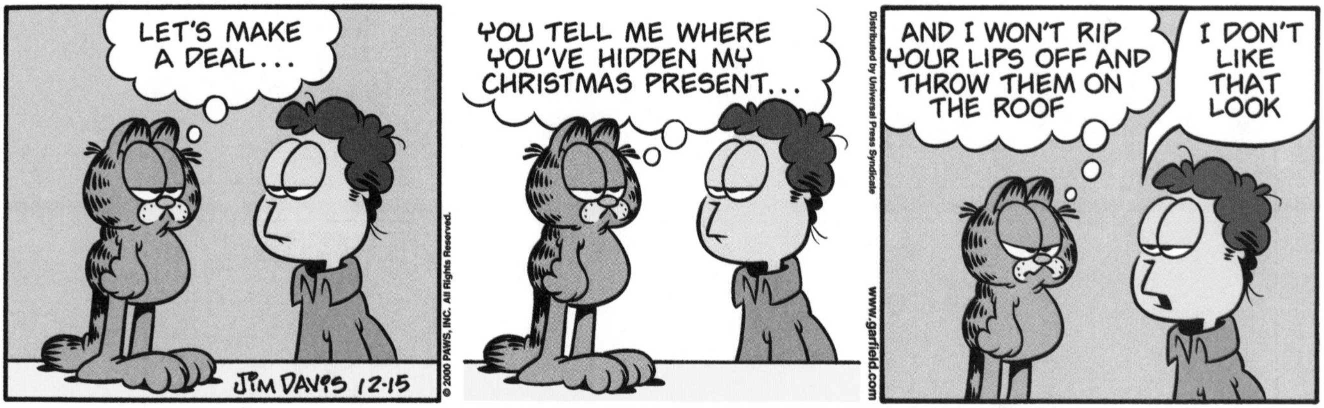
LET'S MAKE A DEAL...
YOU TELL ME WHERE YOU'VE HIDDEN MY CHRISTMAS PRESENT...
AND I WON'T RIP YOUR LIPS OFF AND THROW THEM ON THE ROOF
I DON'T LIKE THAT LOOK
© 2000 PAWS, INC. All Rights Reserved.
Distributed by Universal Press Syndicate
www.garfield.com
JIM DAVIS 12-15

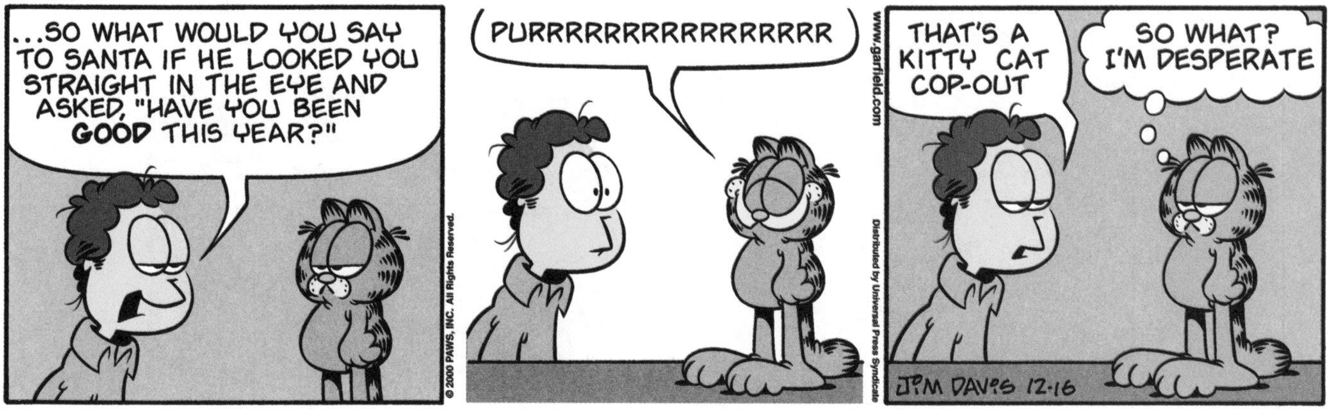
...SO WHAT WOULD YOU SAY TO SANTA IF HE LOOKED YOU STRAIGHT IN THE EYE AND ASKED, "HAVE YOU BEEN **GOOD** THIS YEAR?"
PURRRRRRRRRRRRRRRR
THAT'S A KITTY CAT COP-OUT
SO WHAT? I'M DESPERATE
© 2000 PAWS, INC. All Rights Reserved.
www.garfield.com
Distributed by Universal Press Syndicate
JIM DAVIS 12-16

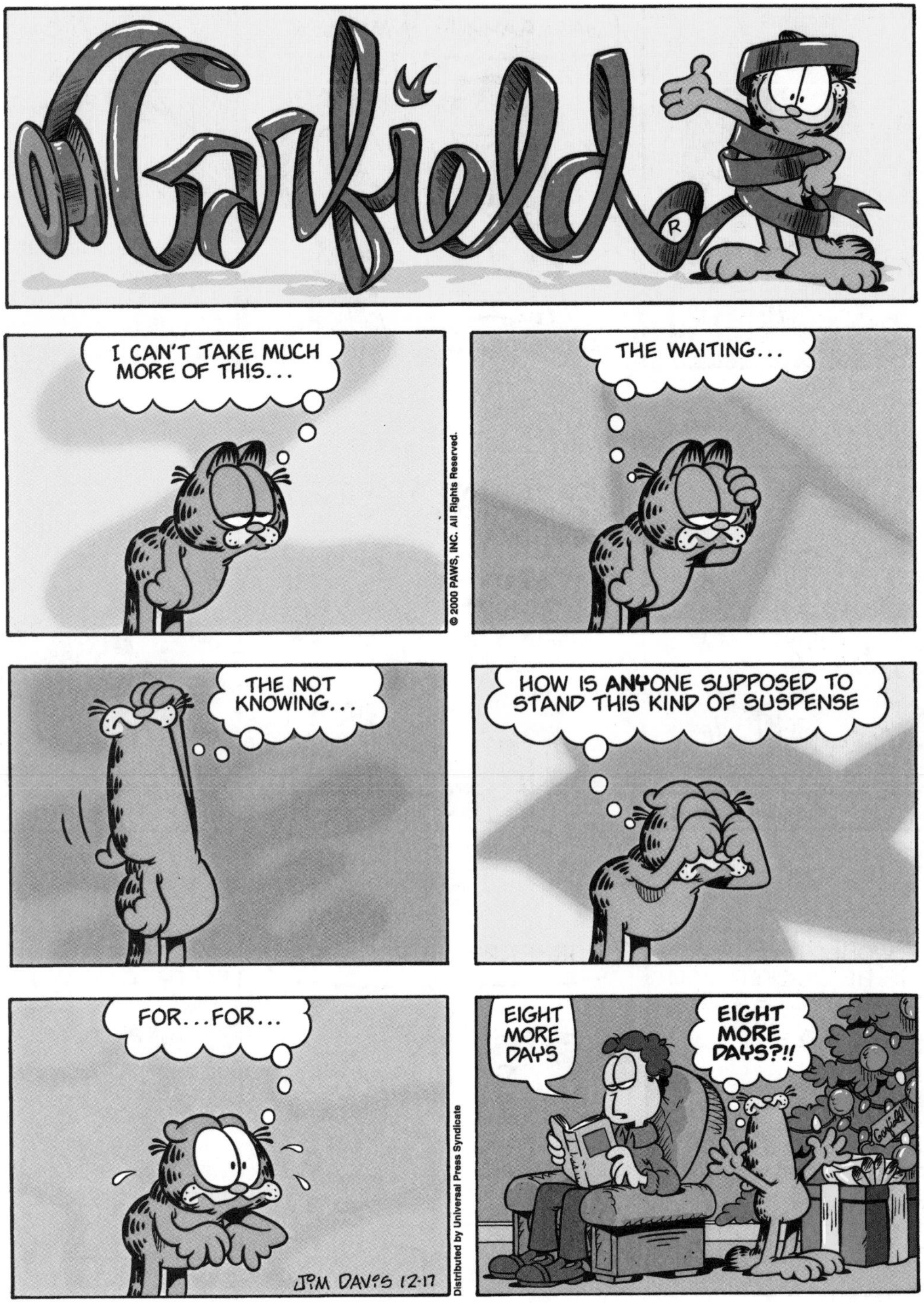
Garfield
I CAN'T TAKE MUCH MORE OF THIS...
© 2000 PAWS, INC. All Rights Reserved.
THE WAITING...
THE NOT KNOWING...
HOW IS ANYONE SUPPOSED TO STAND THIS KIND OF SUSPENSE
FOR...FOR...
JIM DAVIS 12-17
Distributed by Universal Press Syndicate
EIGHT MORE DAYS
EIGHT MORE DAYS?!!

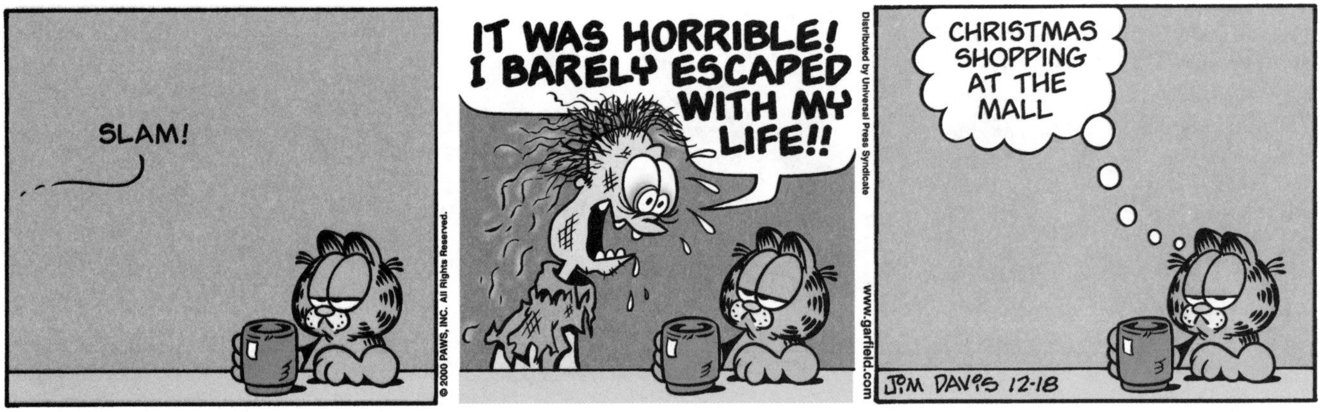
SLAM!
IT WAS HORRIBLE! I BARELY ESCAPED WITH MY LIFE!!
CHRISTMAS SHOPPING AT THE MALL
JIM DAVIS 12-18
© 2000 PAWS, INC. All Rights Reserved.
Distributed by Universal Press Syndicate
www.garfield.com

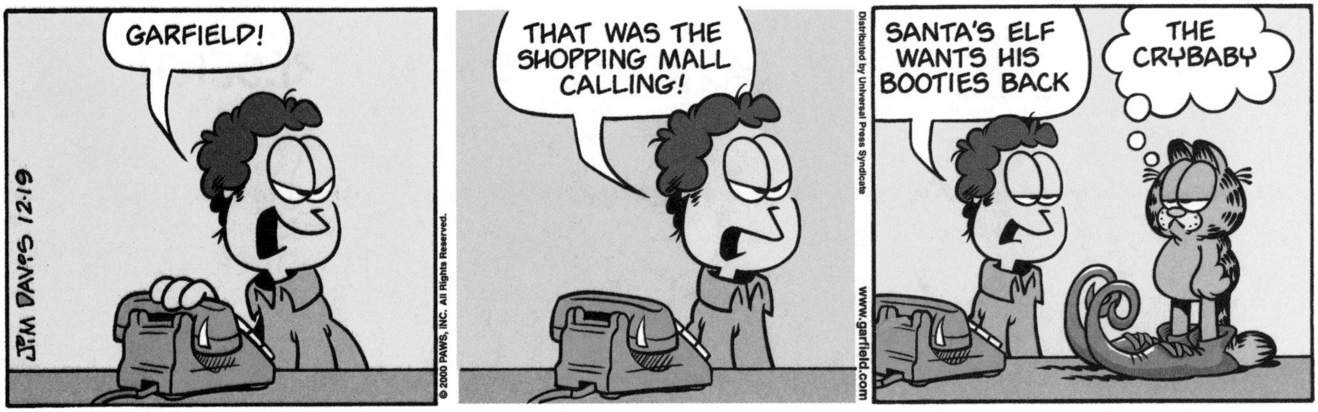
GARFIELD!
JIM DAVIS 12-19
THAT WAS THE SHOPPING MALL CALLING!
SANTA'S ELF WANTS HIS BOOTIES BACK
THE CRYBABY
© 2000 PAWS, INC. All Rights Reserved.
Distributed by Universal Press Syndicate
www.garfield.com

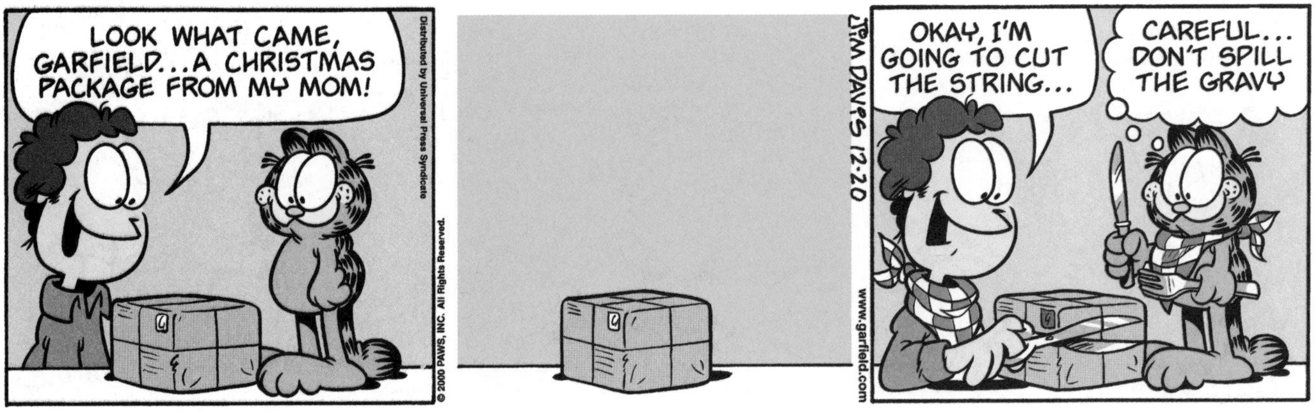
LOOK WHAT CAME, GARFIELD...A CHRISTMAS PACKAGE FROM MY MOM!
JIM DAVIS 12-20
OKAY, I'M GOING TO CUT THE STRING...
CAREFUL... DON'T SPILL THE GRAVY
© 2000 PAWS, INC. All Rights Reserved.
Distributed by Universal Press Syndicate
www.garfield.com

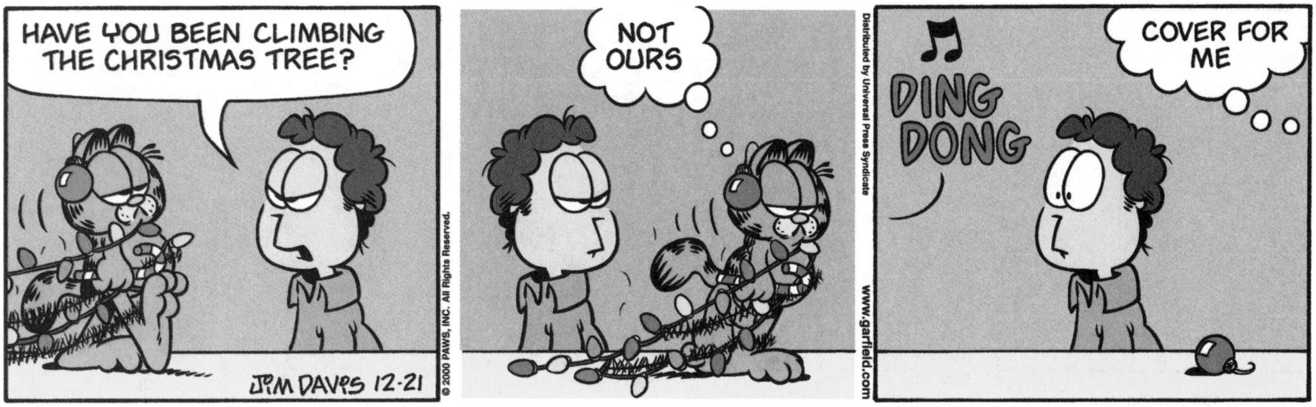
HAVE YOU BEEN CLIMBING THE CHRISTMAS TREE?
JIM DAVIS 12-21
© 2000 PAWS, INC. All Rights Reserved.
NOT OURS
Distributed by Universal Press Syndicate
www.garfield.com
DING DONG
COVER FOR ME

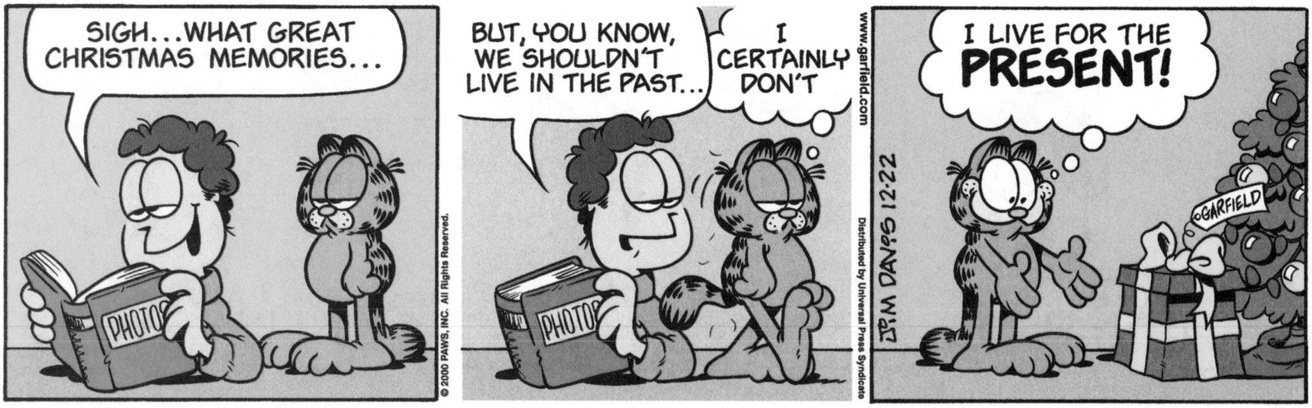
SIGH...WHAT GREAT CHRISTMAS MEMORIES...
PHOTOS
© 2000 PAWS, INC. All Rights Reserved.
BUT, YOU KNOW, WE SHOULDN'T LIVE IN THE PAST...
I CERTAINLY DON'T
PHOTOS
www.garfield.com
Distributed by Universal Press Syndicate
JIM DAVIS 12-22
I LIVE FOR THE PRESENT!
GARFIELD

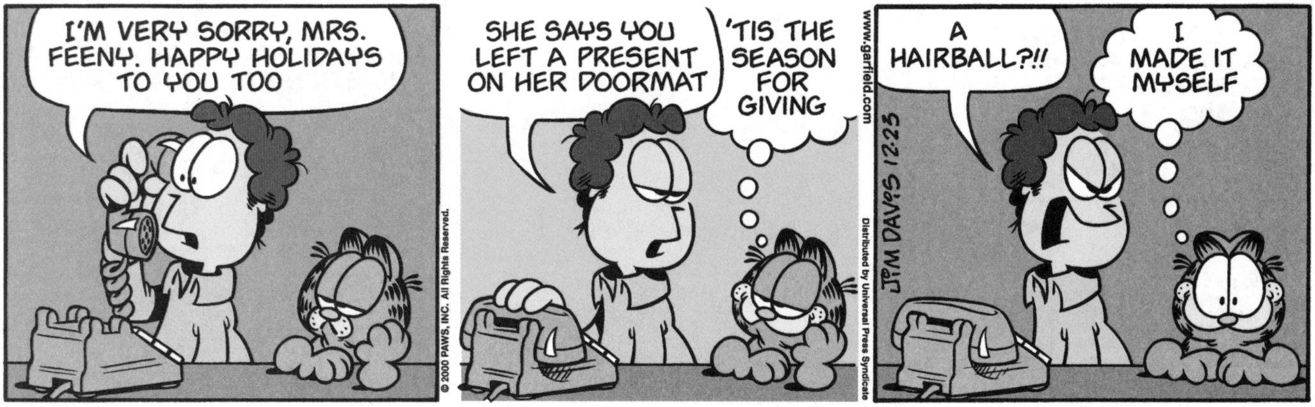
I'M VERY SORRY, MRS. FEENY. HAPPY HOLIDAYS TO YOU TOO
© 2000 PAWS, INC. All Rights Reserved.
SHE SAYS YOU LEFT A PRESENT ON HER DOORMAT
'TIS THE SEASON FOR GIVING
www.garfield.com
JIM DAVIS 12-23
Distributed by Universal Press Syndicate
A HAIRBALL?!!
I MADE IT MYSELF

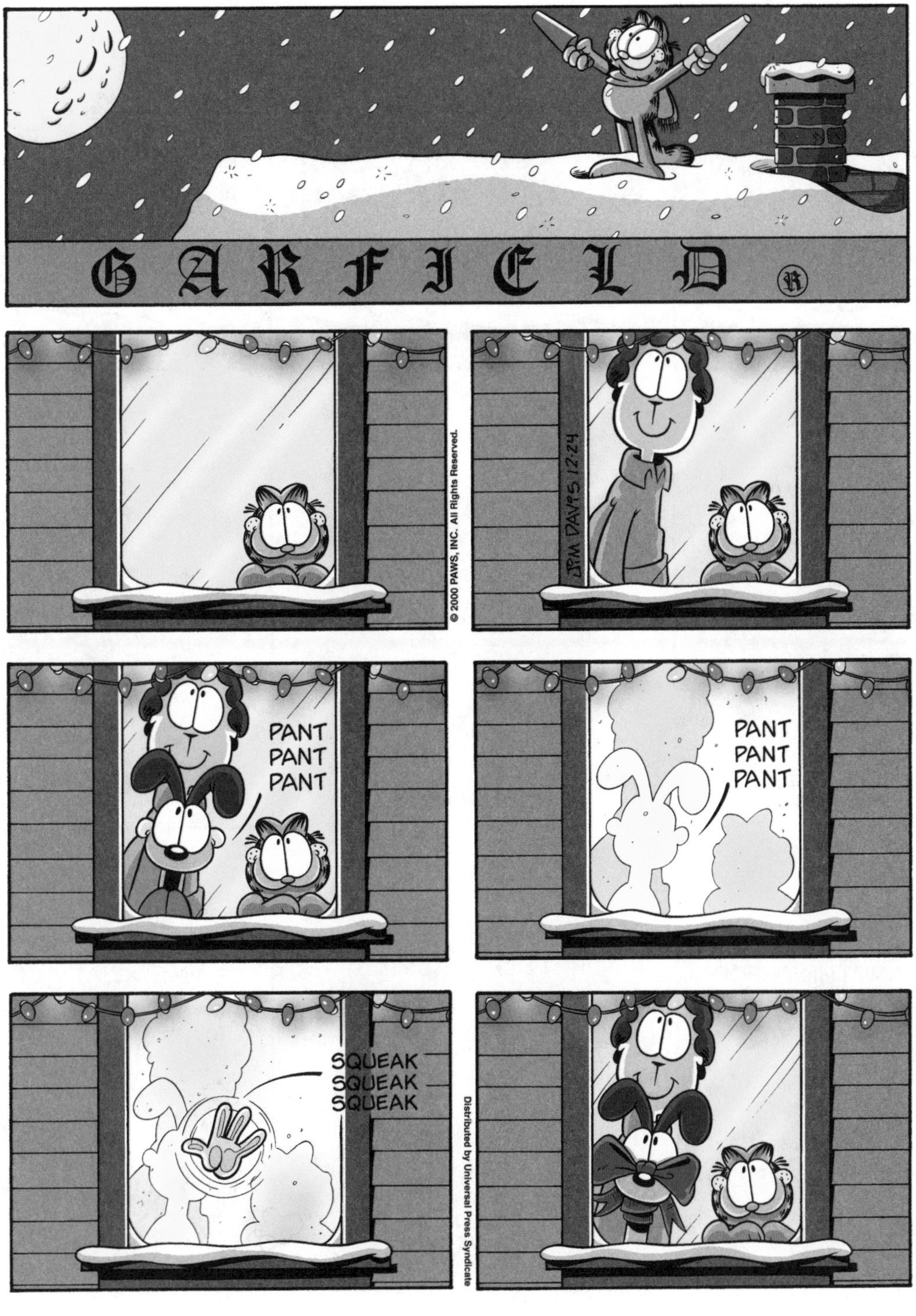
GARFIELD
© 2000 PAWS, INC. All Rights Reserved.
JPM DAVIS 12-24
PANT
PANT
PANT
PANT
PANT
PANT
SQUEAK
SQUEAK
SQUEAK
Distributed by Universal Press Syndicate

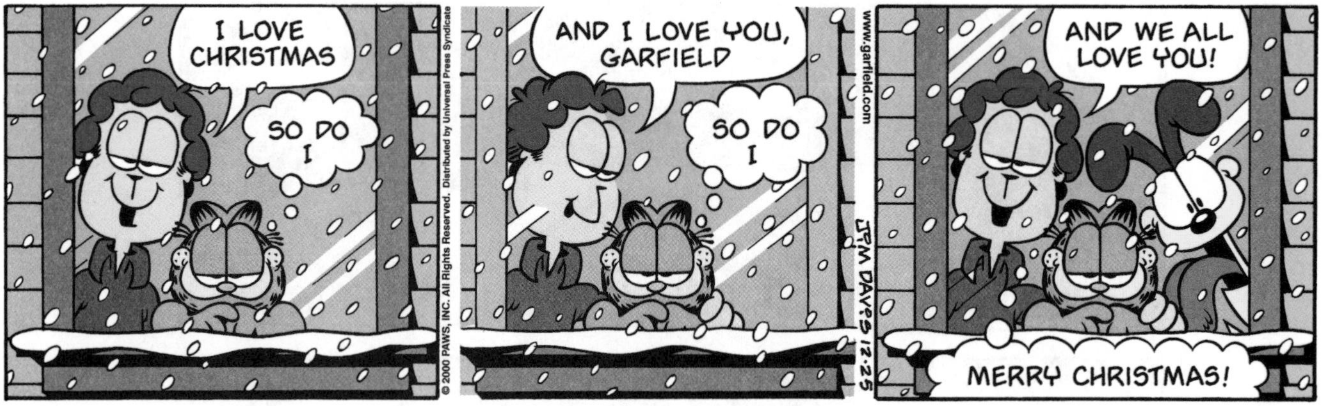
I LOVE CHRISTMAS
SO DO I
© 2000 PAWS, INC. All Rights Reserved. Distributed by Universal Press Syndicate
AND I LOVE YOU, GARFIELD
SO DO I
www.garfield.com
JIM DAVIS 12-25
AND WE ALL LOVE YOU!
MERRY CHRISTMAS!

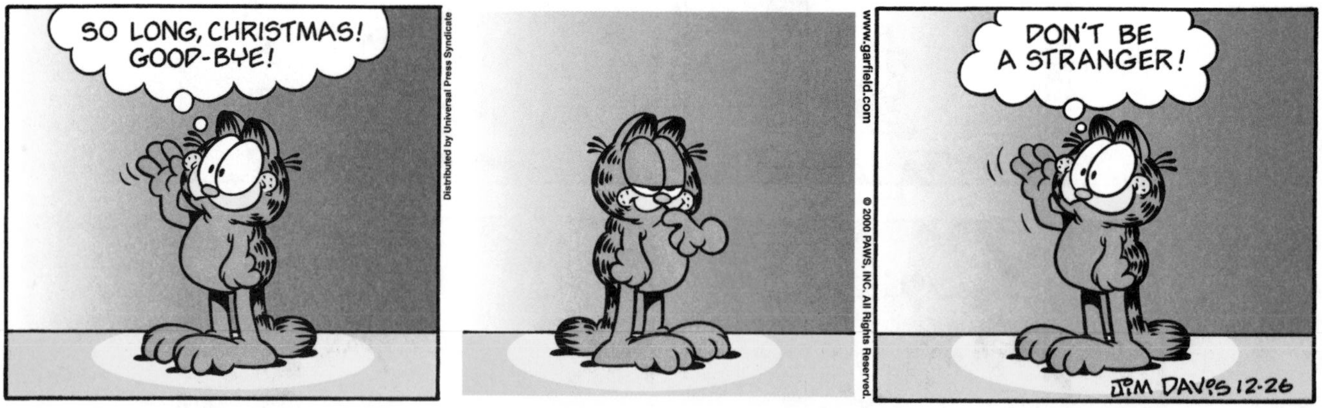
SO LONG, CHRISTMAS! GOOD-BYE!
Distributed by Universal Press Syndicate
www.garfield.com © 2000 PAWS, INC. All Rights Reserved.
DON'T BE A STRANGER!
JIM DAVIS 12-26

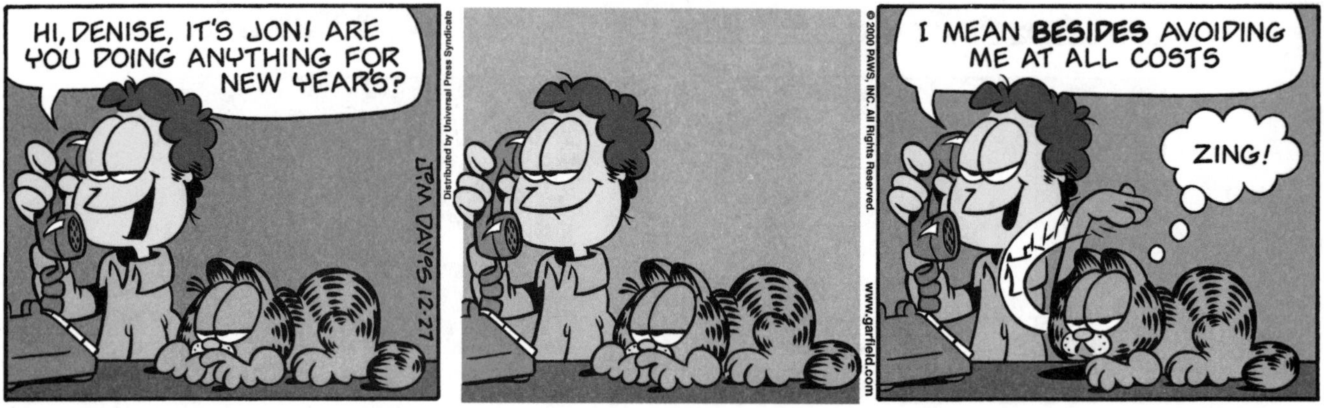
HI, DENISE, IT'S JON! ARE YOU DOING ANYTHING FOR NEW YEAR'S?
JIM DAVIS 12-27
Distributed by Universal Press Syndicate
© 2000 PAWS, INC. All Rights Reserved. www.garfield.com
I MEAN **BESIDES** AVOIDING ME AT ALL COSTS
ZING!

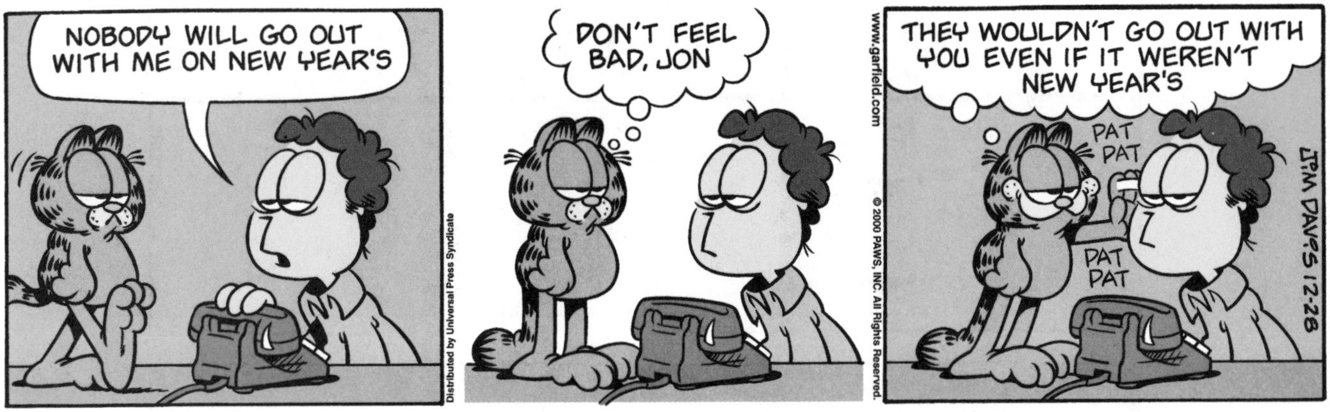
NOBODY WILL GO OUT WITH ME ON NEW YEAR'S
Distributed by Universal Press Syndicate
DON'T FEEL BAD, JON
www.garfield.com
© 2000 PAWS, INC. All Rights Reserved.
THEY WOULDN'T GO OUT WITH YOU EVEN IF IT WEREN'T NEW YEAR'S
PAT PAT
PAT PAT
JIM DAVIS 12-28

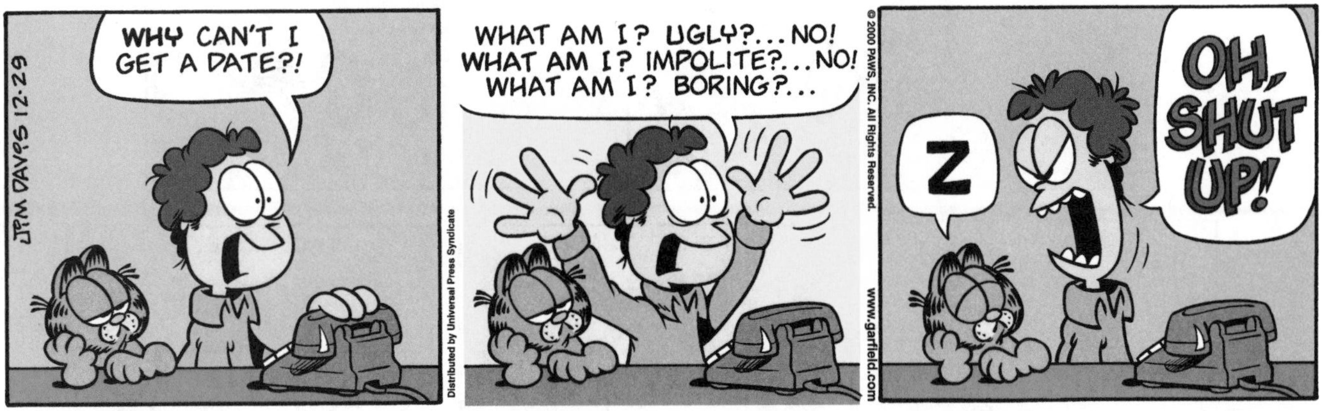
JIM DAVIS 12-29
WHY CAN'T I GET A DATE?!
Distributed by Universal Press Syndicate
WHAT AM I? UGLY?...NO! WHAT AM I? IMPOLITE?...NO! WHAT AM I? BORING?...
© 2000 PAWS, INC. All Rights Reserved.
www.garfield.com
Z
OH, SHUT UP!

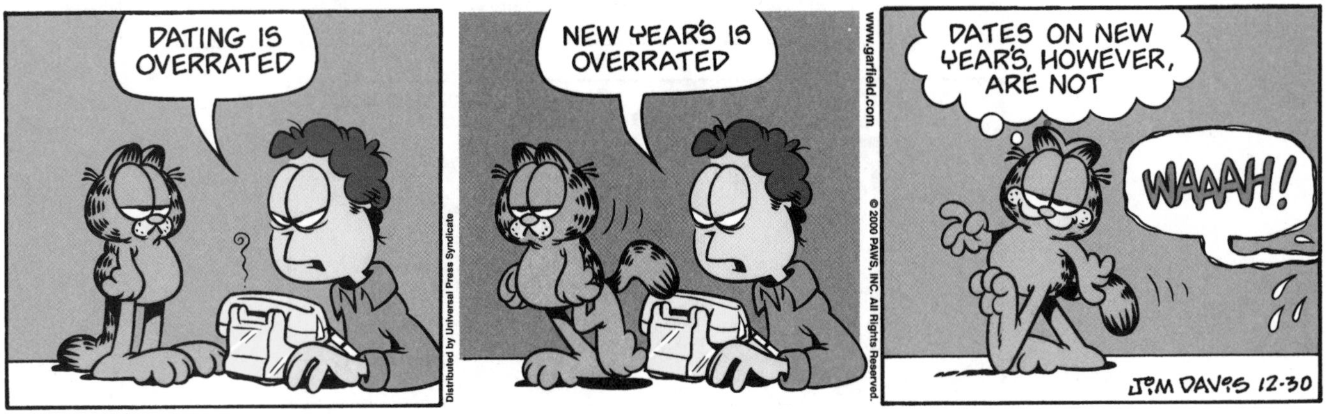
DATING IS OVERRATED
Distributed by Universal Press Syndicate
NEW YEAR'S IS OVERRATED
www.garfield.com
© 2000 PAWS, INC. All Rights Reserved.
DATES ON NEW YEAR'S, HOWEVER, ARE NOT
WAAAH!
JIM DAVIS 12-30

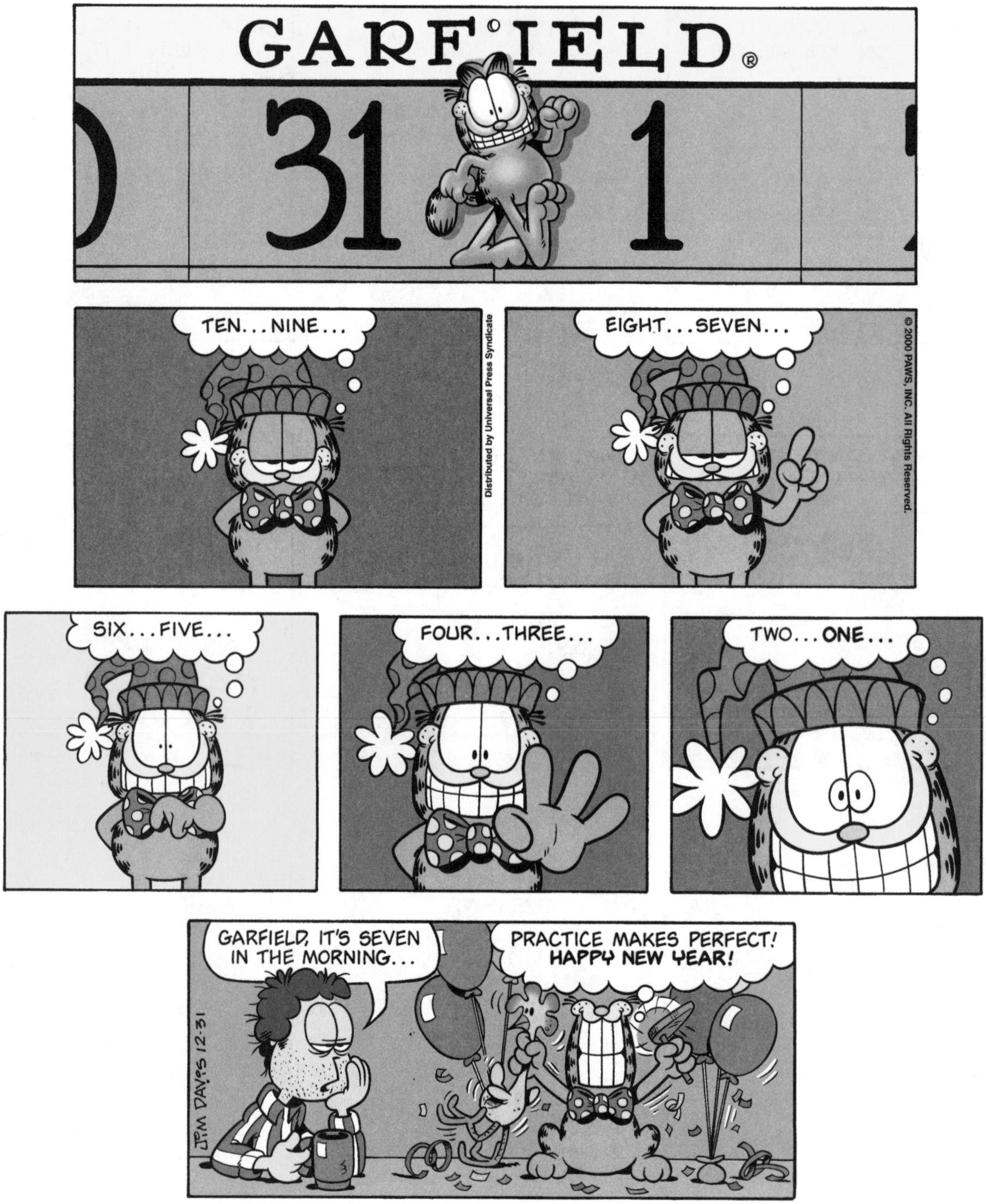
GARFIELD®
31
1
Distributed by Universal Press Syndicate
TEN...NINE...
EIGHT...SEVEN...
© 2000 PAWS, INC. All Rights Reserved.
SIX...FIVE...
FOUR...THREE...
TWO...ONE...
JPM DAVPS 12·31
GARFIELD, IT'S SEVEN IN THE MORNING...
PRACTICE MAKES PERFECT! HAPPY NEW YEAR!

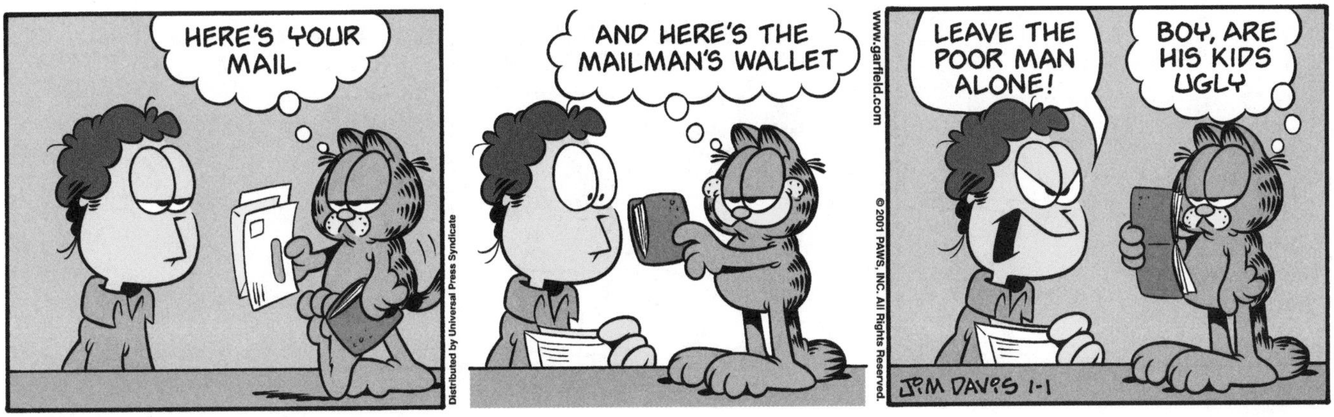
HERE'S YOUR MAIL
Distributed by Universal Press Syndicate
AND HERE'S THE MAILMAN'S WALLET
www.garfield.com
© 2001 PAWS, INC. All Rights Reserved.
LEAVE THE POOR MAN ALONE!
BOY, ARE HIS KIDS UGLY
JIM DAVIS 1-1

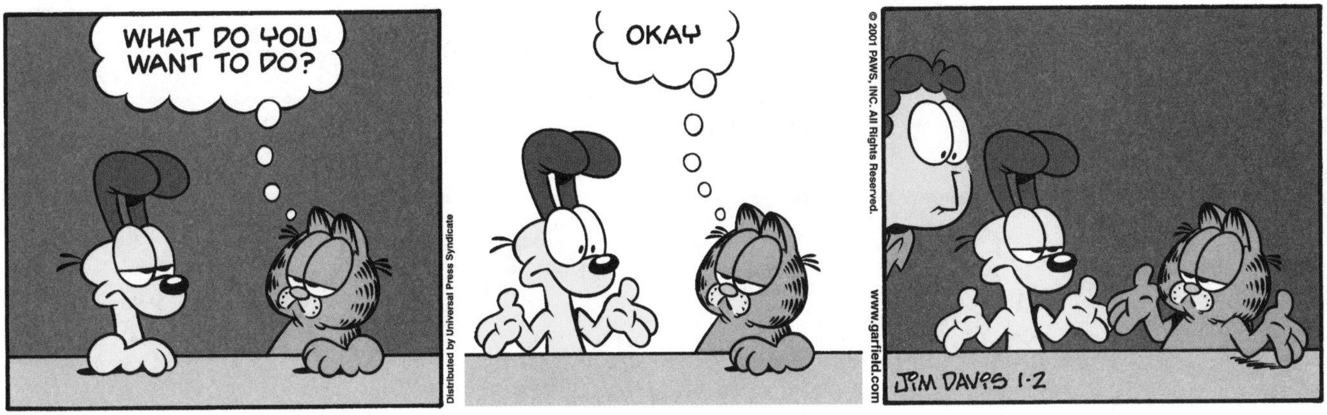
WHAT DO YOU WANT TO DO?
Distributed by Universal Press Syndicate
OKAY
© 2001 PAWS, INC. All Rights Reserved.
www.garfield.com
JIM DAVIS 1-2

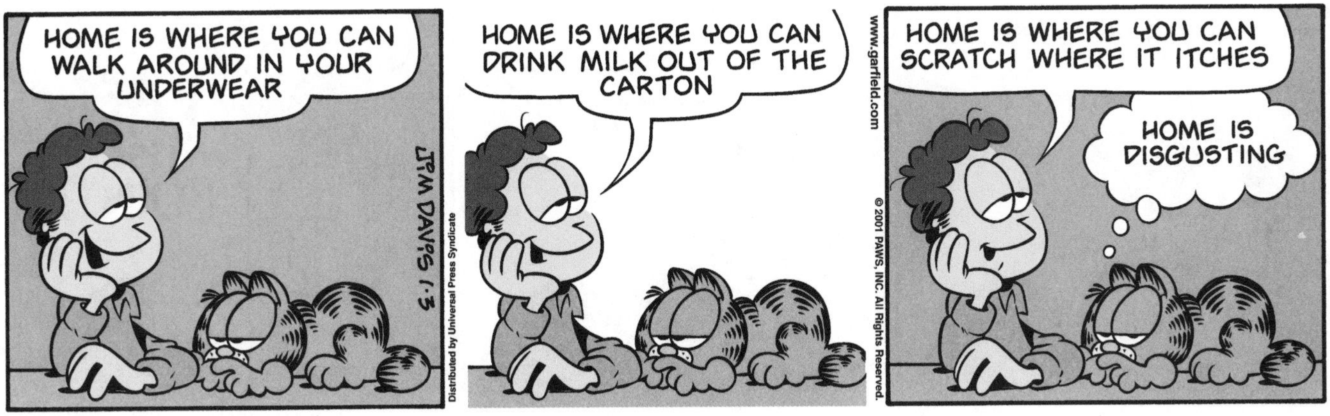
HOME IS WHERE YOU CAN WALK AROUND IN YOUR UNDERWEAR
JIM DAVIS 1-3
Distributed by Universal Press Syndicate
HOME IS WHERE YOU CAN DRINK MILK OUT OF THE CARTON
www.garfield.com
© 2001 PAWS, INC. All Rights Reserved.
HOME IS WHERE YOU CAN SCRATCH WHERE IT ITCHES
HOME IS DISGUSTING

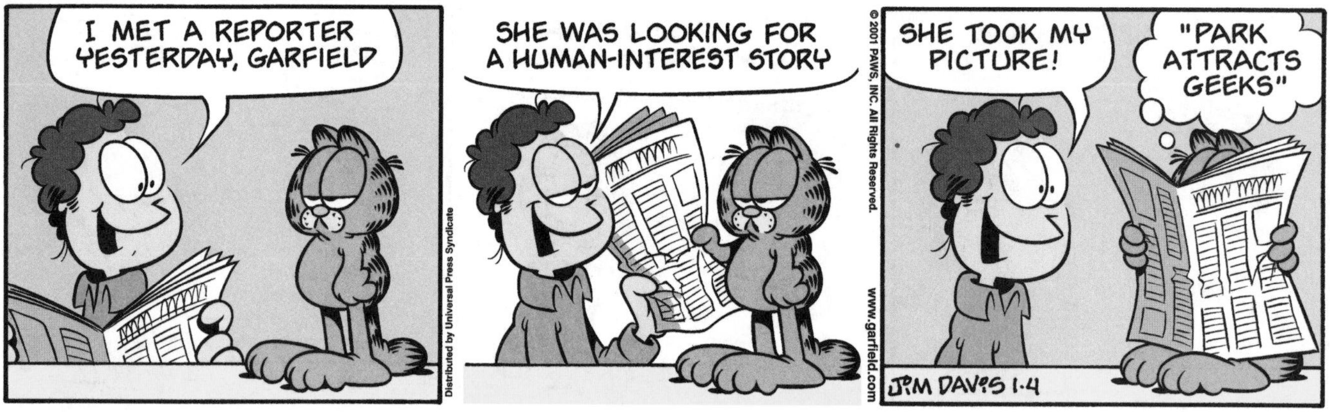
I MET A REPORTER YESTERDAY, GARFIELD
Distributed by Universal Press Syndicate
SHE WAS LOOKING FOR A HUMAN-INTEREST STORY
© 2001 PAWS, INC. All Rights Reserved.
www.garfield.com
SHE TOOK MY PICTURE!
"PARK ATTRACTS GEEKS"
JIM DAVIS 1-4

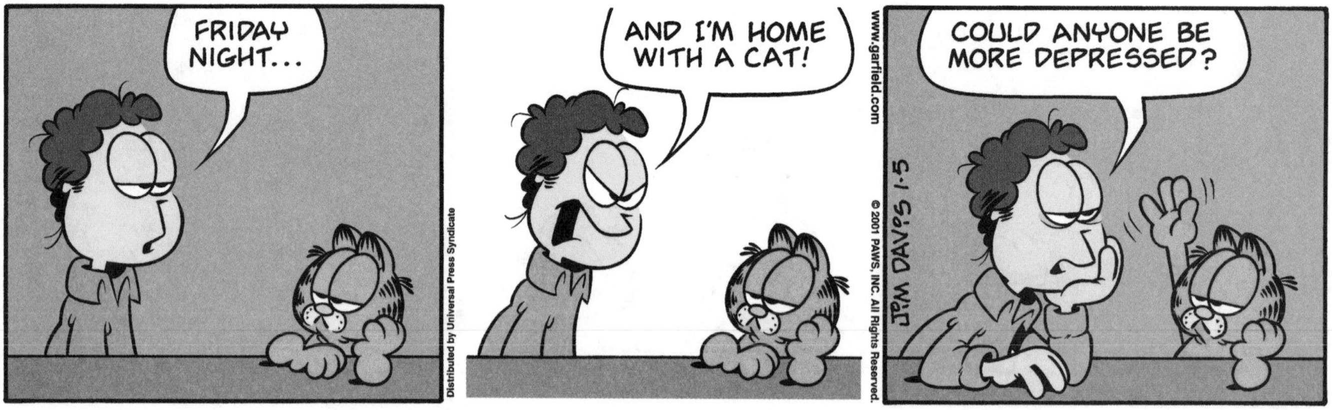
FRIDAY NIGHT...
Distributed by Universal Press Syndicate
AND I'M HOME WITH A CAT!
www.garfield.com
© 2001 PAWS, INC. All Rights Reserved.
JIM DAVIS 1-5
COULD ANYONE BE MORE DEPRESSED?

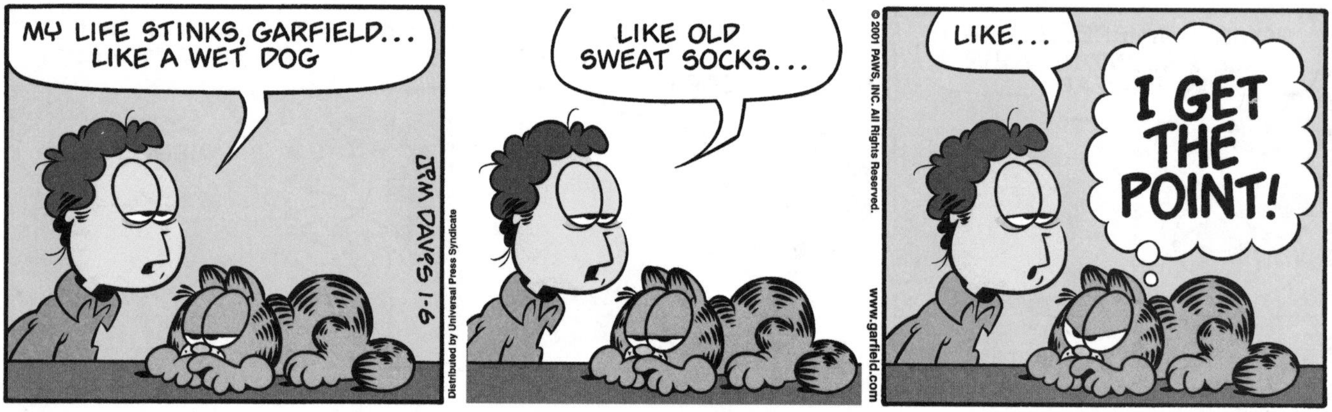
MY LIFE STINKS, GARFIELD... LIKE A WET DOG
JIM DAVIS 1-6
Distributed by Universal Press Syndicate
LIKE OLD SWEAT SOCKS...
© 2001 PAWS, INC. All Rights Reserved.
www.garfield.com
LIKE...
I GET THE POINT!

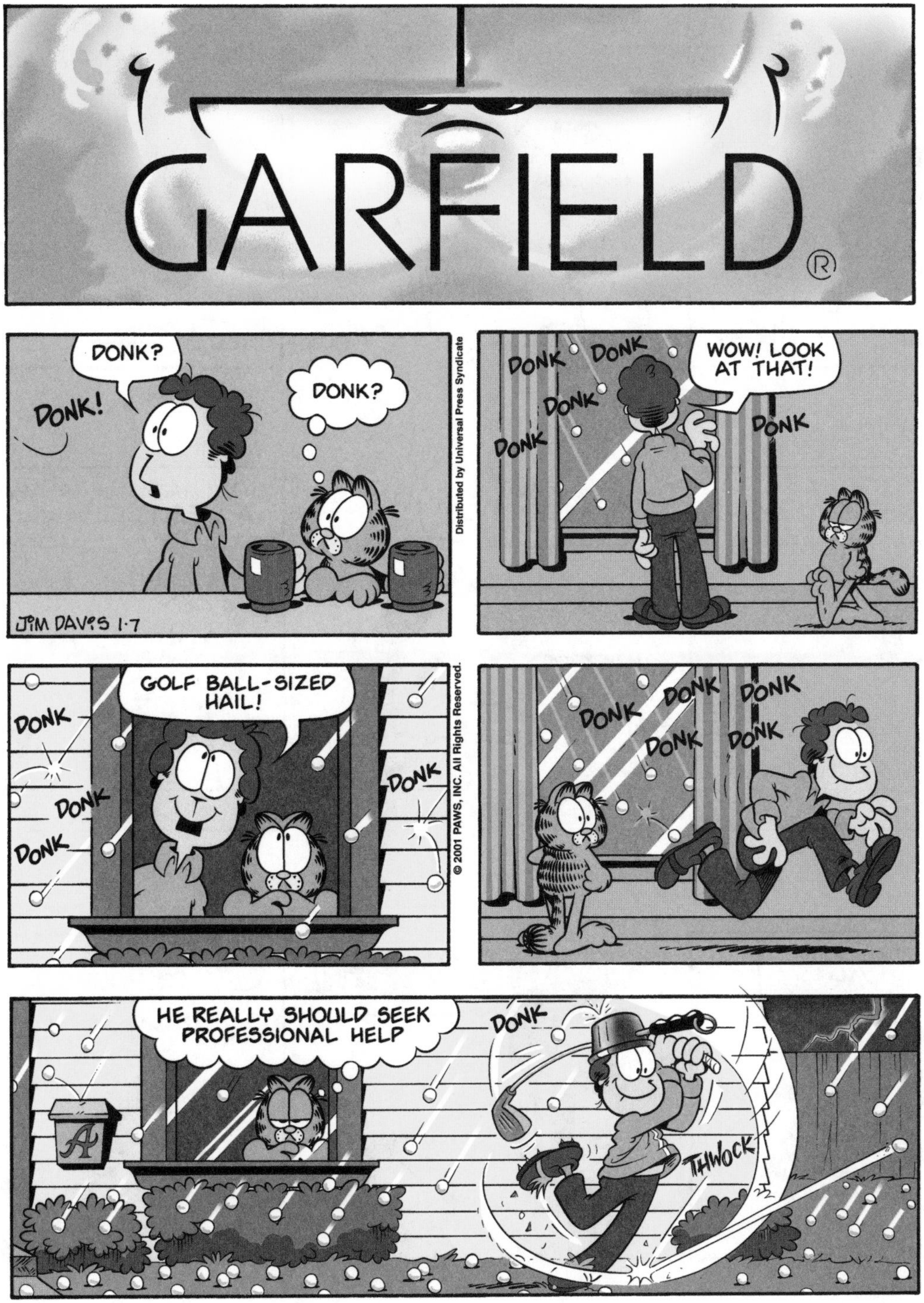
GARFIELD®
DONK!
DONK?
DONK?
JIM DAVIS 1·7
Distributed by Universal Press Syndicate
DONK DONK
DONK
DONK
WOW! LOOK AT THAT!
DONK
GOLF BALL-SIZED HAIL!
DONK
DONK
DONK
DONK
© 2001 PAWS, INC. All Rights Reserved.
DONK DONK DONK
DONK DONK
HE REALLY SHOULD SEEK PROFESSIONAL HELP
DONK
THWOCK

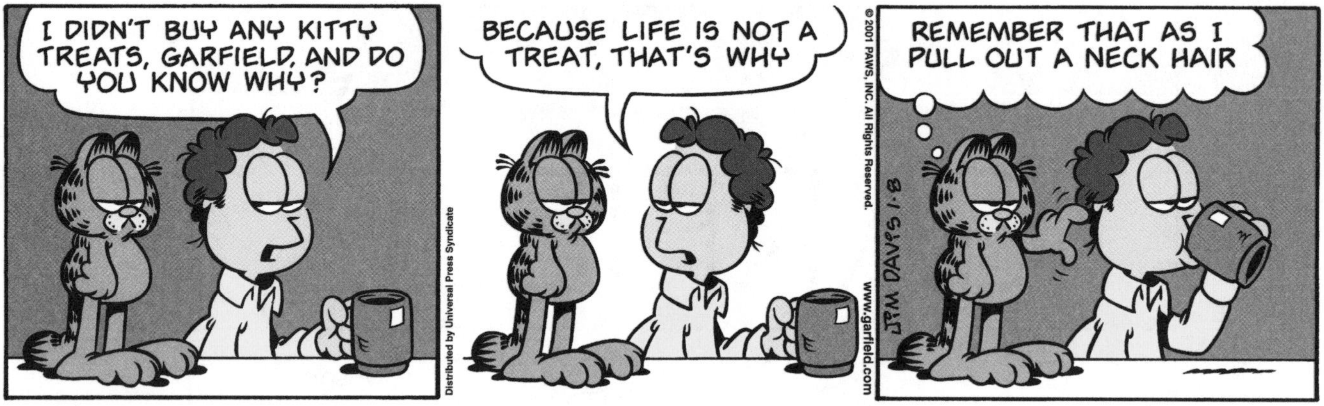
I DIDN'T BUY ANY KITTY TREATS, GARFIELD, AND DO YOU KNOW WHY?
BECAUSE LIFE IS NOT A TREAT, THAT'S WHY
REMEMBER THAT AS I PULL OUT A NECK HAIR
Distributed by Universal Press Syndicate
© 2001 PAWS, INC. All Rights Reserved.
www.garfield.com
JIM DAVIS 1-8

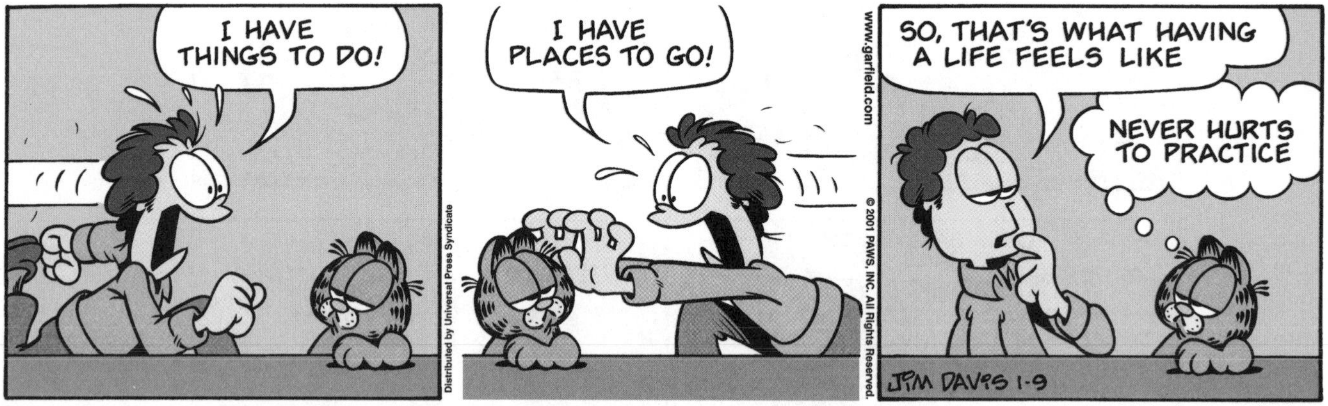
I HAVE THINGS TO DO!
I HAVE PLACES TO GO!
SO, THAT'S WHAT HAVING A LIFE FEELS LIKE
NEVER HURTS TO PRACTICE
Distributed by Universal Press Syndicate
www.garfield.com
© 2001 PAWS, INC. All Rights Reserved.
JIM DAVIS 1-9

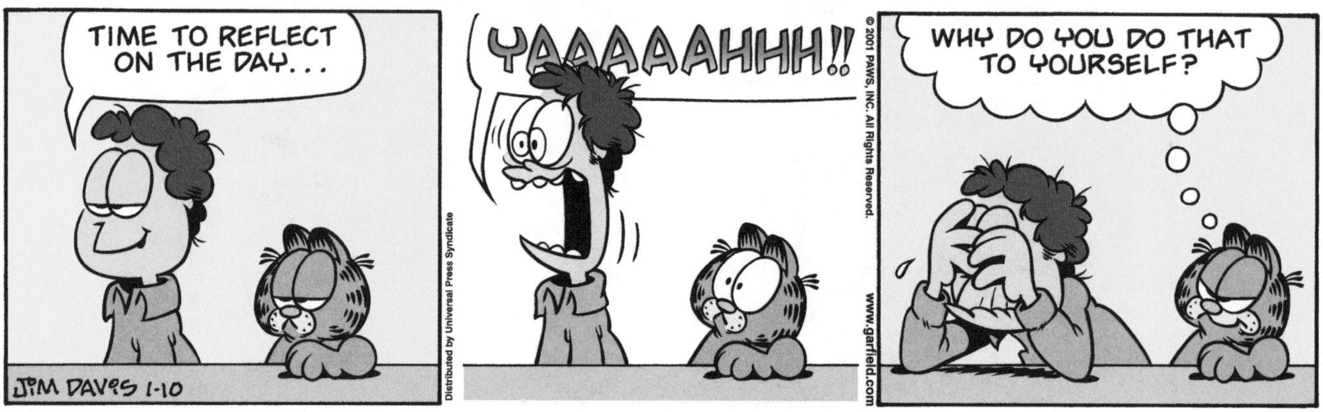
TIME TO REFLECT ON THE DAY...
YAAAAAHHH!!
WHY DO YOU DO THAT TO YOURSELF?
JIM DAVIS 1-10
Distributed by Universal Press Syndicate
© 2001 PAWS, INC. All Rights Reserved.
www.garfield.com

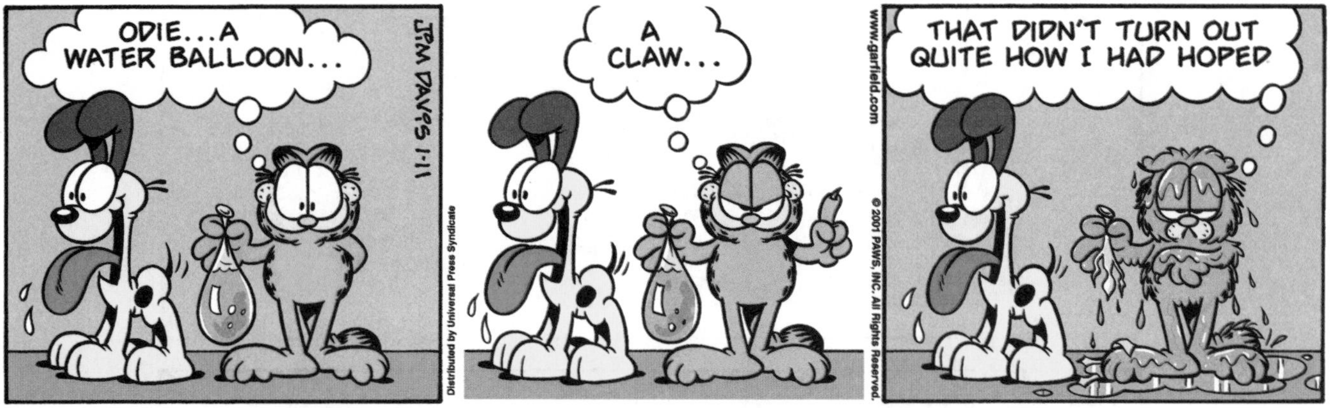
ODIE...A WATER BALLOON...
JIM DAVIS 1-11
Distributed by Universal Press Syndicate
A CLAW...
www.garfield.com
© 2001 PAWS, INC. All Rights Reserved.
THAT DIDN'T TURN OUT QUITE HOW I HAD HOPED

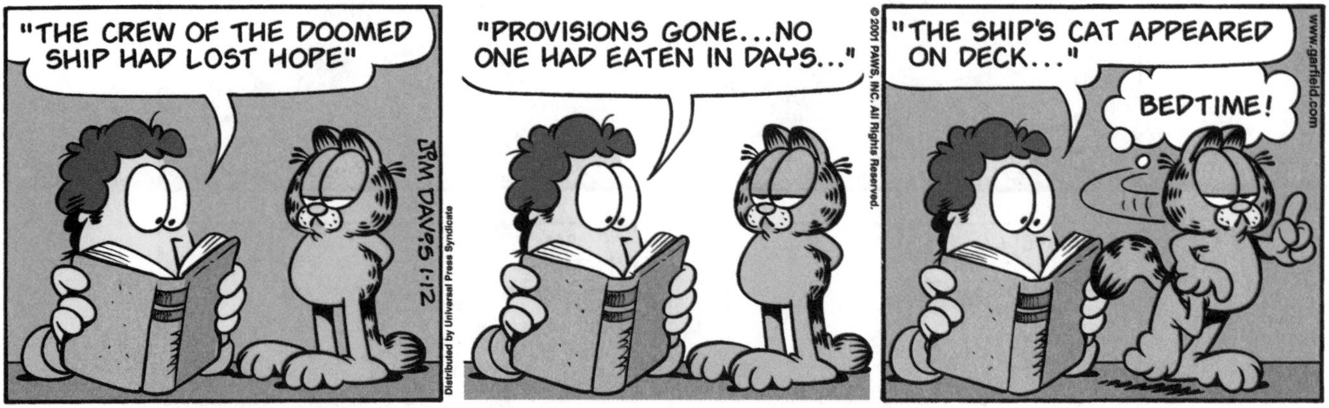
"THE CREW OF THE DOOMED SHIP HAD LOST HOPE"
JIM DAVIS 1-12
Distributed by Universal Press Syndicate
"PROVISIONS GONE...NO ONE HAD EATEN IN DAYS..."
© 2001 PAWS, INC. All Rights Reserved.
"THE SHIP'S CAT APPEARED ON DECK..."
BEDTIME!
www.garfield.com

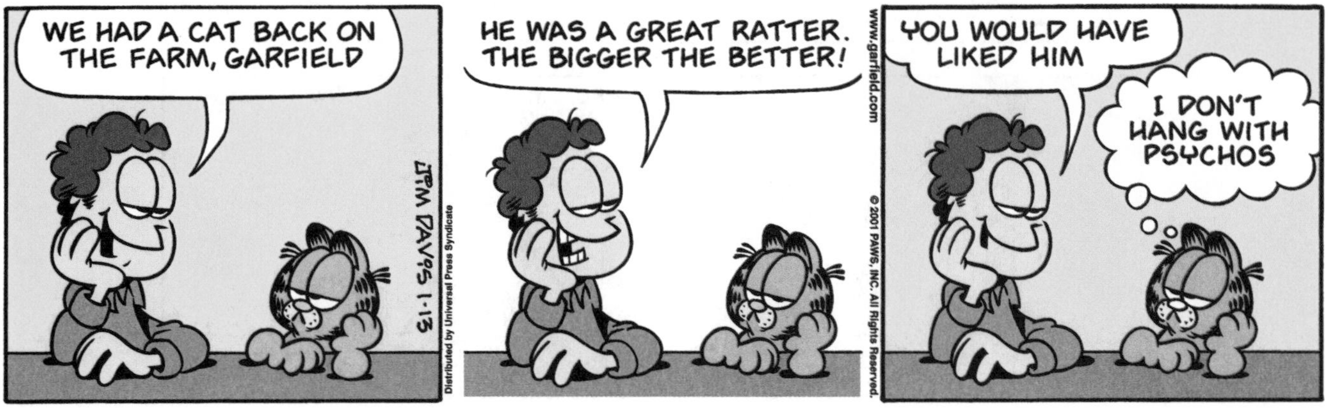
WE HAD A CAT BACK ON THE FARM, GARFIELD
JIM DAVIS 1-13
Distributed by Universal Press Syndicate
HE WAS A GREAT RATTER. THE BIGGER THE BETTER!
www.garfield.com
© 2001 PAWS, INC. All Rights Reserved.
YOU WOULD HAVE LIKED HIM
I DON'T HANG WITH PSYCHOS

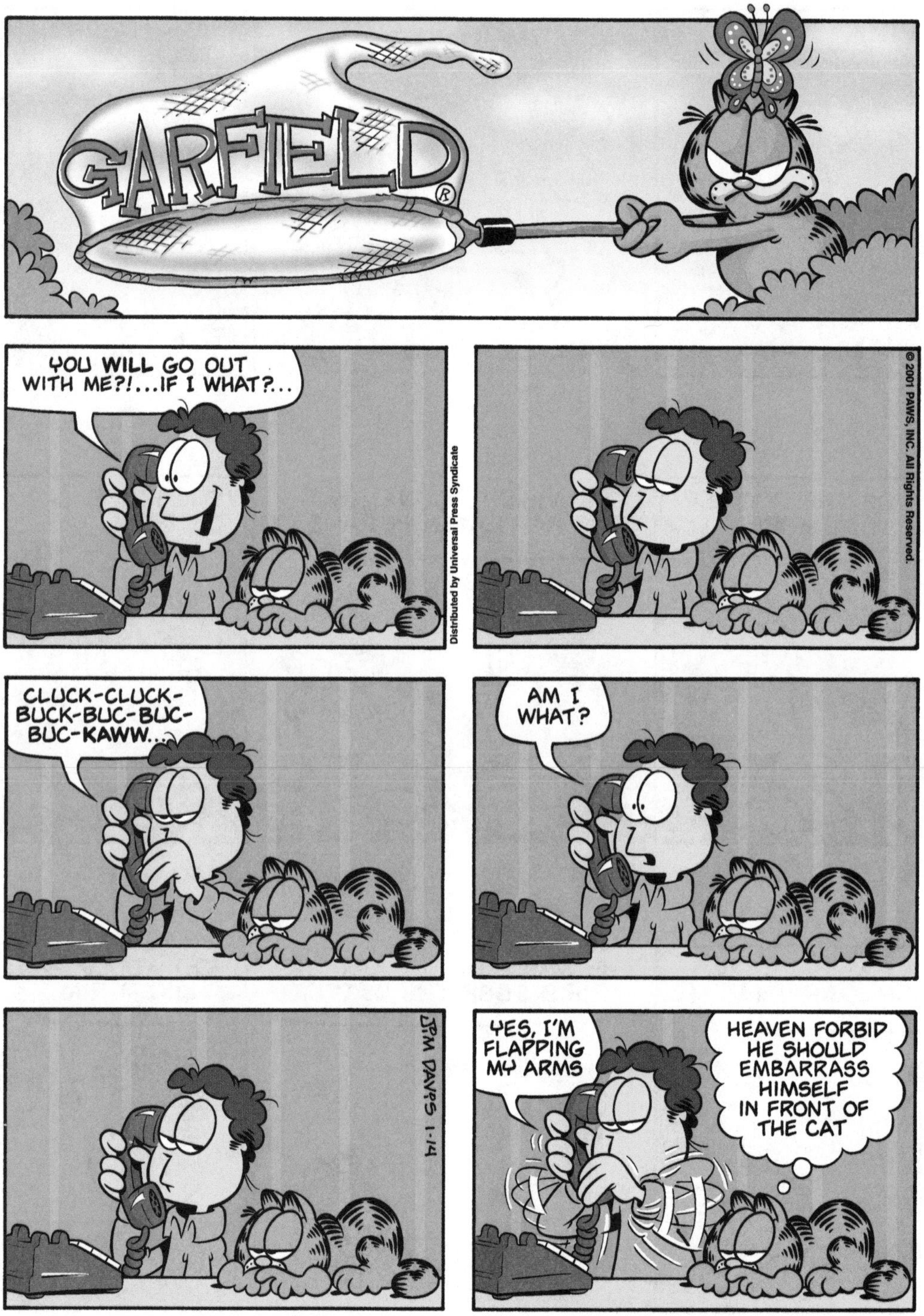
GARFIELD®
YOU WILL GO OUT WITH ME?!...IF I WHAT?...
Distributed by Universal Press Syndicate
© 2001 PAWS, INC. All Rights Reserved.
CLUCK-CLUCK-BUCK-BUC-BUC-BUC-KAWW...
AM I WHAT?
JPM DAVPS 1-14
YES, I'M FLAPPING MY ARMS
HEAVEN FORBID HE SHOULD EMBARRASS HIMSELF IN FRONT OF THE CAT

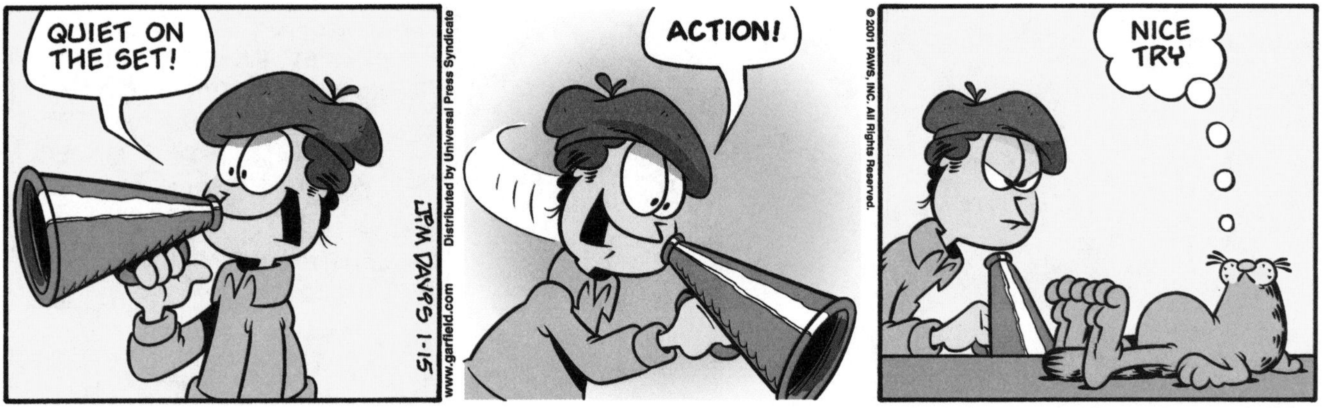
QUIET ON THE SET!
JIM DAVIS 1-15
Distributed by Universal Press Syndicate www.garfield.com
ACTION!
© 2001 PAWS, INC. All Rights Reserved.
NICE TRY

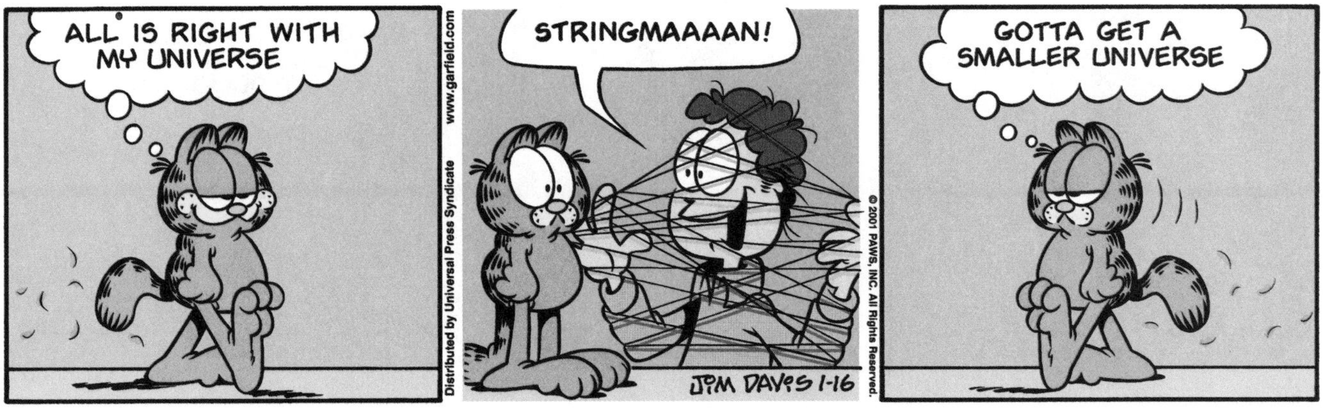
ALL IS RIGHT WITH MY UNIVERSE
Distributed by Universal Press Syndicate www.garfield.com
STRINGMAAAAN!
JIM DAVIS 1-16
© 2001 PAWS, INC. All Rights Reserved.
GOTTA GET A SMALLER UNIVERSE

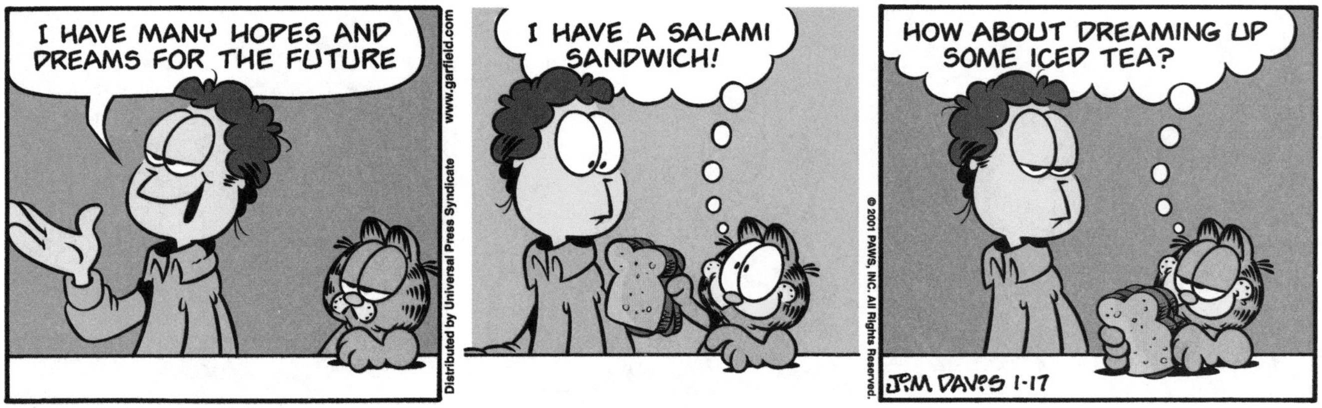
I HAVE MANY HOPES AND DREAMS FOR THE FUTURE
Distributed by Universal Press Syndicate www.garfield.com
I HAVE A SALAMI SANDWICH!
© 2001 PAWS, INC. All Rights Reserved.
HOW ABOUT DREAMING UP SOME ICED TEA?
JIM DAVIS 1-17

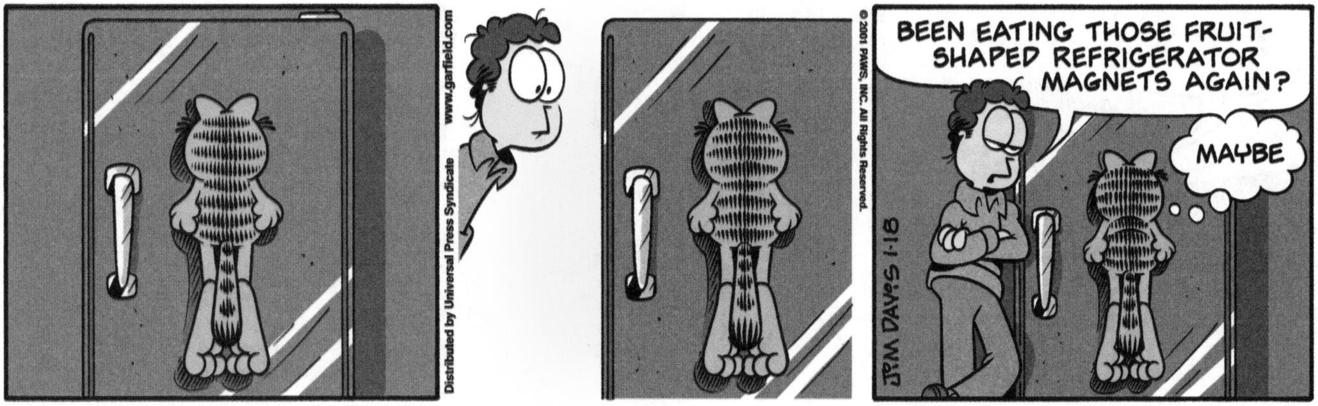
www.garfield.com
Distributed by Universal Press Syndicate
© 2001 PAWS, INC. All Rights Reserved.
JIM DAVIS 1-18
BEEN EATING THOSE FRUIT-SHAPED REFRIGERATOR MAGNETS AGAIN?
MAYBE

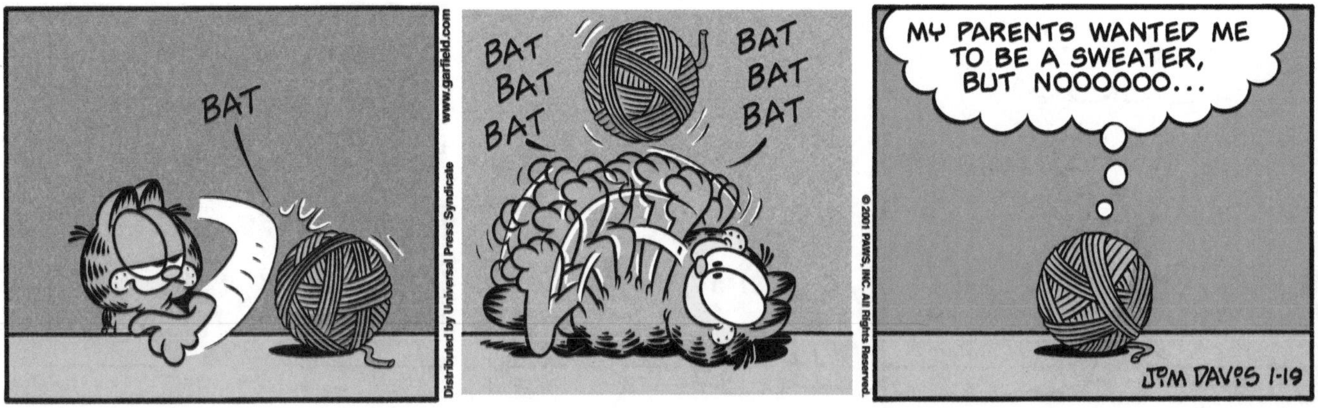
BAT
www.garfield.com
Distributed by Universal Press Syndicate
BAT BAT BAT
BAT BAT BAT
© 2001 PAWS, INC. All Rights Reserved.
MY PARENTS WANTED ME TO BE A SWEATER, BUT NOOOOOO...
JIM DAVIS 1-19

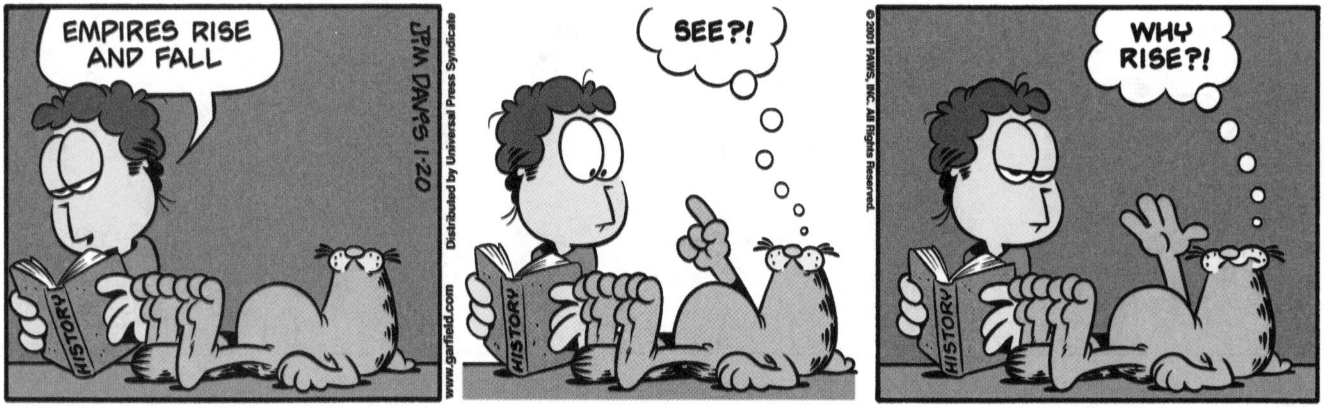
EMPIRES RISE AND FALL
HISTORY
JIM DAVIS 1-20
Distributed by Universal Press Syndicate
www.garfield.com
SEE?!
HISTORY
© 2001 PAWS, INC. All Rights Reserved.
WHY RISE?!
HISTORY

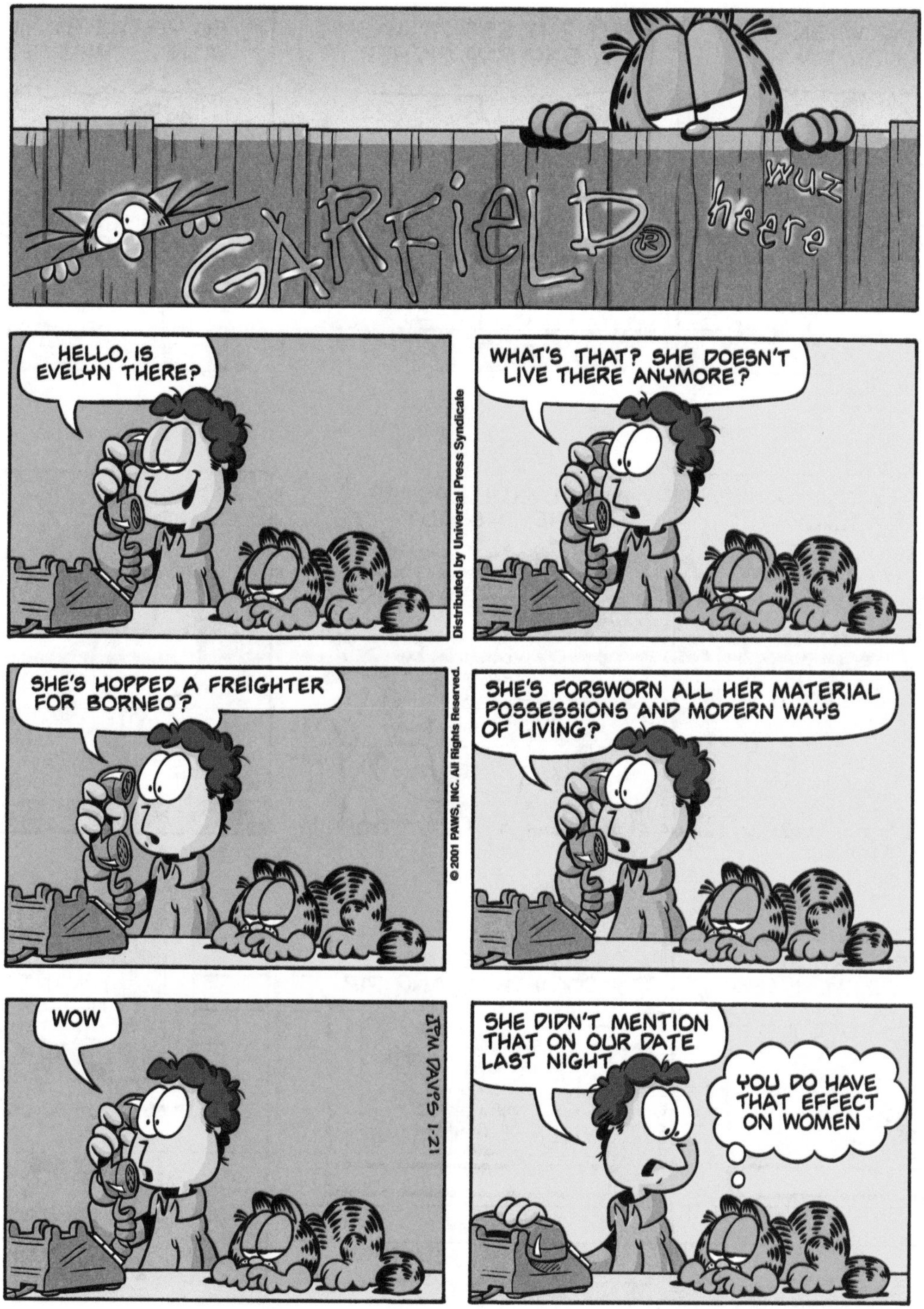
GARFIELD®
wuz heere
HELLO, IS EVELYN THERE?
WHAT'S THAT? SHE DOESN'T LIVE THERE ANYMORE?
SHE'S HOPPED A FREIGHTER FOR BORNEO?
SHE'S FORSWORN ALL HER MATERIAL POSSESSIONS AND MODERN WAYS OF LIVING?
WOW
SHE DIDN'T MENTION THAT ON OUR DATE LAST NIGHT
YOU DO HAVE THAT EFFECT ON WOMEN
JPM DAVPS 1-21
© 2001 PAWS, INC. All Rights Reserved. Distributed by Universal Press Syndicate

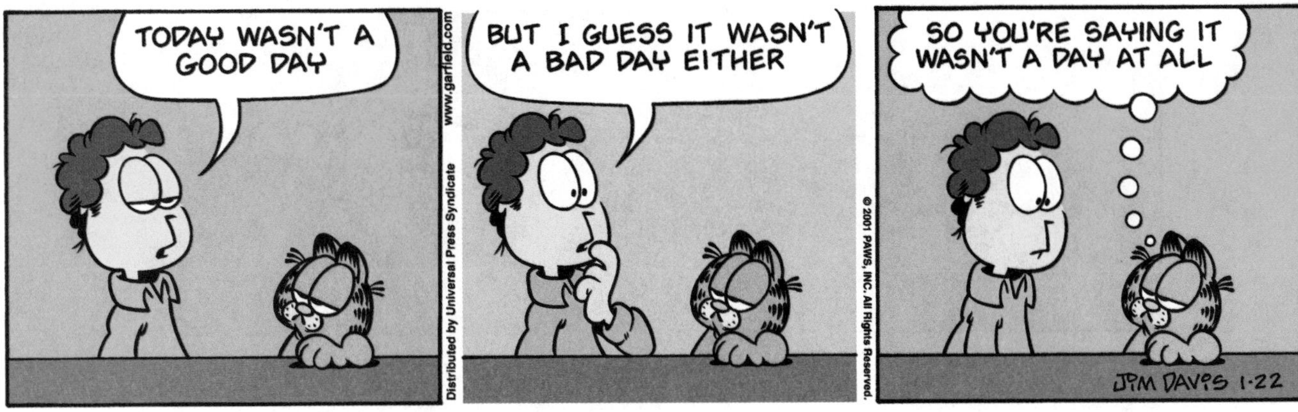
TODAY WASN'T A GOOD DAY
BUT I GUESS IT WASN'T A BAD DAY EITHER
SO YOU'RE SAYING IT WASN'T A DAY AT ALL
JIM DAVIS 1·22
Distributed by Universal Press Syndicate www.garfield.com
© 2001 PAWS, INC. All Rights Reserved.

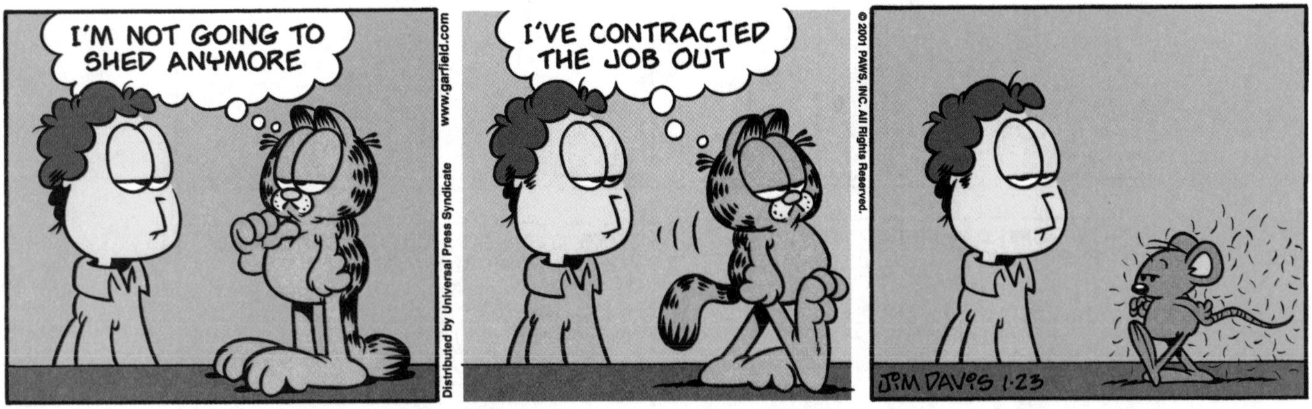
I'M NOT GOING TO SHED ANYMORE
I'VE CONTRACTED THE JOB OUT
JIM DAVIS 1·23
Distributed by Universal Press Syndicate www.garfield.com
© 2001 PAWS, INC. All Rights Reserved.

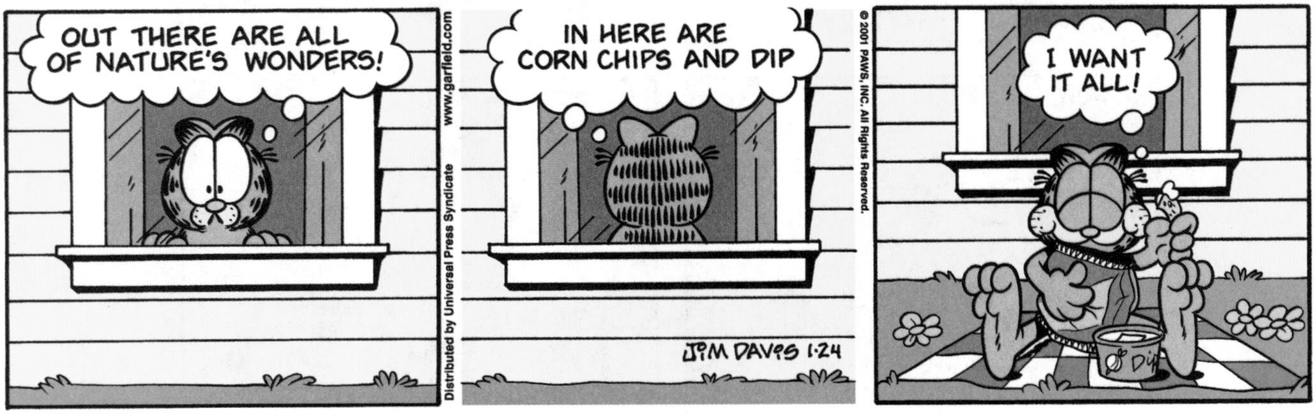
OUT THERE ARE ALL OF NATURE'S WONDERS!
IN HERE ARE CORN CHIPS AND DIP
I WANT IT ALL!
JIM DAVIS 1·24
Distributed by Universal Press Syndicate www.garfield.com
© 2001 PAWS, INC. All Rights Reserved.

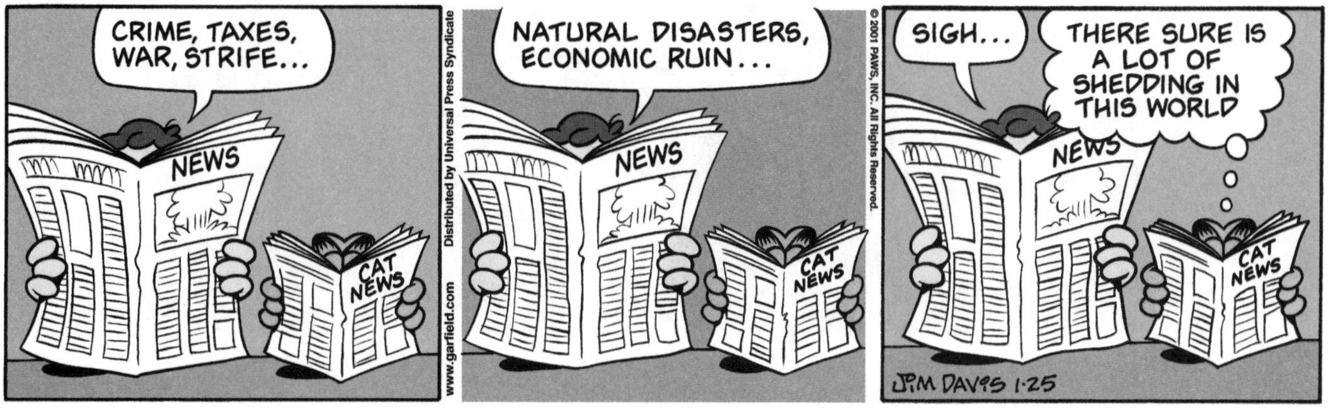
CRIME, TAXES, WAR, STRIFE...
NEWS
CAT NEWS
www.garfield.com
Distributed by Universal Press Syndicate
NATURAL DISASTERS, ECONOMIC RUIN...
NEWS
CAT NEWS
© 2001 PAWS, INC. All Rights Reserved.
SIGH...
THERE SURE IS A LOT OF SHEDDING IN THIS WORLD
NEWS
CAT NEWS
JIM DAVIS 1·25

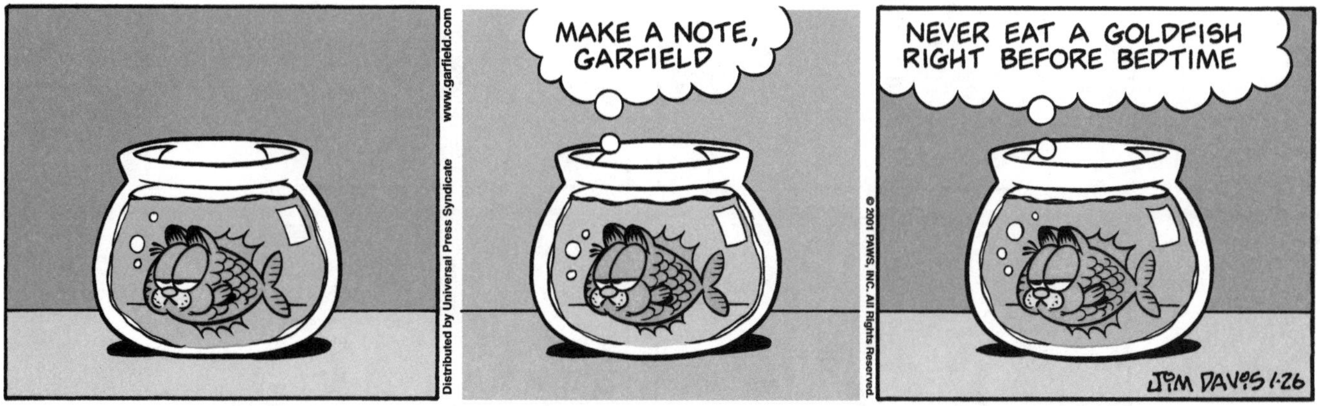
Distributed by Universal Press Syndicate
www.garfield.com
MAKE A NOTE, GARFIELD
© 2001 PAWS, INC. All Rights Reserved.
NEVER EAT A GOLDFISH RIGHT BEFORE BEDTIME
JIM DAVIS 1·26

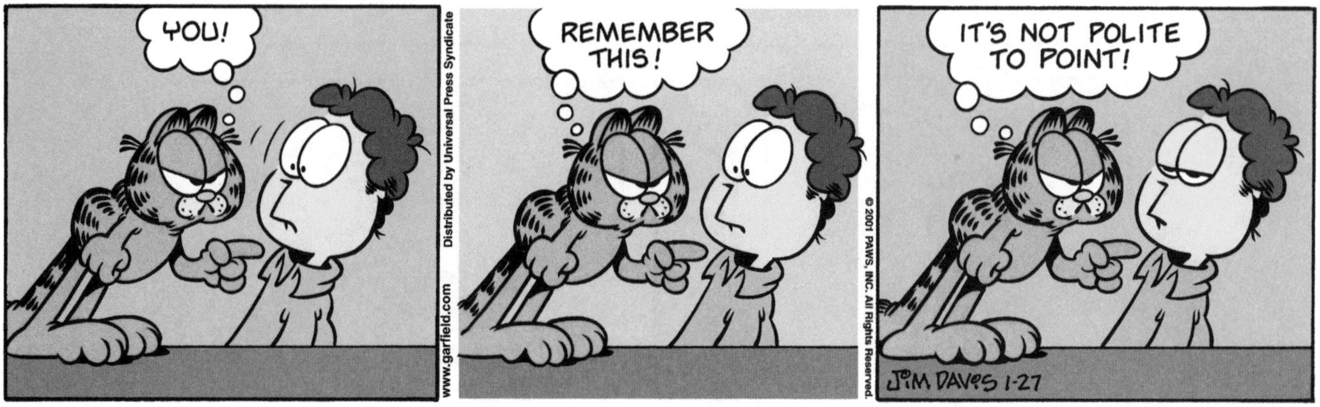
YOU!
www.garfield.com
Distributed by Universal Press Syndicate
REMEMBER THIS!
© 2001 PAWS, INC. All Rights Reserved.
IT'S NOT POLITE TO POINT!
JIM DAVIS 1·27

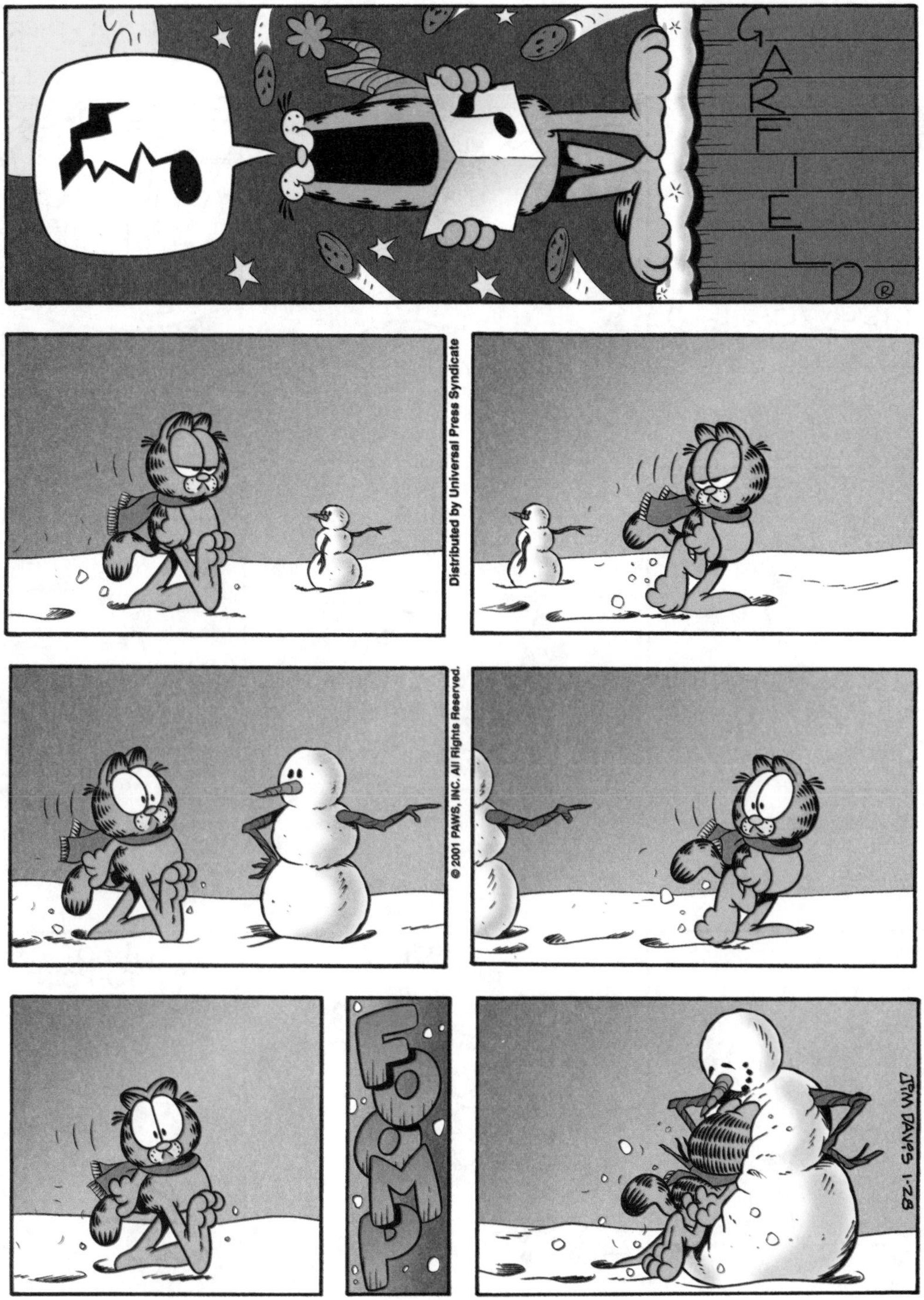
GARFIELD®
Distributed by Universal Press Syndicate
© 2001 PAWS, INC. All Rights Reserved.
FOMP
JIM DAVIS 1-28

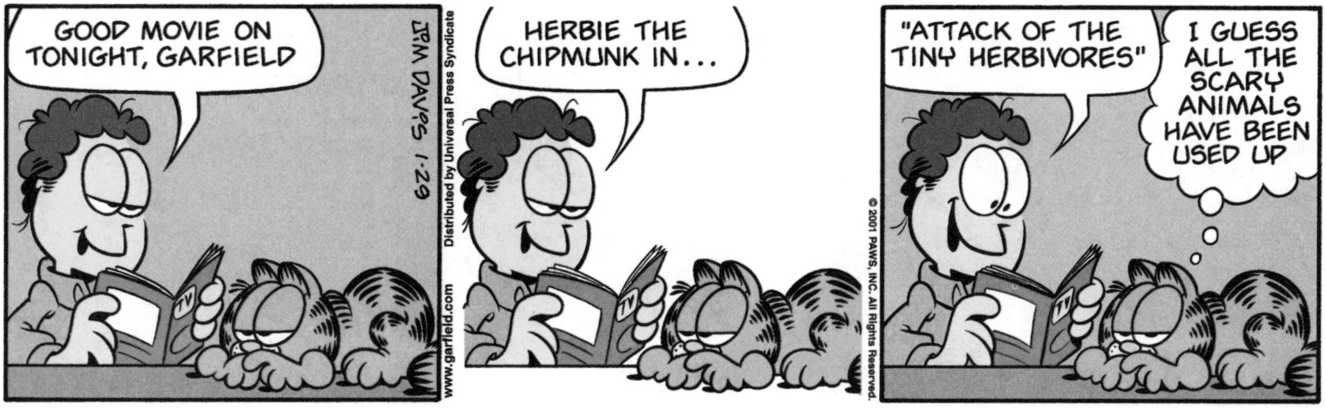
GOOD MOVIE ON TONIGHT, GARFIELD
JIM DAVIS 1-29
HERBIE THE CHIPMUNK IN...
"ATTACK OF THE TINY HERBIVORES"
I GUESS ALL THE SCARY ANIMALS HAVE BEEN USED UP
Distributed by Universal Press Syndicate
www.garfield.com
© 2001 PAWS, INC. All Rights Reserved.

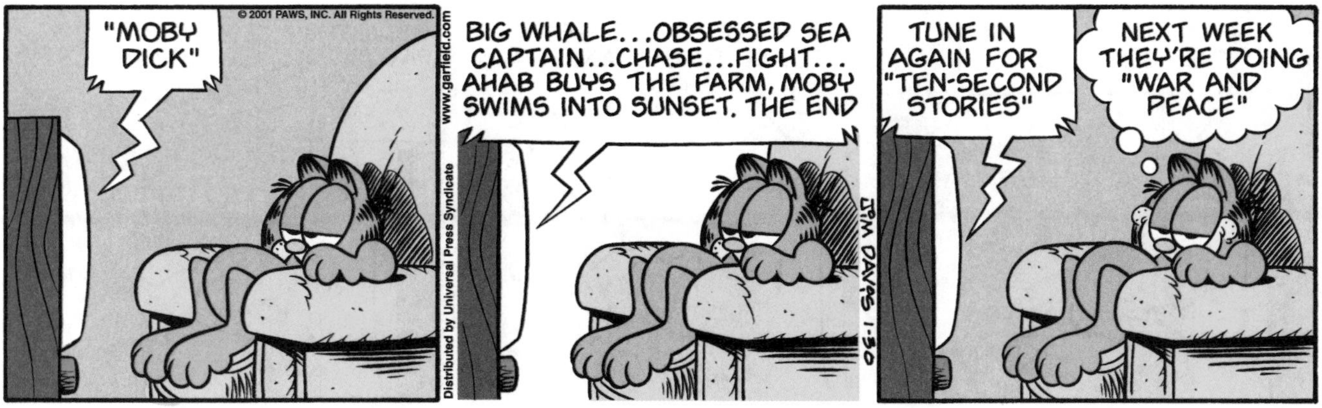
"MOBY DICK"
© 2001 PAWS, INC. All Rights Reserved.
BIG WHALE...OBSESSED SEA CAPTAIN...CHASE...FIGHT... AHAB BUYS THE FARM, MOBY SWIMS INTO SUNSET. THE END
TUNE IN AGAIN FOR "TEN-SECOND STORIES"
NEXT WEEK THEY'RE DOING "WAR AND PEACE"
JIM DAVIS 1-30
www.garfield.com
Distributed by Universal Press Syndicate

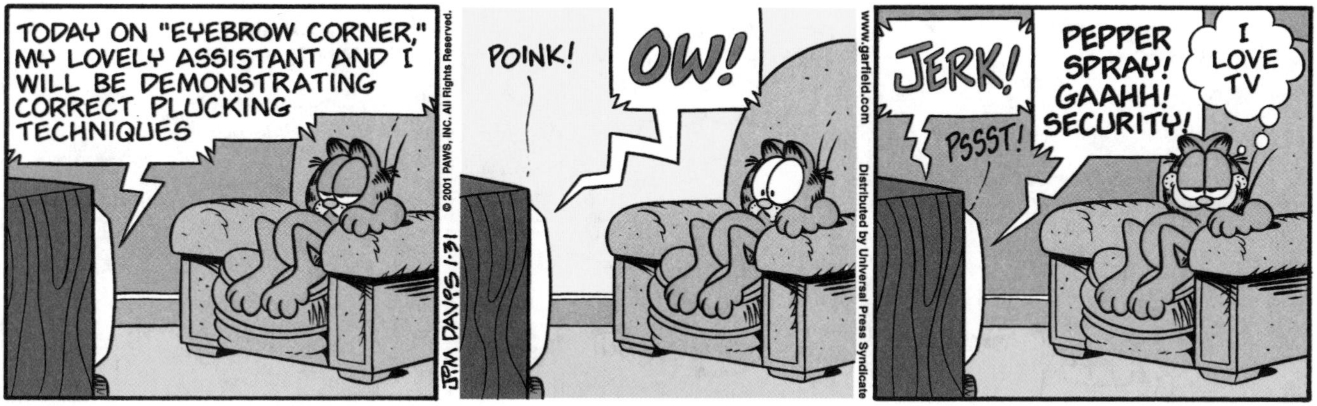
TODAY ON "EYEBROW CORNER," MY LOVELY ASSISTANT AND I WILL BE DEMONSTRATING CORRECT PLUCKING TECHNIQUES
JIM DAVIS 1-31
© 2001 PAWS, INC. All Rights Reserved.
POINK!
OW!
JERK!
PSSST!
PEPPER SPRAY! GAAHH! SECURITY!
I LOVE TV
www.garfield.com
Distributed by Universal Press Syndicate

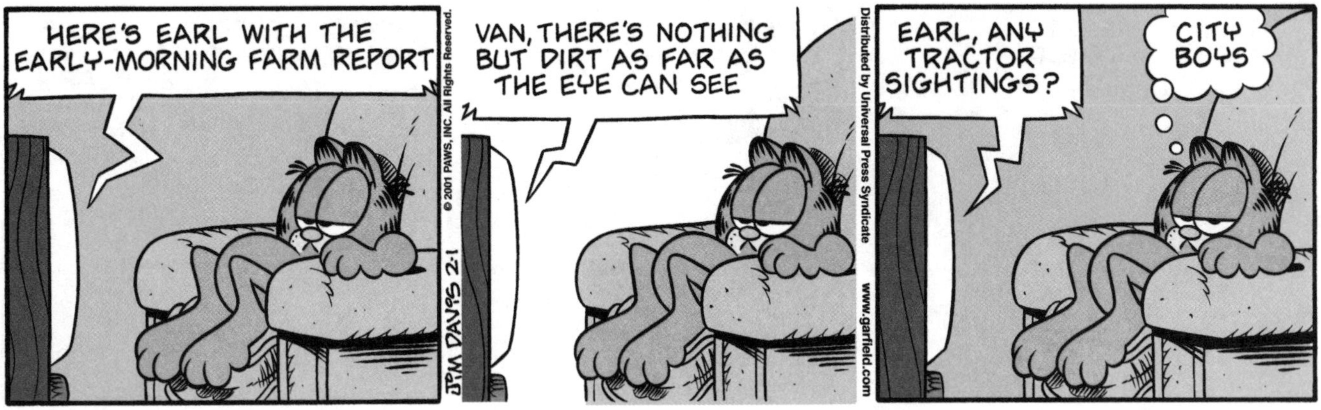
HERE'S EARL WITH THE EARLY-MORNING FARM REPORT
© 2001 PAWS, INC. All Rights Reserved.
JIM DAVIS 2·1
VAN, THERE'S NOTHING BUT DIRT AS FAR AS THE EYE CAN SEE
Distributed by Universal Press Syndicate www.garfield.com
EARL, ANY TRACTOR SIGHTINGS?
CITY BOYS

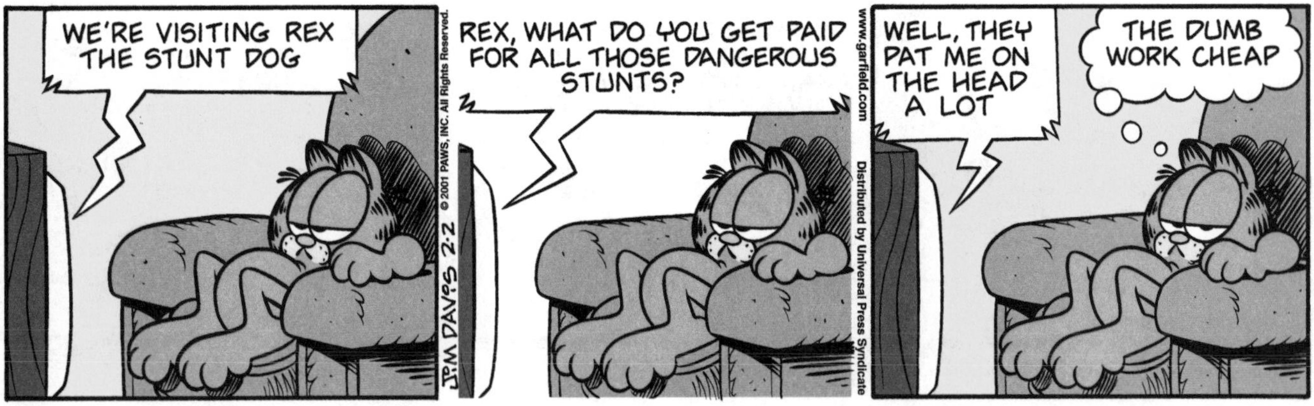
WE'RE VISITING REX THE STUNT DOG
© 2001 PAWS, INC. All Rights Reserved.
JIM DAVIS 2·2
REX, WHAT DO YOU GET PAID FOR ALL THOSE DANGEROUS STUNTS?
www.garfield.com Distributed by Universal Press Syndicate
WELL, THEY PAT ME ON THE HEAD A LOT
THE DUMB WORK CHEAP

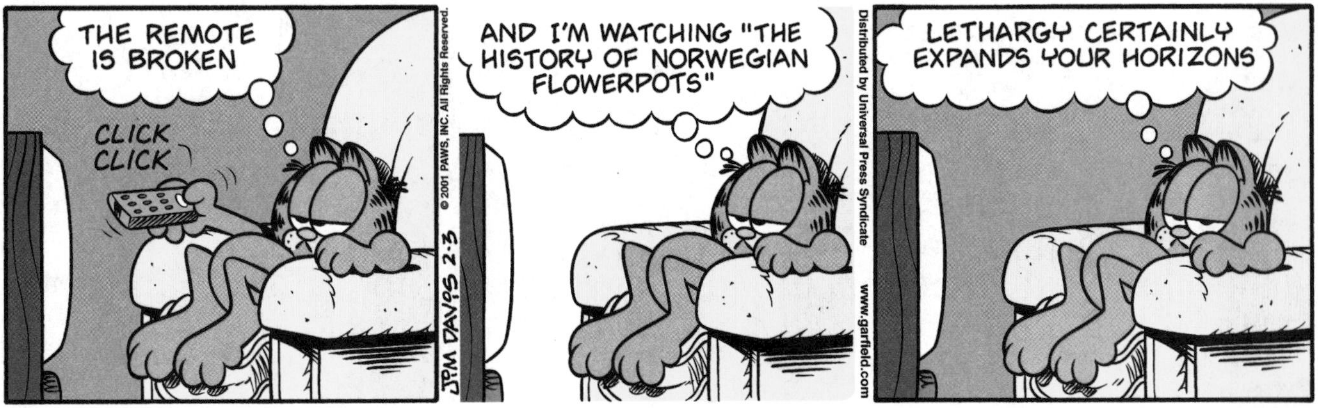
THE REMOTE IS BROKEN
CLICK CLICK
© 2001 PAWS, INC. All Rights Reserved.
JIM DAVIS 2·3
AND I'M WATCHING "THE HISTORY OF NORWEGIAN FLOWERPOTS"
Distributed by Universal Press Syndicate www.garfield.com
LETHARGY CERTAINLY EXPANDS YOUR HORIZONS

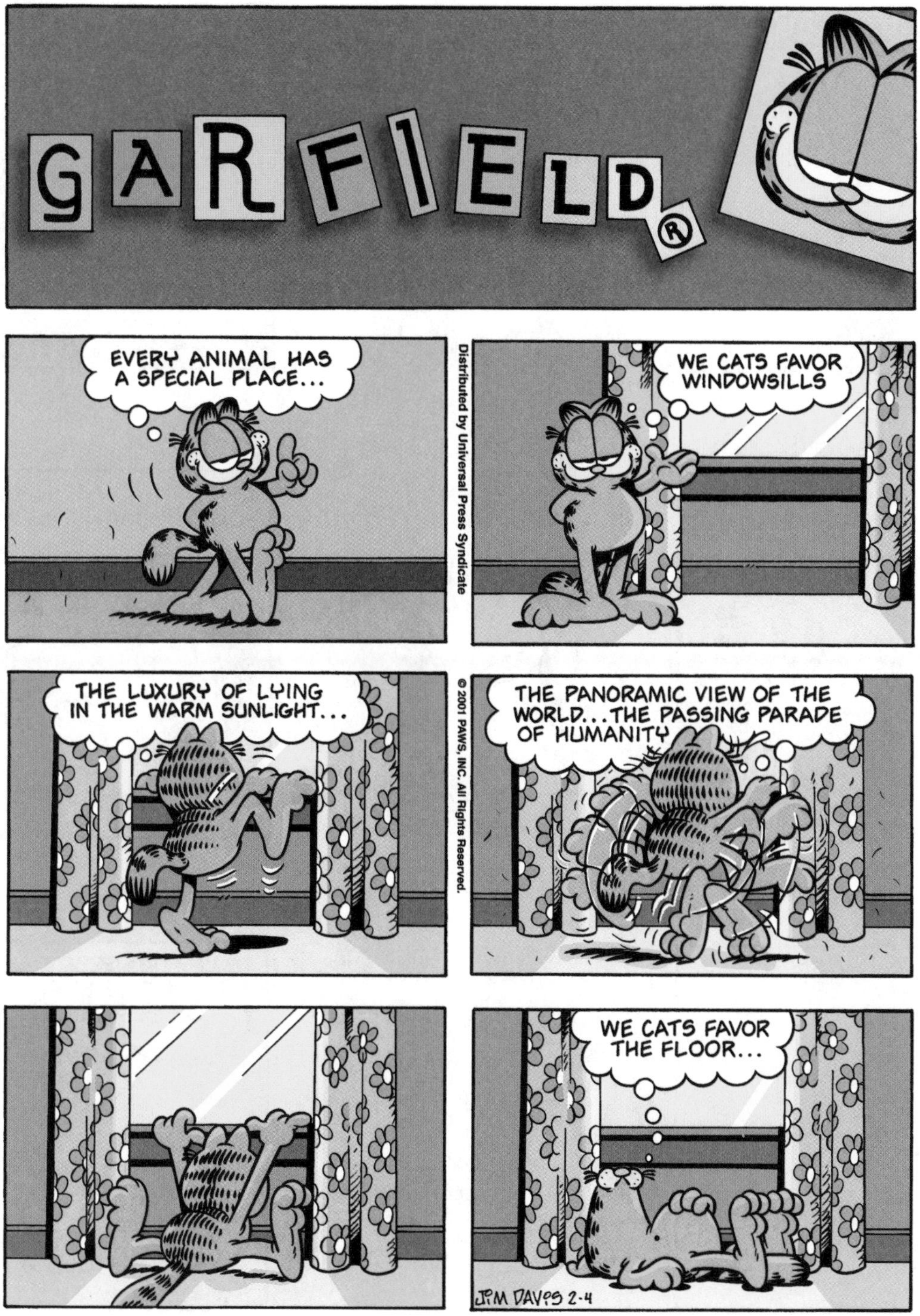
GARFIELD®
EVERY ANIMAL HAS A SPECIAL PLACE...
WE CATS FAVOR WINDOWSILLS
THE LUXURY OF LYING IN THE WARM SUNLIGHT...
THE PANORAMIC VIEW OF THE WORLD...THE PASSING PARADE OF HUMANITY
WE CATS FAVOR THE FLOOR...
JIM DAVIS 2-4
Distributed by Universal Press Syndicate
© 2001 PAWS, INC. All Rights Reserved.

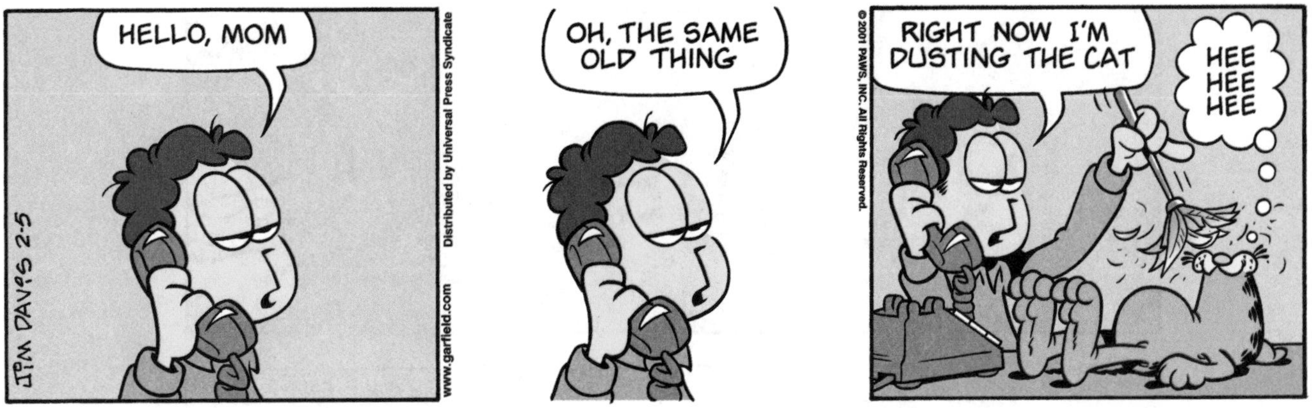
HELLO, MOM
OH, THE SAME OLD THING
RIGHT NOW I'M DUSTING THE CAT
HEE HEE HEE
JIM DAVIS 2-5
www.garfield.com Distributed by Universal Press Syndicate
© 2001 PAWS, INC. All Rights Reserved.

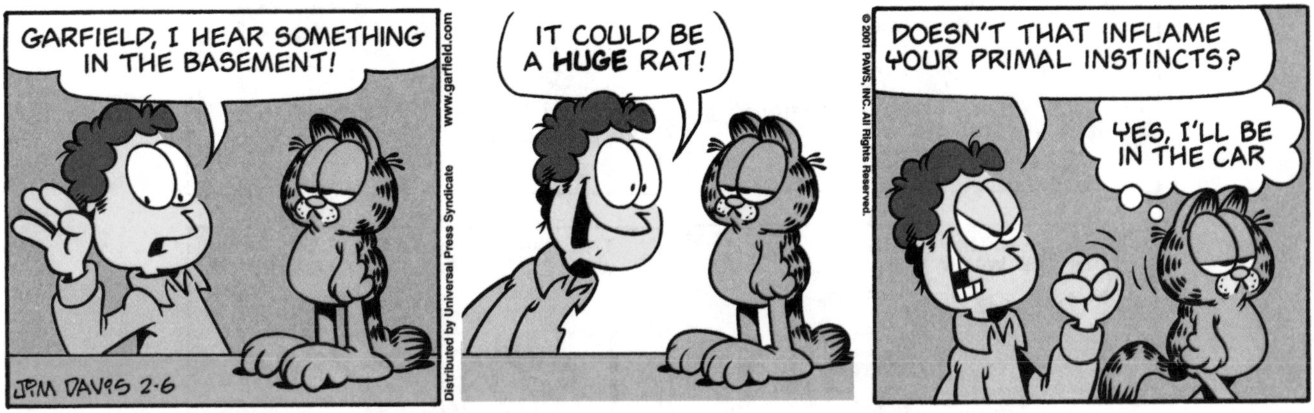
GARFIELD, I HEAR SOMETHING IN THE BASEMENT!
IT COULD BE A **HUGE** RAT!
DOESN'T THAT INFLAME YOUR PRIMAL INSTINCTS?
YES, I'LL BE IN THE CAR
JIM DAVIS 2-6
www.garfield.com Distributed by Universal Press Syndicate
© 2001 PAWS, INC. All Rights Reserved.

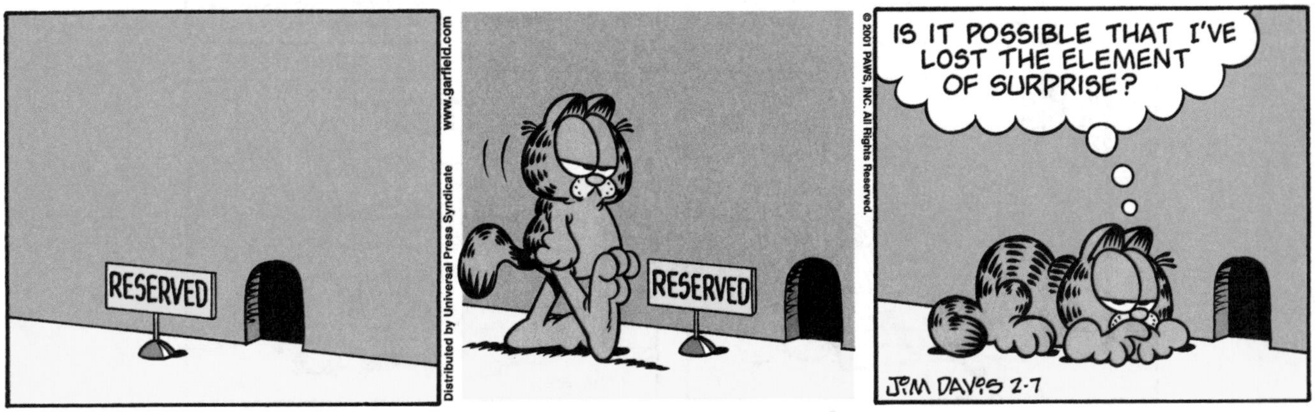
RESERVED
RESERVED
IS IT POSSIBLE THAT I'VE LOST THE ELEMENT OF SURPRISE?
JIM DAVIS 2-7
www.garfield.com Distributed by Universal Press Syndicate
© 2001 PAWS, INC. All Rights Reserved.

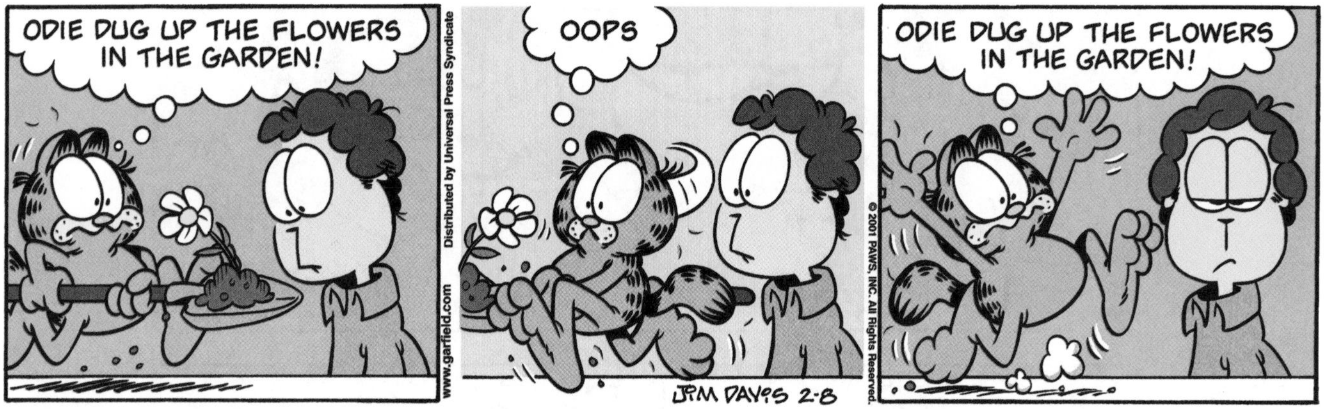
ODIE DUG UP THE FLOWERS IN THE GARDEN!
OOPS
ODIE DUG UP THE FLOWERS IN THE GARDEN!
JIM DAVIS 2-8
www.garfield.com Distributed by Universal Press Syndicate
© 2001 PAWS, INC. All Rights Reserved.

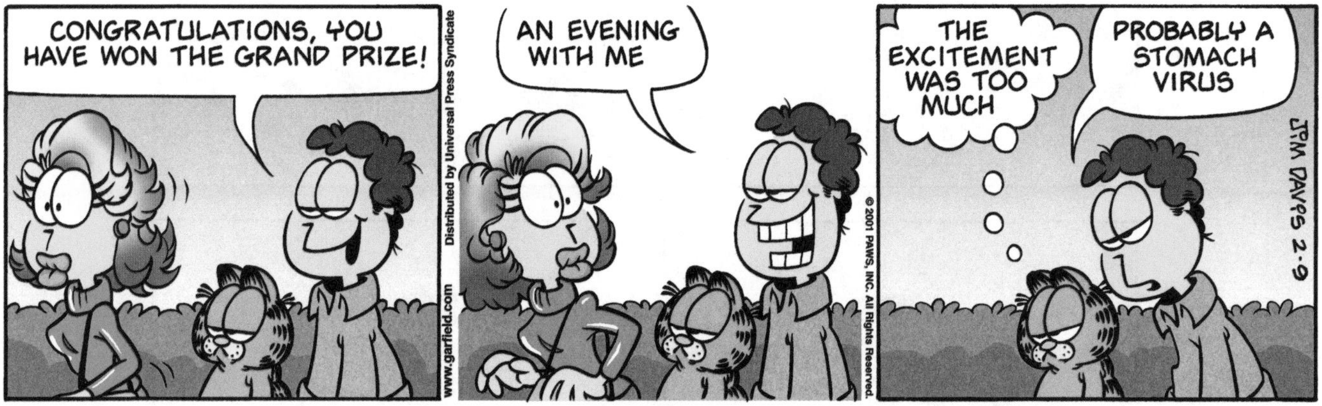
CONGRATULATIONS, YOU HAVE WON THE GRAND PRIZE!
AN EVENING WITH ME
THE EXCITEMENT WAS TOO MUCH
PROBABLY A STOMACH VIRUS
JIM DAVIS 2-9
www.garfield.com Distributed by Universal Press Syndicate
© 2001 PAWS, INC. All Rights Reserved.

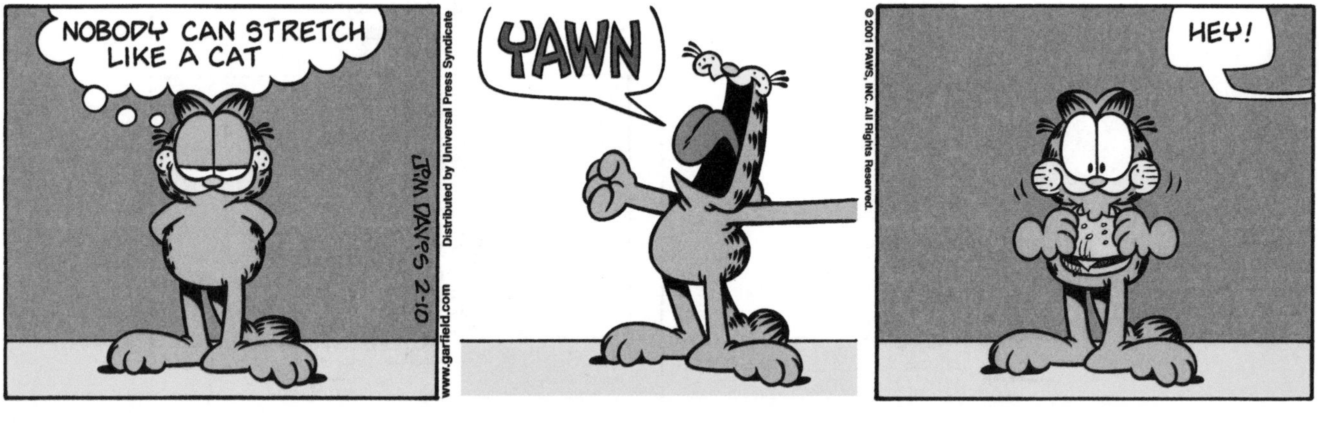
NOBODY CAN STRETCH LIKE A CAT
YAWN
HEY!
JIM DAVIS 2-10
www.garfield.com Distributed by Universal Press Syndicate
© 2001 PAWS, INC. All Rights Reserved.

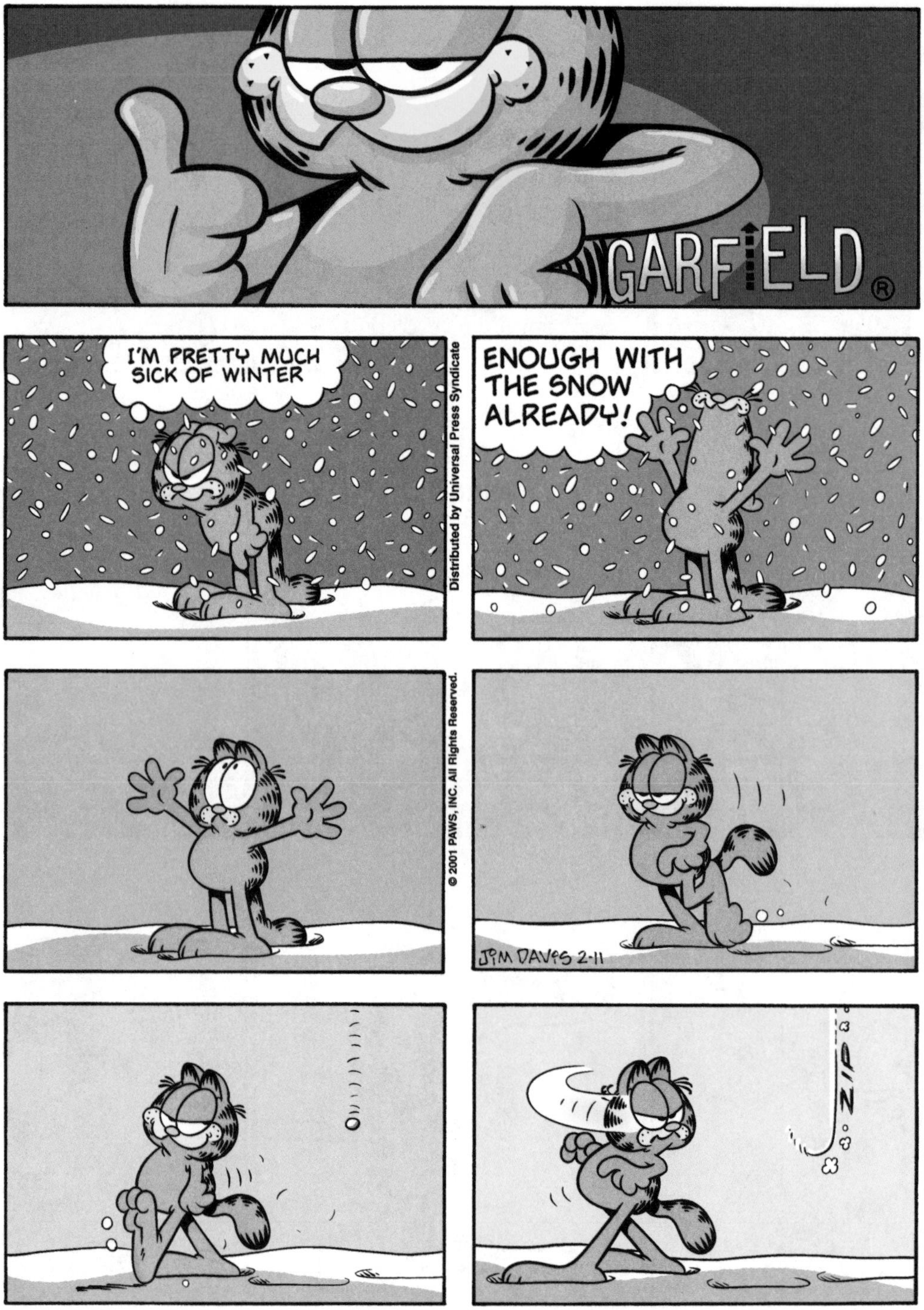
GARFIELD®
I'M PRETTY MUCH SICK OF WINTER
Distributed by Universal Press Syndicate
ENOUGH WITH THE SNOW ALREADY!
© 2001 PAWS, INC. All Rights Reserved.
JIM DAVIS 2-11
ZIP

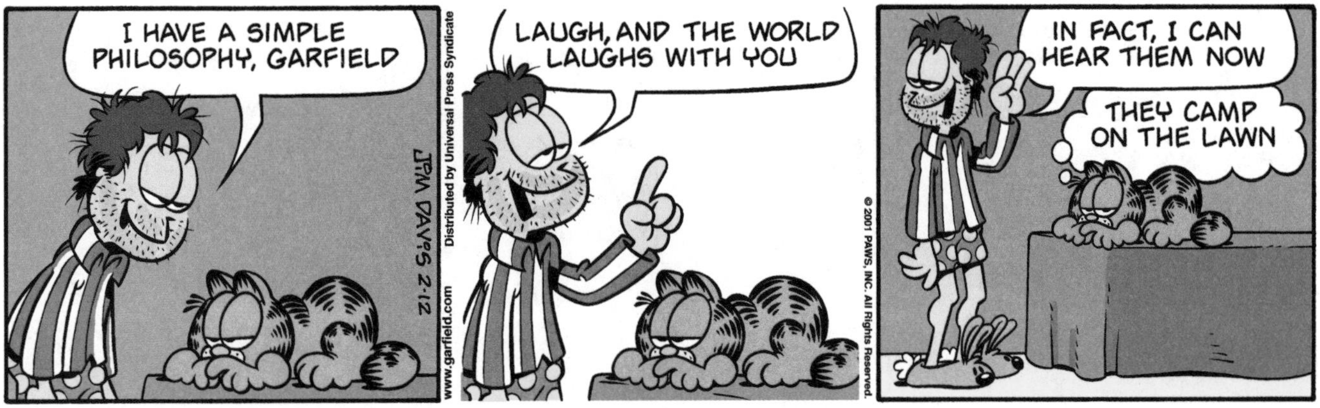
I HAVE A SIMPLE PHILOSOPHY, GARFIELD
JIM DAVIS 2-12
Distributed by Universal Press Syndicate
www.garfield.com
LAUGH, AND THE WORLD LAUGHS WITH YOU
© 2001 PAWS, INC. All Rights Reserved.
IN FACT, I CAN HEAR THEM NOW
THEY CAMP ON THE LAWN

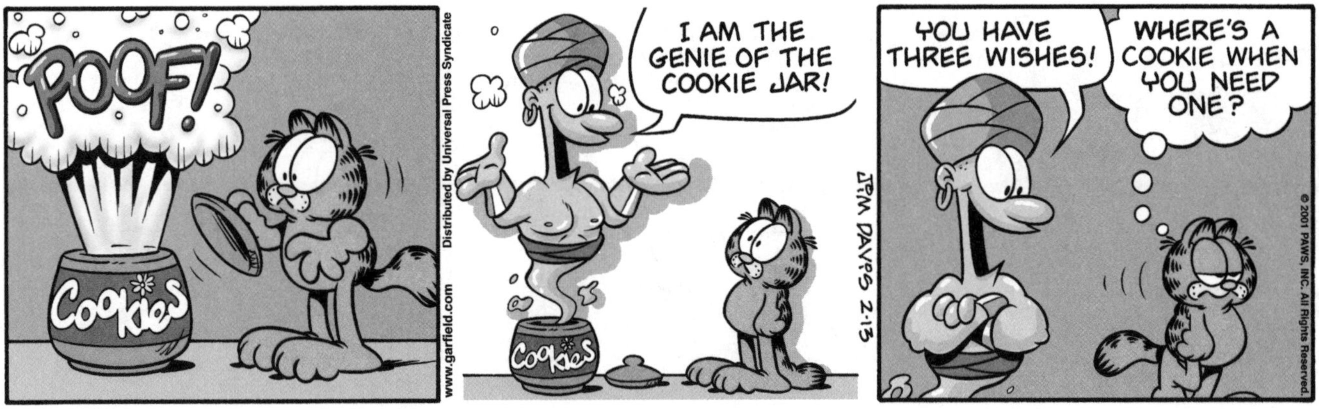
POOF!
COOKIES
Distributed by Universal Press Syndicate
www.garfield.com
I AM THE GENIE OF THE COOKIE JAR!
COOKIES
JIM DAVIS 2-13
YOU HAVE THREE WISHES!
WHERE'S A COOKIE WHEN YOU NEED ONE?
© 2001 PAWS, INC. All Rights Reserved.

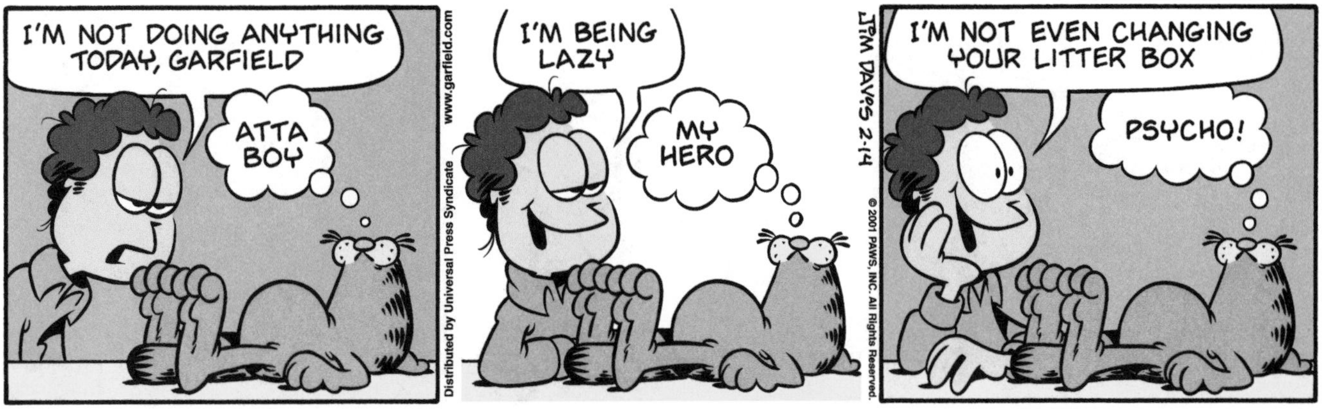
I'M NOT DOING ANYTHING TODAY, GARFIELD
ATTA BOY
www.garfield.com
Distributed by Universal Press Syndicate
I'M BEING LAZY
MY HERO
JIM DAVIS 2-14
© 2001 PAWS, INC. All Rights Reserved.
I'M NOT EVEN CHANGING YOUR LITTER BOX
PSYCHO!

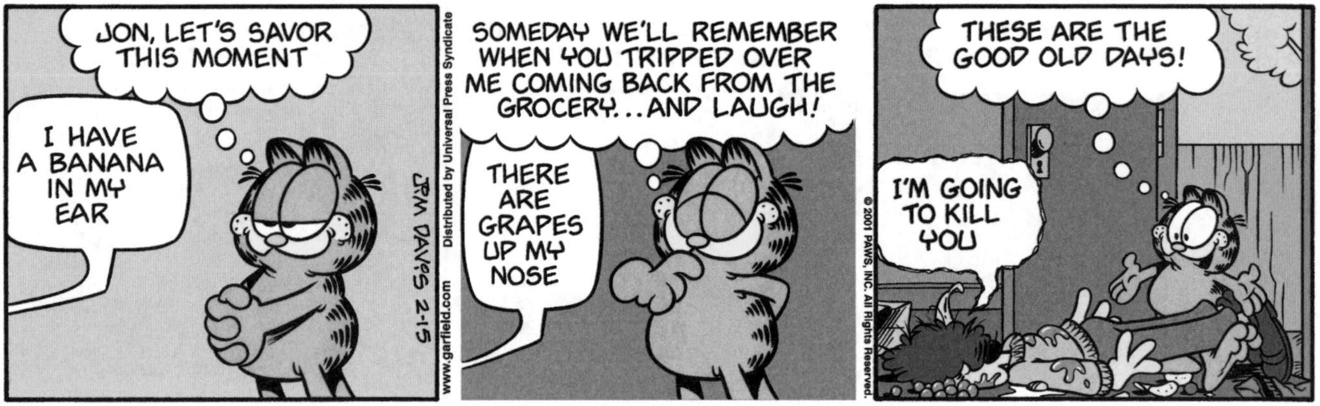
JON, LET'S SAVOR THIS MOMENT
I HAVE A BANANA IN MY EAR
JIM DAVIS 2-15
Distributed by Universal Press Syndicate
www.garfield.com
SOMEDAY WE'LL REMEMBER WHEN YOU TRIPPED OVER ME COMING BACK FROM THE GROCERY... AND LAUGH!
THERE ARE GRAPES UP MY NOSE
© 2001 PAWS, INC. All Rights Reserved.
THESE ARE THE GOOD OLD DAYS!
I'M GOING TO KILL YOU

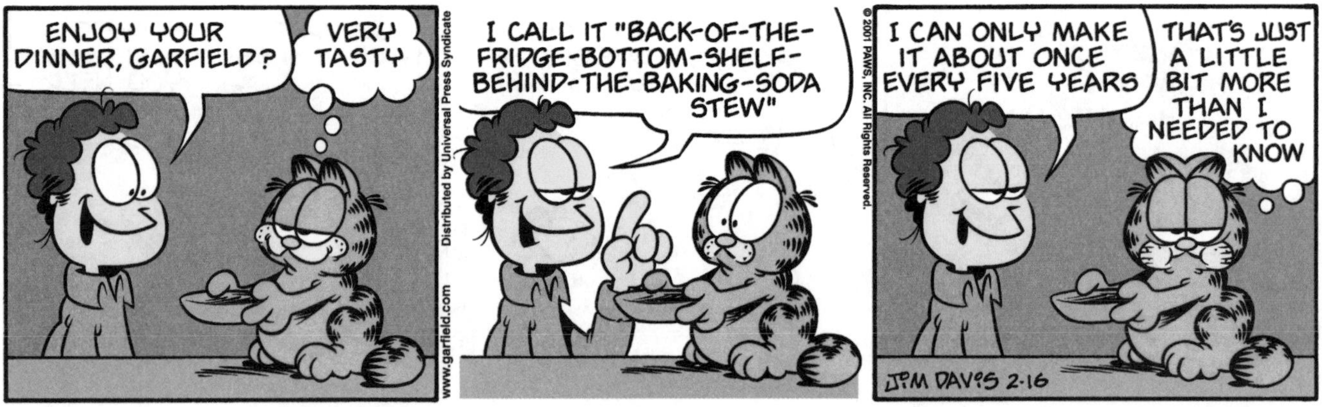
ENJOY YOUR DINNER, GARFIELD?
VERY TASTY
Distributed by Universal Press Syndicate
www.garfield.com
I CALL IT "BACK-OF-THE-FRIDGE-BOTTOM-SHELF-BEHIND-THE-BAKING-SODA STEW"
© 2001 PAWS, INC. All Rights Reserved.
I CAN ONLY MAKE IT ABOUT ONCE EVERY FIVE YEARS
THAT'S JUST A LITTLE BIT MORE THAN I NEEDED TO KNOW
JIM DAVIS 2-16

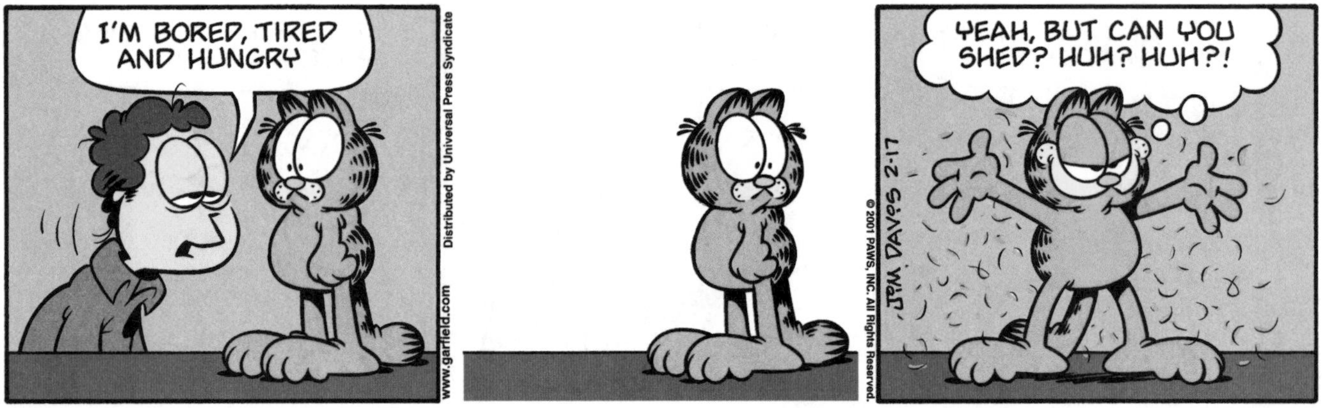
I'M BORED, TIRED AND HUNGRY
Distributed by Universal Press Syndicate
www.garfield.com
© 2001 PAWS, INC. All Rights Reserved.
JIM DAVIS 2-17
YEAH, BUT CAN YOU SHED? HUH? HUH?!

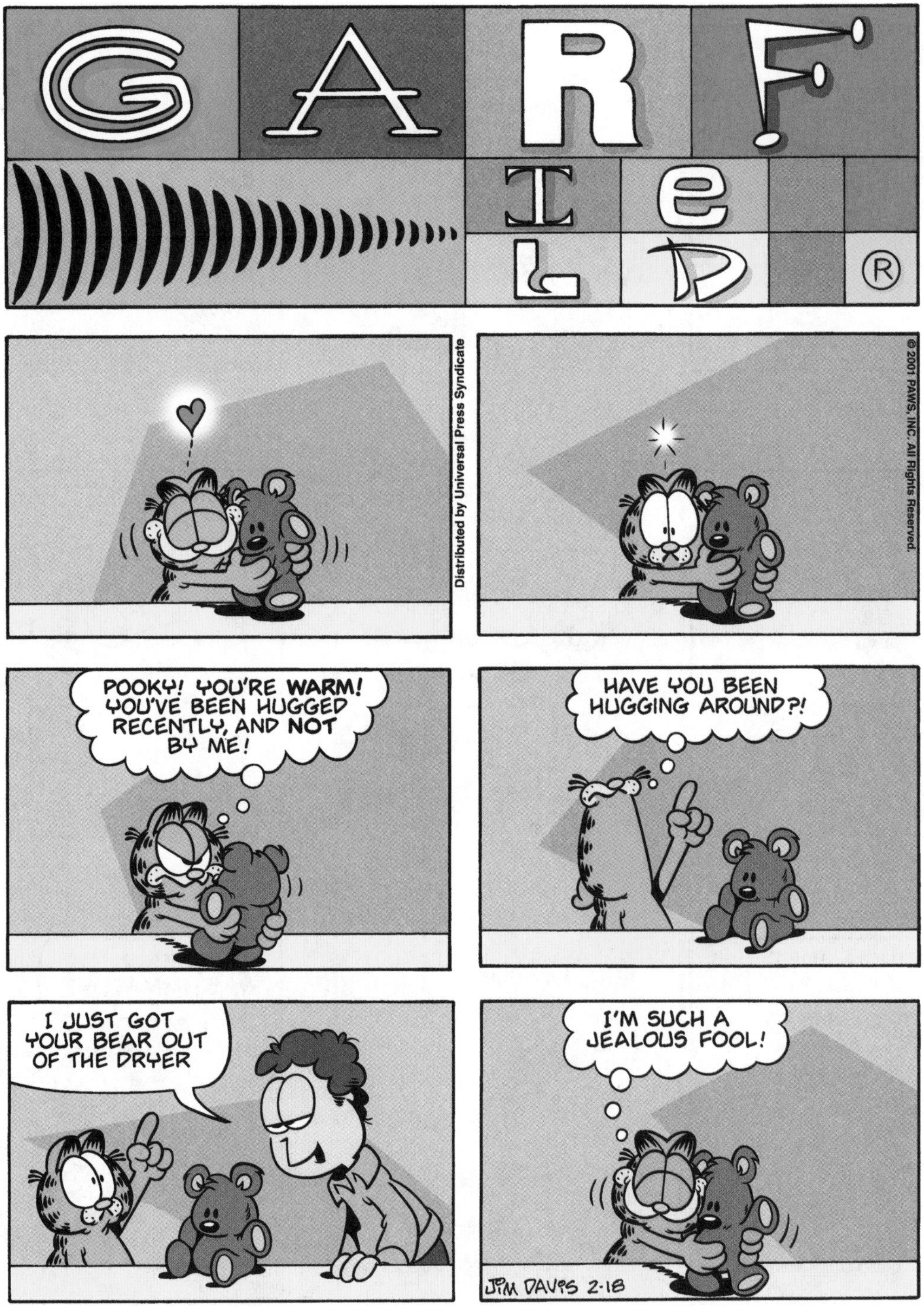
GARFIELD®
Distributed by Universal Press Syndicate
© 2001 PAWS, INC. All Rights Reserved.
POOKY! YOU'RE WARM! YOU'VE BEEN HUGGED RECENTLY, AND NOT BY ME!
HAVE YOU BEEN HUGGING AROUND?!
I JUST GOT YOUR BEAR OUT OF THE DRYER
I'M SUCH A JEALOUS FOOL!
JIM DAVIS 2-18

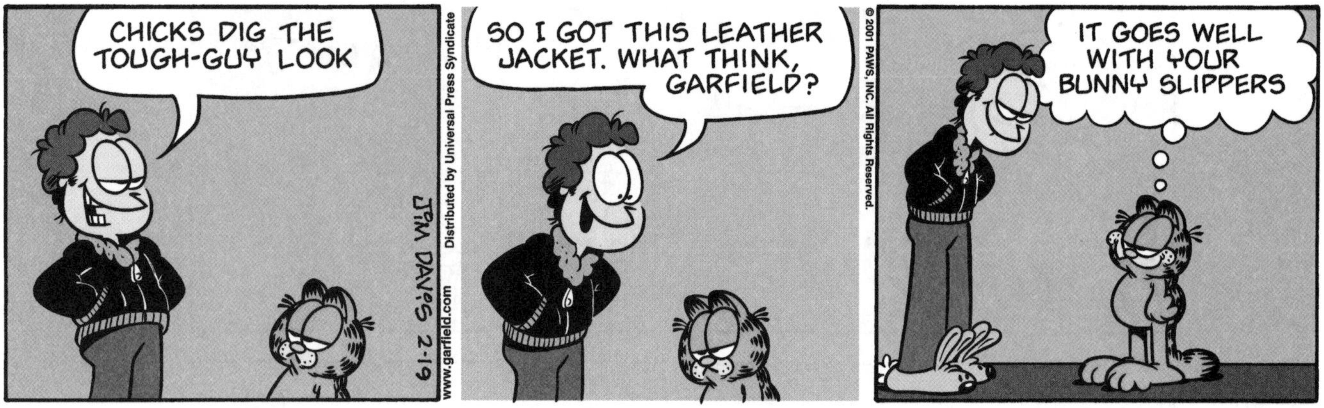
CHICKS DIG THE TOUGH-GUY LOOK
SO I GOT THIS LEATHER JACKET. WHAT THINK, GARFIELD?
IT GOES WELL WITH YOUR BUNNY SLIPPERS
JIM DAVIS 2-19
www.garfield.com Distributed by Universal Press Syndicate
© 2001 PAWS, INC. All Rights Reserved.

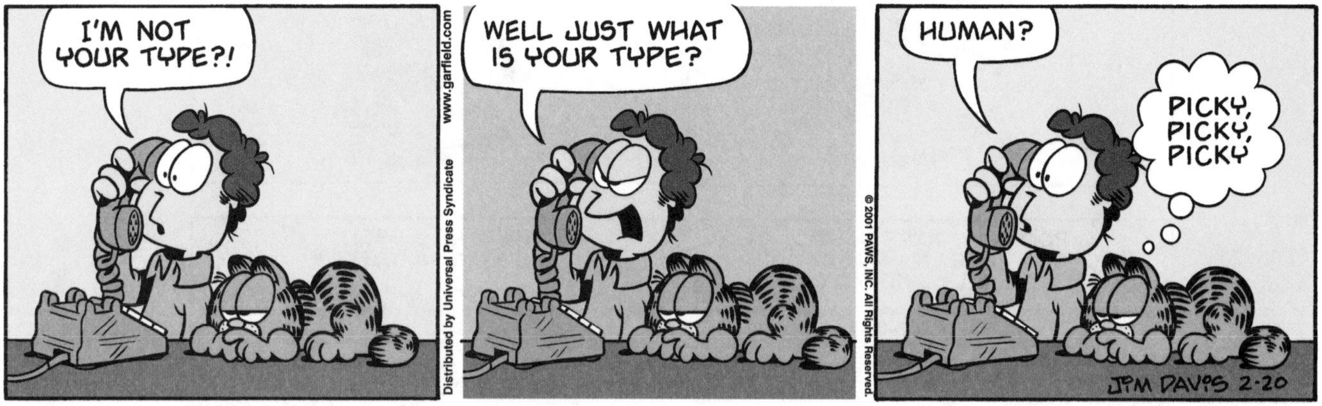
I'M NOT YOUR TYPE?!
WELL JUST WHAT IS YOUR TYPE?
HUMAN?
PICKY, PICKY, PICKY
JIM DAVIS 2-20
www.garfield.com Distributed by Universal Press Syndicate
© 2001 PAWS, INC. All Rights Reserved.

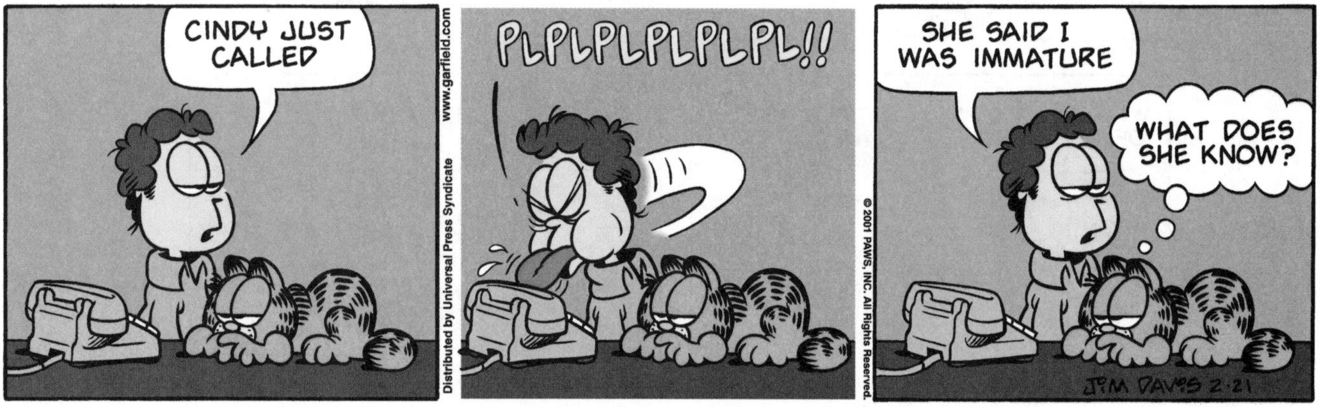
CINDY JUST CALLED
PLPLPLPLPLPL!!
SHE SAID I WAS IMMATURE
WHAT DOES SHE KNOW?
JIM DAVIS 2-21
www.garfield.com Distributed by Universal Press Syndicate
© 2001 PAWS, INC. All Rights Reserved.

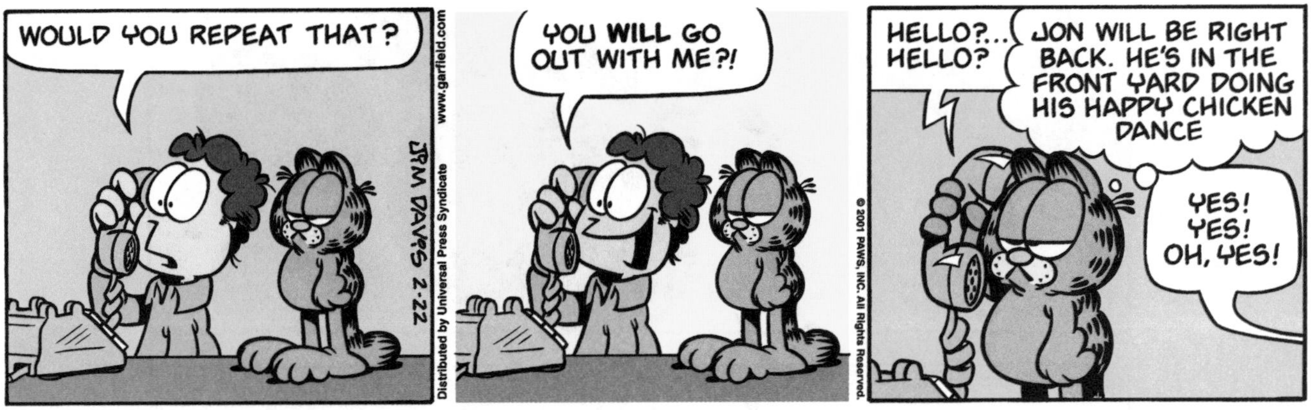
WOULD YOU REPEAT THAT?
JIM DAVIS 2-22
Distributed by Universal Press Syndicate www.garfield.com
YOU **WILL** GO OUT WITH ME?!
© 2001 PAWS, INC. All Rights Reserved.
HELLO?... HELLO?
JON WILL BE RIGHT BACK. HE'S IN THE FRONT YARD DOING HIS HAPPY CHICKEN DANCE
YES! YES! OH, YES!

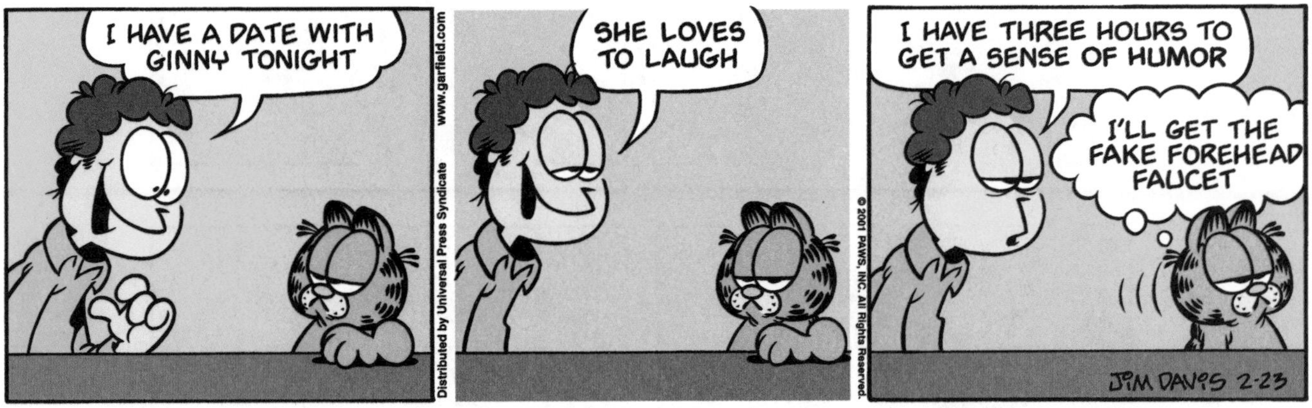
I HAVE A DATE WITH GINNY TONIGHT
Distributed by Universal Press Syndicate www.garfield.com
SHE LOVES TO LAUGH
© 2001 PAWS, INC. All Rights Reserved.
I HAVE THREE HOURS TO GET A SENSE OF HUMOR
I'LL GET THE FAKE FOREHEAD FAUCET
JIM DAVIS 2-23

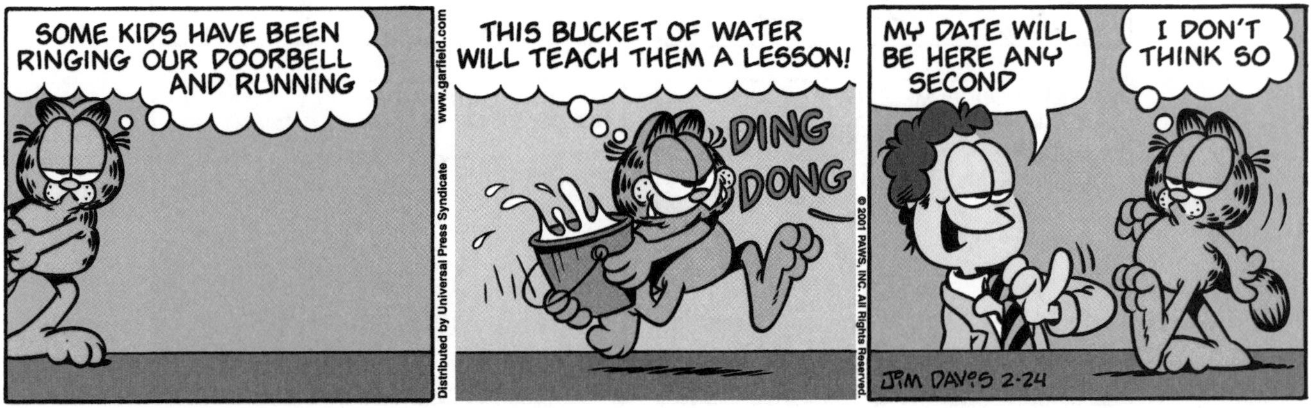
SOME KIDS HAVE BEEN RINGING OUR DOORBELL AND RUNNING
Distributed by Universal Press Syndicate www.garfield.com
THIS BUCKET OF WATER WILL TEACH THEM A LESSON!
DING DONG
© 2001 PAWS, INC. All Rights Reserved.
MY DATE WILL BE HERE ANY SECOND
I DON'T THINK SO
JIM DAVIS 2-24

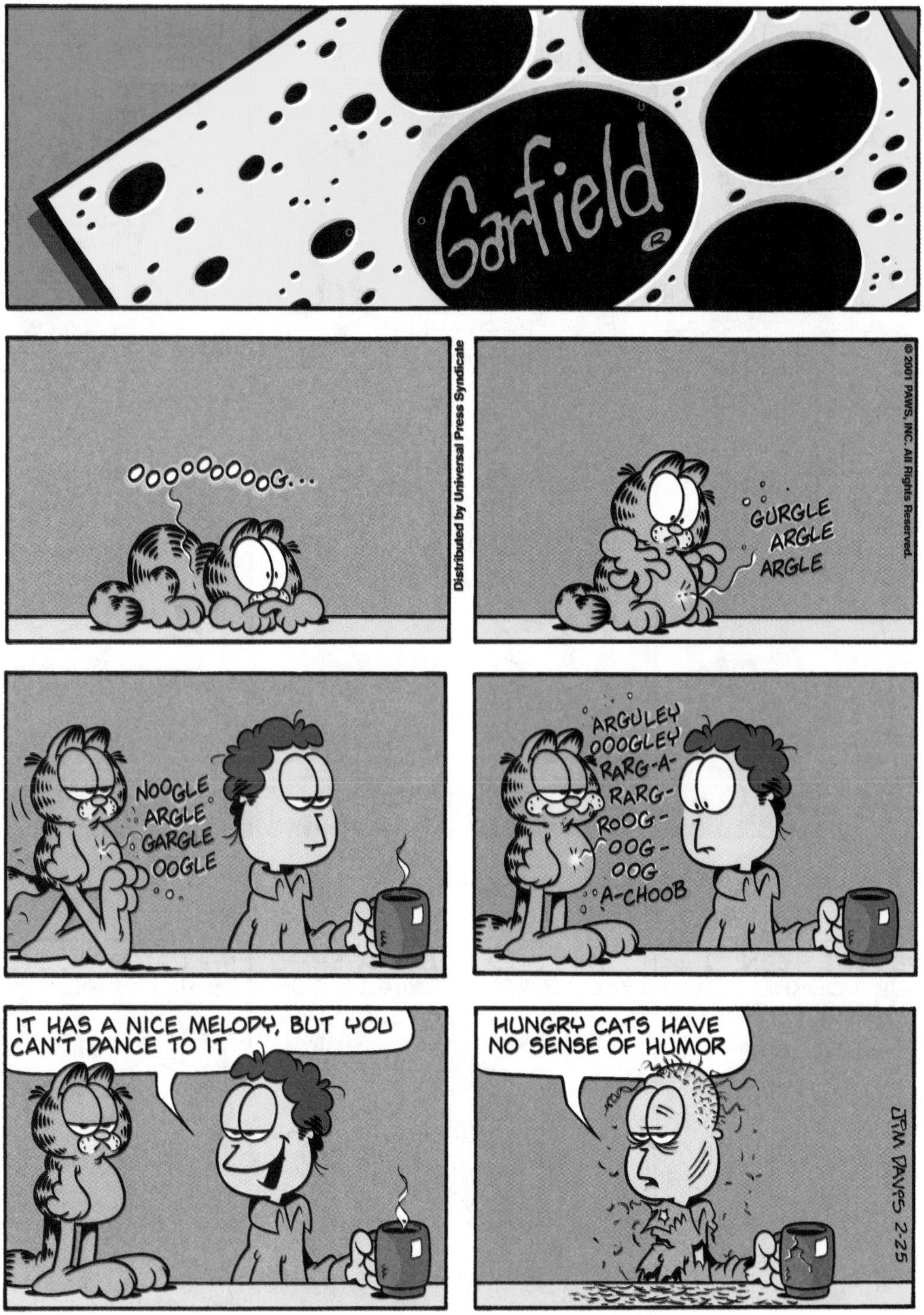
Garfield
OOOOOOOOOG...
Distributed by Universal Press Syndicate
GURGLE ARGLE ARGLE
© 2001 PAWS, INC. All Rights Reserved.
NOOGLE ARGLE GARGLE OOGLE
ARGULEY OOOGLEY RARG-A-RARG-ROOG-OOG-OOG A-CHOOB
IT HAS A NICE MELODY, BUT YOU CAN'T DANCE TO IT
HUNGRY CATS HAVE NO SENSE OF HUMOR
JIM DAVIS 2-25

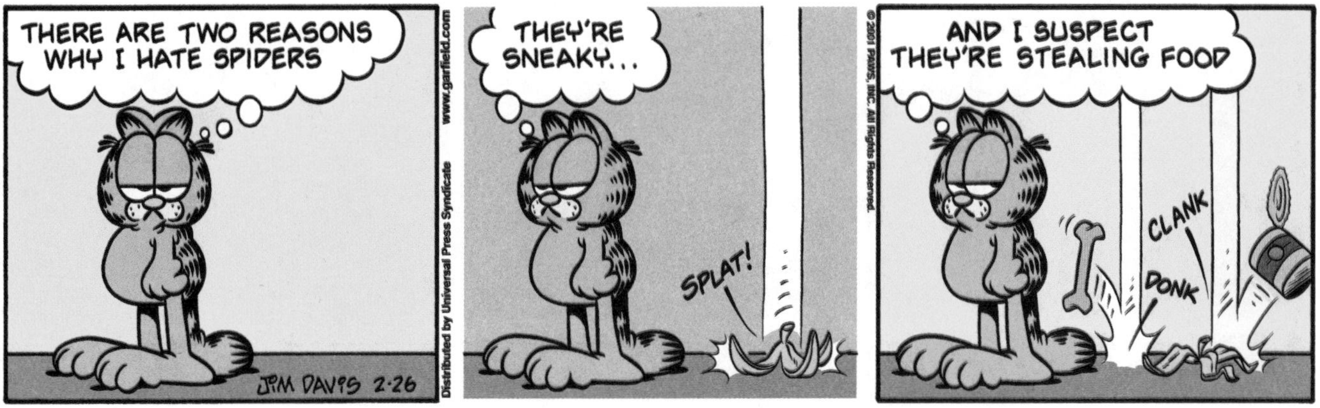
THERE ARE TWO REASONS WHY I HATE SPIDERS
JIM DAVIS 2·26
Distributed by Universal Press Syndicate www.garfield.com
THEY'RE SNEAKY...
SPLAT!
© 2001 PAWS, INC. All Rights Reserved.
AND I SUSPECT THEY'RE STEALING FOOD
CLANK
DONK

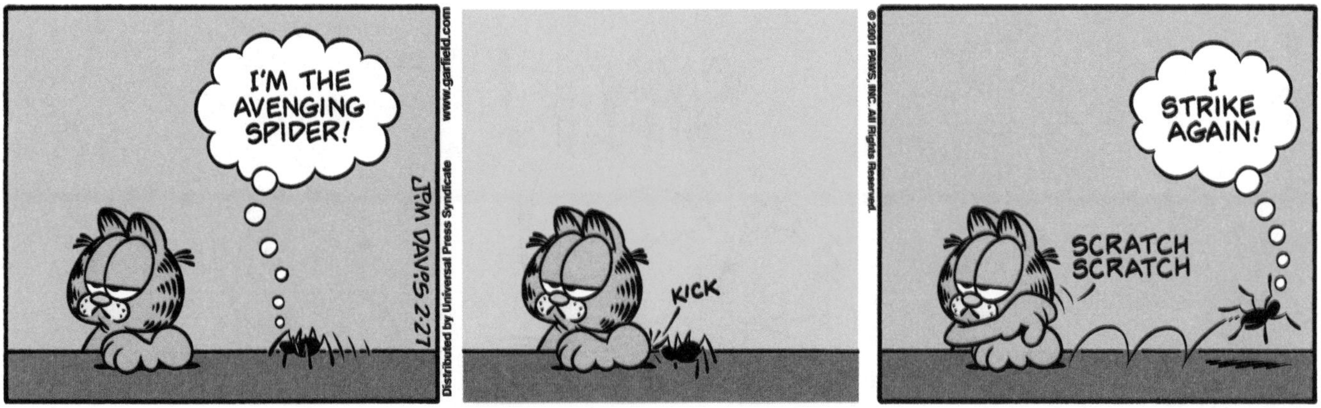
I'M THE AVENGING SPIDER!
JIM DAVIS 2·27
Distributed by Universal Press Syndicate www.garfield.com
KICK
© 2001 PAWS, INC. All Rights Reserved.
I STRIKE AGAIN!
SCRATCH SCRATCH

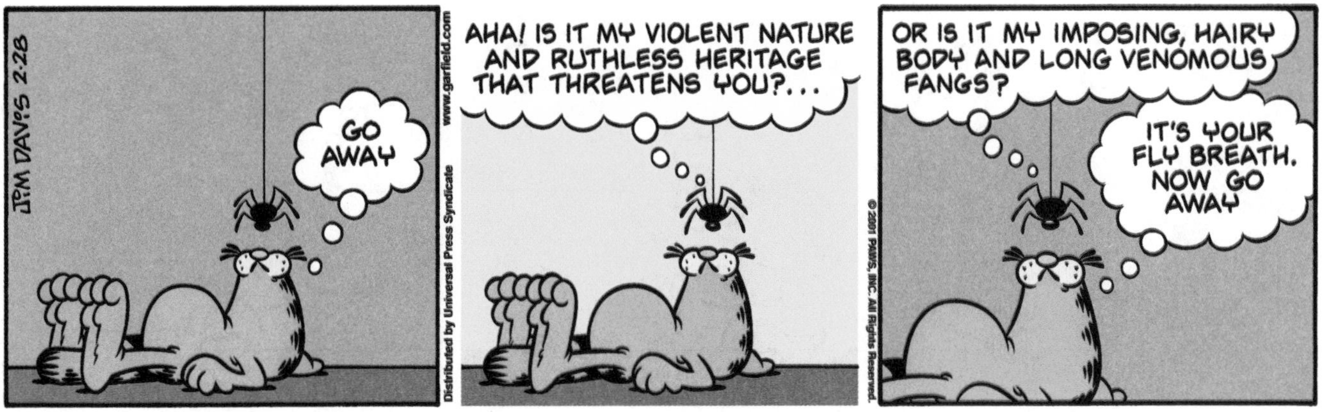
JIM DAVIS 2·28
GO AWAY
Distributed by Universal Press Syndicate www.garfield.com
AHA! IS IT MY VIOLENT NATURE AND RUTHLESS HERITAGE THAT THREATENS YOU?...
© 2001 PAWS, INC. All Rights Reserved.
OR IS IT MY IMPOSING, HAIRY BODY AND LONG VENOMOUS FANGS?
IT'S YOUR FLY BREATH. NOW GO AWAY

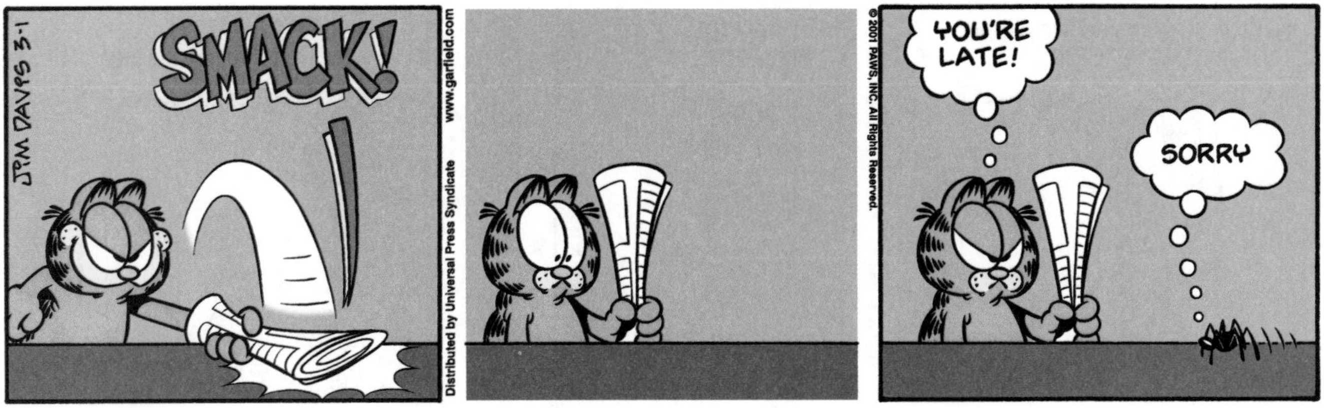
JIM DAVIS 3-1
SMACK!
www.garfield.com
Distributed by Universal Press Syndicate
© 2001 PAWS, INC. All Rights Reserved.
YOU'RE LATE!
SORRY

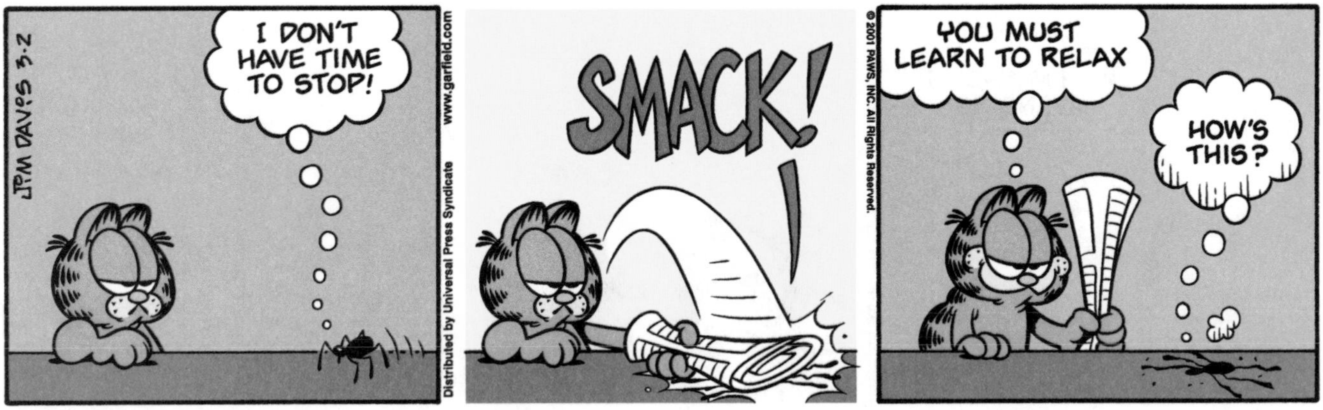
JIM DAVIS 3-2
I DON'T HAVE TIME TO STOP!
www.garfield.com
Distributed by Universal Press Syndicate
SMACK!
© 2001 PAWS, INC. All Rights Reserved.
YOU MUST LEARN TO RELAX
HOW'S THIS?

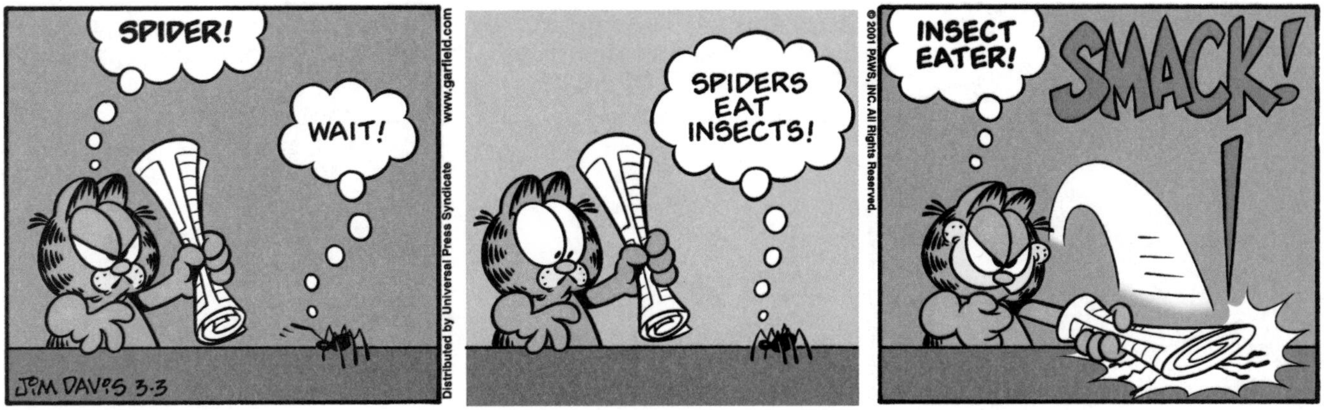
SPIDER!
WAIT!
JIM DAVIS 3-3
www.garfield.com
Distributed by Universal Press Syndicate
SPIDERS EAT INSECTS!
© 2001 PAWS, INC. All Rights Reserved.
INSECT EATER!
SMACK!

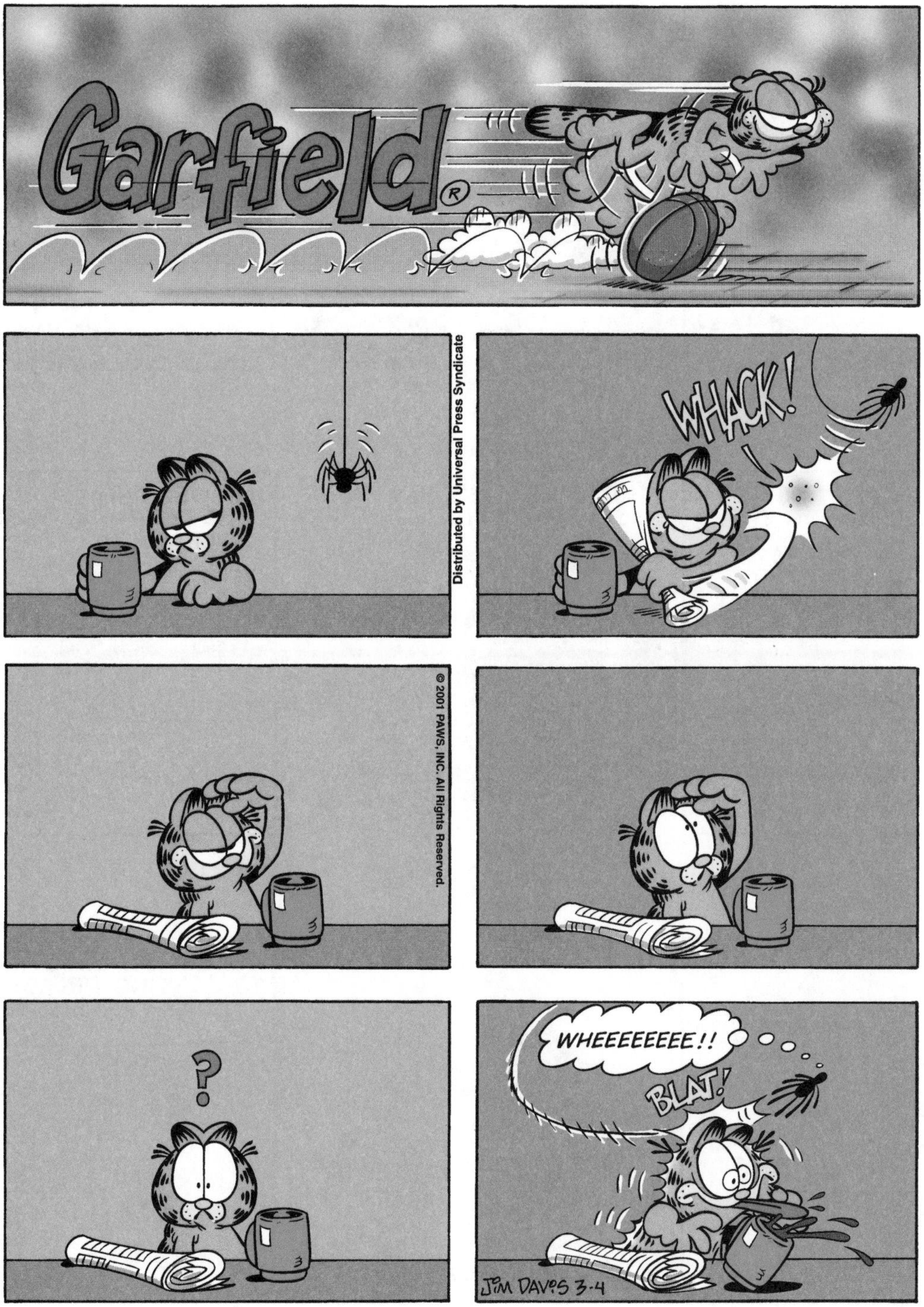
Garfield®
WHACK!
?
WHEEEEEEEEE!!
BLAT!
JIM DAVIS 3-4

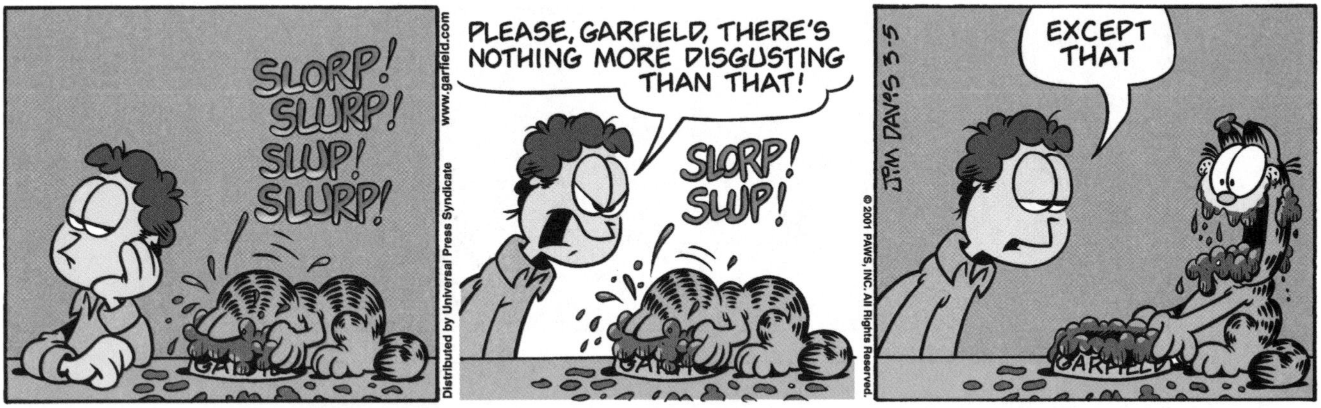
SLORP! SLURP! SLUP! SLURP!
PLEASE, GARFIELD, THERE'S NOTHING MORE DISGUSTING THAN THAT!
SLORP! SLUP!
EXCEPT THAT
JIM DAVIS 3-5
Distributed by Universal Press Syndicate www.garfield.com
© 2001 PAWS, INC. All Rights Reserved.

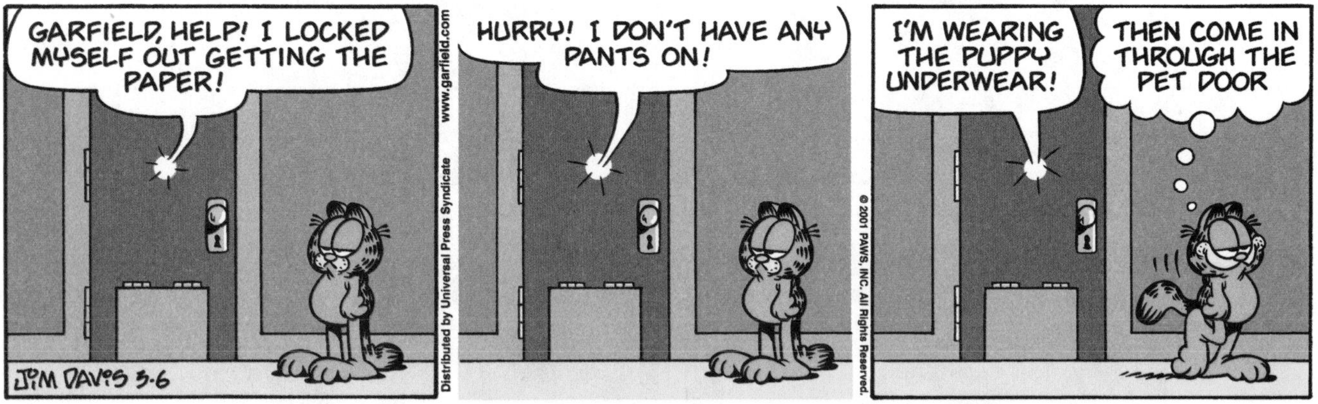
GARFIELD, HELP! I LOCKED MYSELF OUT GETTING THE PAPER!
HURRY! I DON'T HAVE ANY PANTS ON!
I'M WEARING THE PUPPY UNDERWEAR!
THEN COME IN THROUGH THE PET DOOR
JIM DAVIS 3-6
Distributed by Universal Press Syndicate www.garfield.com
© 2001 PAWS, INC. All Rights Reserved.

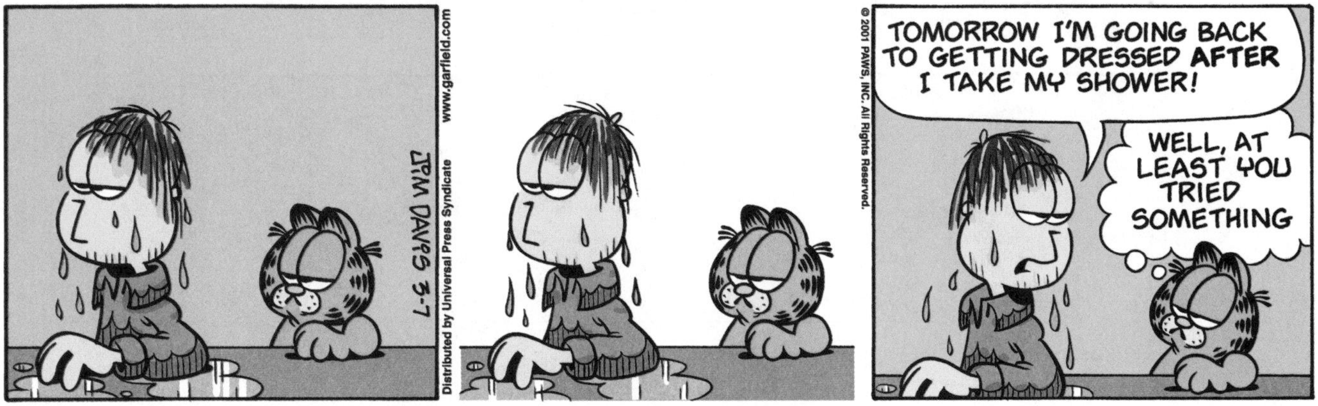
TOMORROW I'M GOING BACK TO GETTING DRESSED AFTER I TAKE MY SHOWER!
WELL, AT LEAST YOU TRIED SOMETHING
JIM DAVIS 3-7
Distributed by Universal Press Syndicate www.garfield.com
© 2001 PAWS, INC. All Rights Reserved.

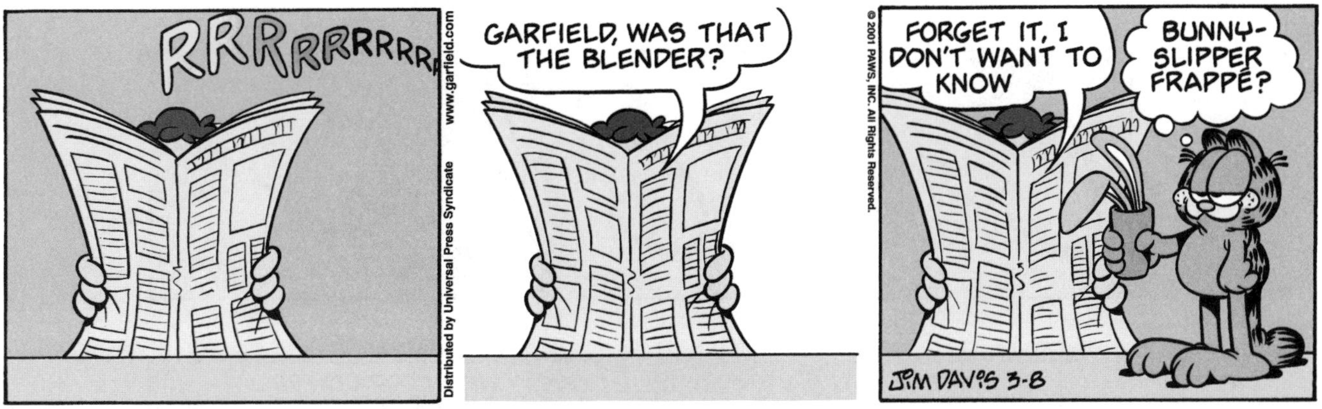
RRRRRRRRR
GARFIELD, WAS THAT THE BLENDER?
FORGET IT, I DON'T WANT TO KNOW
BUNNY-SLIPPER FRAPPÉ?
JIM DAVIS 3-8
Distributed by Universal Press Syndicate www.garfield.com
© 2001 PAWS, INC. All Rights Reserved.

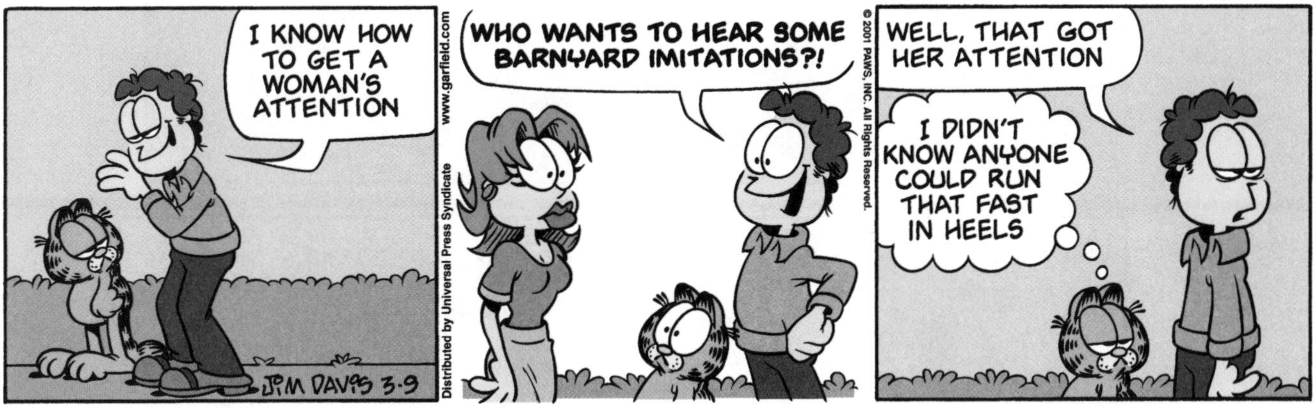
I KNOW HOW TO GET A WOMAN'S ATTENTION
JIM DAVIS 3-9
WHO WANTS TO HEAR SOME BARNYARD IMITATIONS?!
WELL, THAT GOT HER ATTENTION
I DIDN'T KNOW ANYONE COULD RUN THAT FAST IN HEELS
Distributed by Universal Press Syndicate www.garfield.com
© 2001 PAWS, INC. All Rights Reserved.

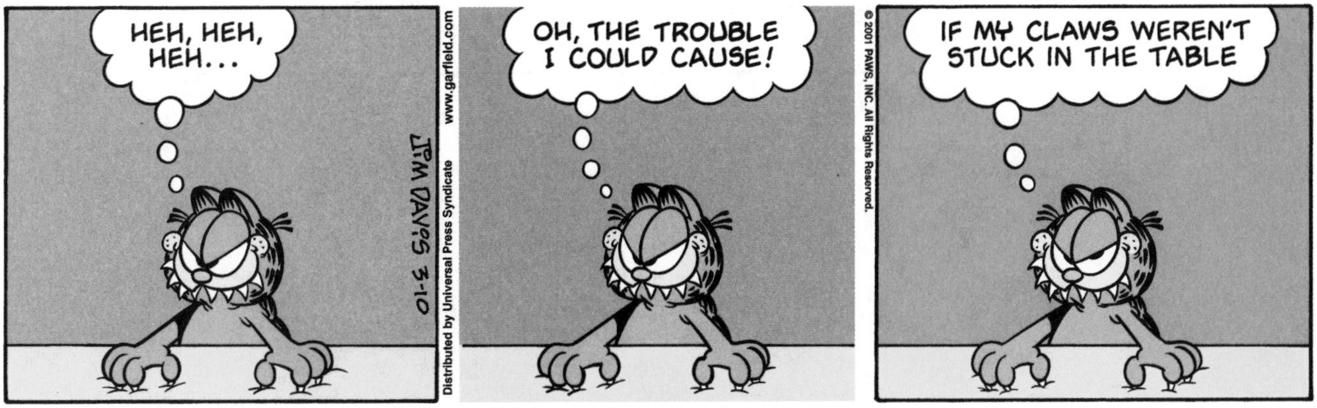
HEH, HEH, HEH...
JIM DAVIS 3-10
OH, THE TROUBLE I COULD CAUSE!
IF MY CLAWS WEREN'T STUCK IN THE TABLE
Distributed by Universal Press Syndicate www.garfield.com
© 2001 PAWS, INC. All Rights Reserved.

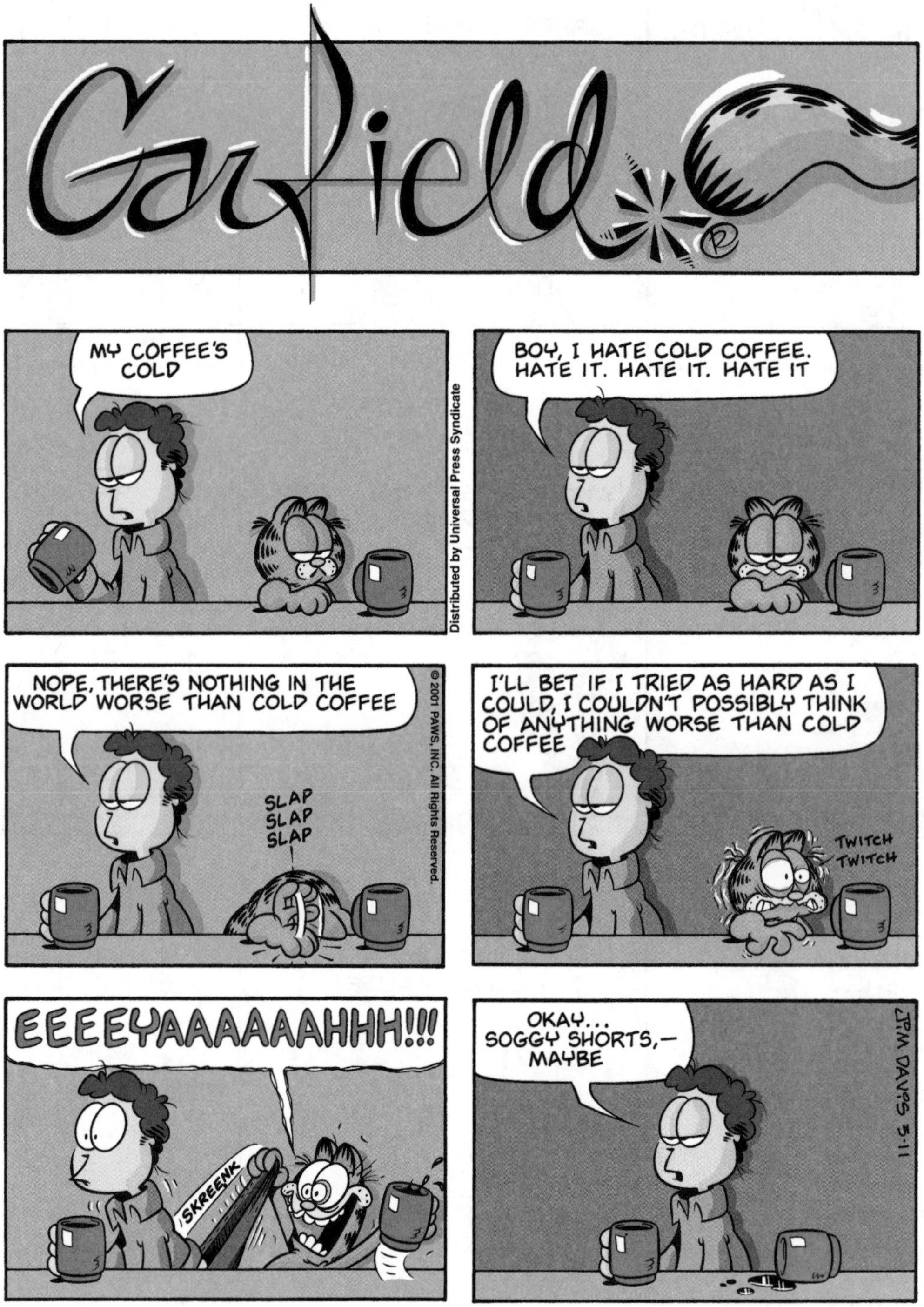
Garfield
MY COFFEE'S COLD
Distributed by Universal Press Syndicate
BOY, I HATE COLD COFFEE. HATE IT. HATE IT. HATE IT
NOPE, THERE'S NOTHING IN THE WORLD WORSE THAN COLD COFFEE
SLAP SLAP SLAP
© 2001 PAWS, INC. All Rights Reserved.
I'LL BET IF I TRIED AS HARD AS I COULD, I COULDN'T POSSIBLY THINK OF ANYTHING WORSE THAN COLD COFFEE
TWITCH TWITCH
EEEEYAAAAAAHHH!!!
SKREENK
OKAY... SOGGY SHORTS, — MAYBE
JIM DAVIS 3-11

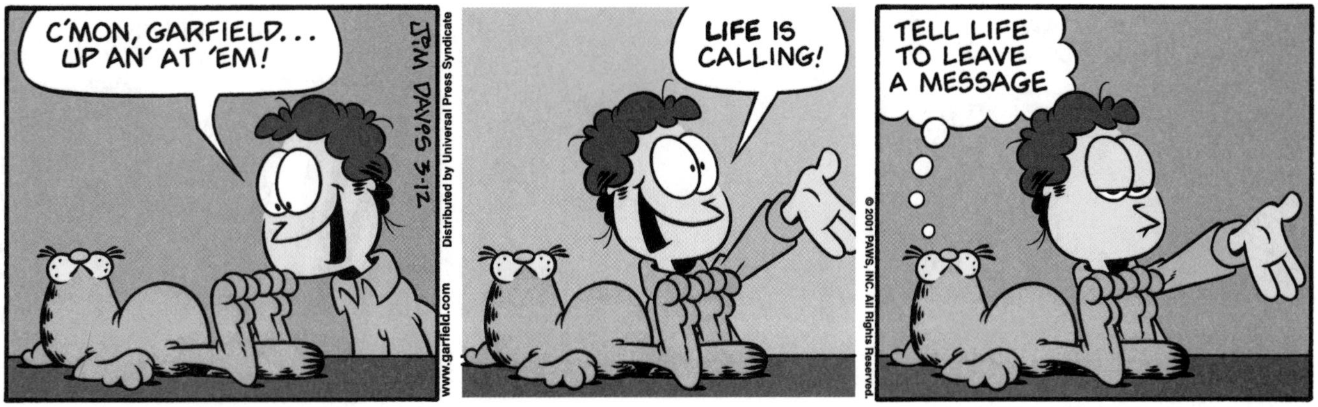
C'MON, GARFIELD... UP AN' AT 'EM!
JIM DAVIS 3-12
www.garfield.com Distributed by Universal Press Syndicate
LIFE IS CALLING!
© 2001 PAWS, INC. All Rights Reserved.
TELL LIFE TO LEAVE A MESSAGE

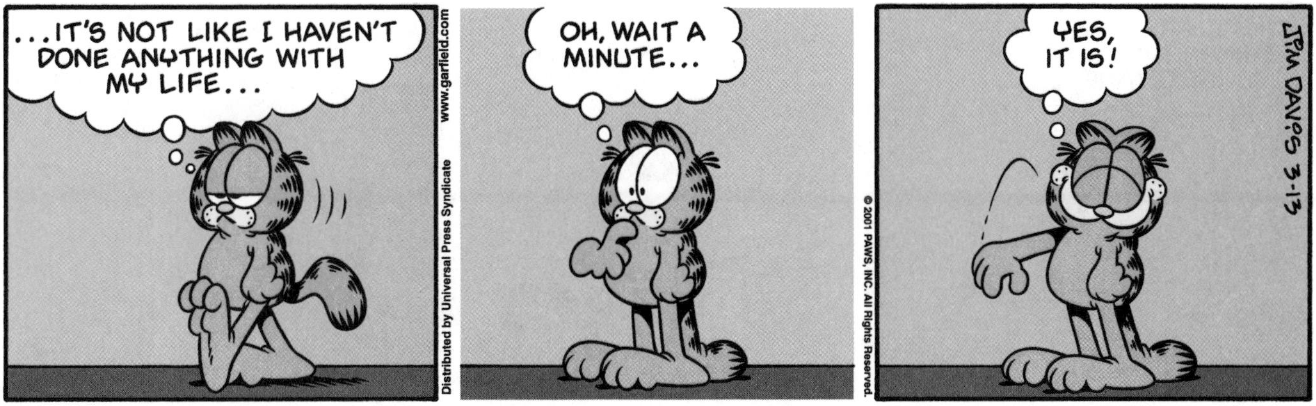
...IT'S NOT LIKE I HAVEN'T DONE ANYTHING WITH MY LIFE...
Distributed by Universal Press Syndicate www.garfield.com
OH, WAIT A MINUTE...
© 2001 PAWS, INC. All Rights Reserved.
YES, IT IS!
JIM DAVIS 3-13

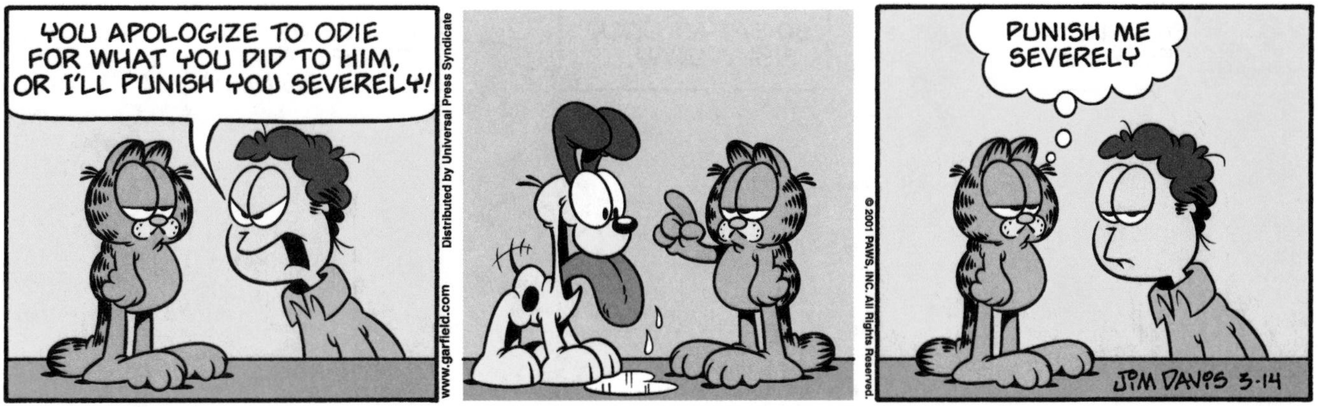
YOU APOLOGIZE TO ODIE FOR WHAT YOU DID TO HIM, OR I'LL PUNISH YOU SEVERELY!
www.garfield.com Distributed by Universal Press Syndicate
© 2001 PAWS, INC. All Rights Reserved.
PUNISH ME SEVERELY
JIM DAVIS 3-14

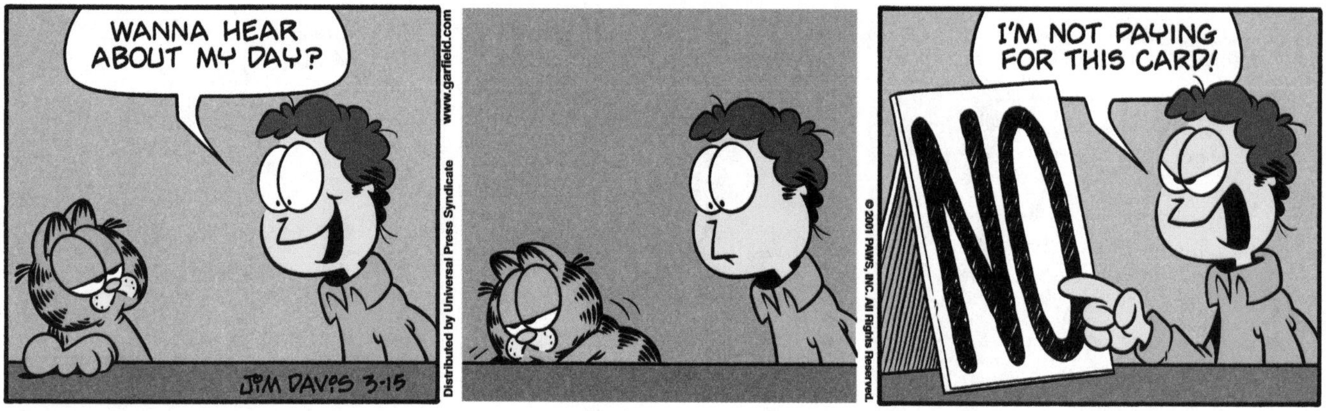
WANNA HEAR ABOUT MY DAY?
JIM DAVIS 3-15
www.garfield.com
Distributed by Universal Press Syndicate
© 2001 PAWS, INC. All Rights Reserved.
I'M NOT PAYING FOR THIS CARD!
NO

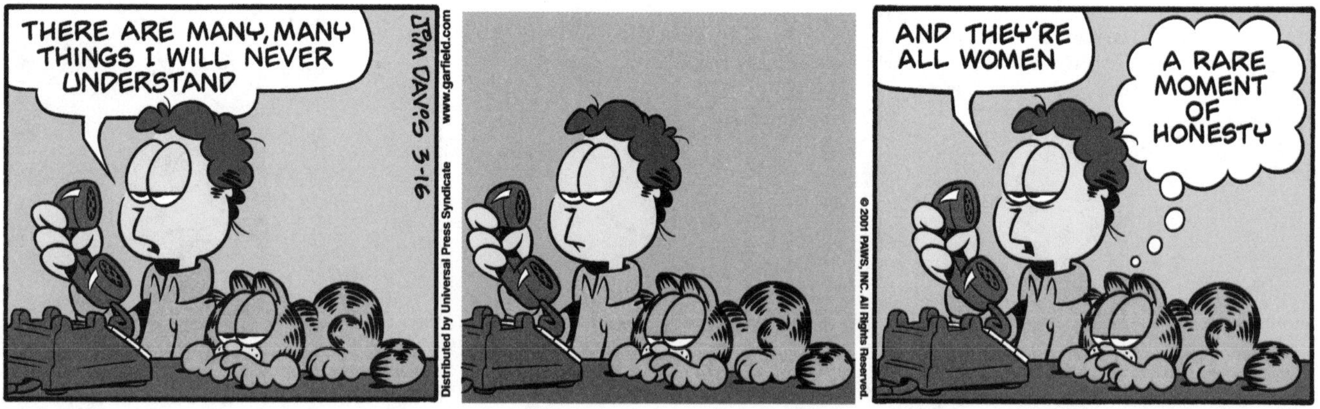
THERE ARE MANY, MANY THINGS I WILL NEVER UNDERSTAND
JIM DAVIS 3-16
www.garfield.com
Distributed by Universal Press Syndicate
© 2001 PAWS, INC. All Rights Reserved.
AND THEY'RE ALL WOMEN
A RARE MOMENT OF HONESTY

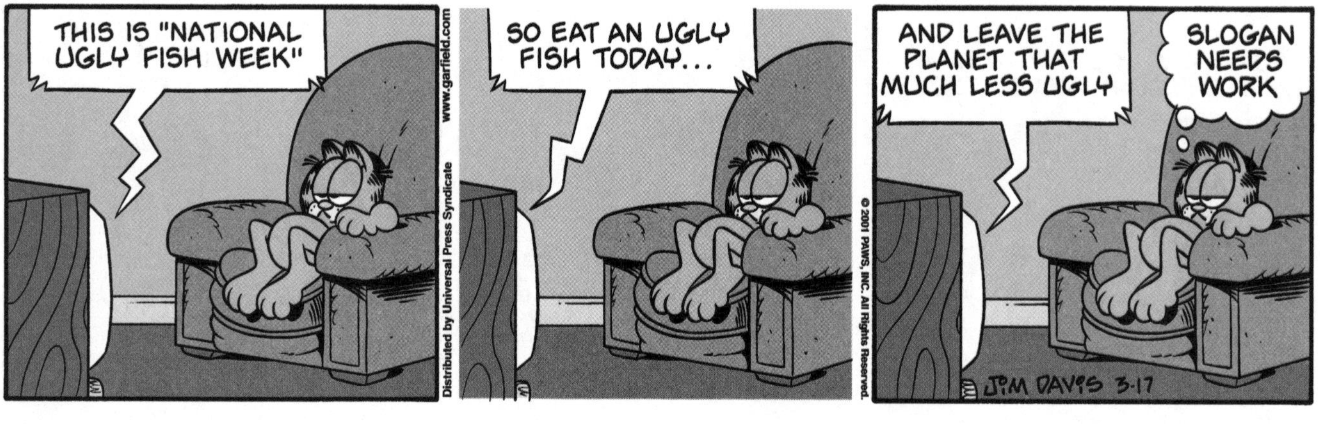
THIS IS "NATIONAL UGLY FISH WEEK"
www.garfield.com
Distributed by Universal Press Syndicate
SO EAT AN UGLY FISH TODAY...
© 2001 PAWS, INC. All Rights Reserved.
AND LEAVE THE PLANET THAT MUCH LESS UGLY
SLOGAN NEEDS WORK
JIM DAVIS 3-17

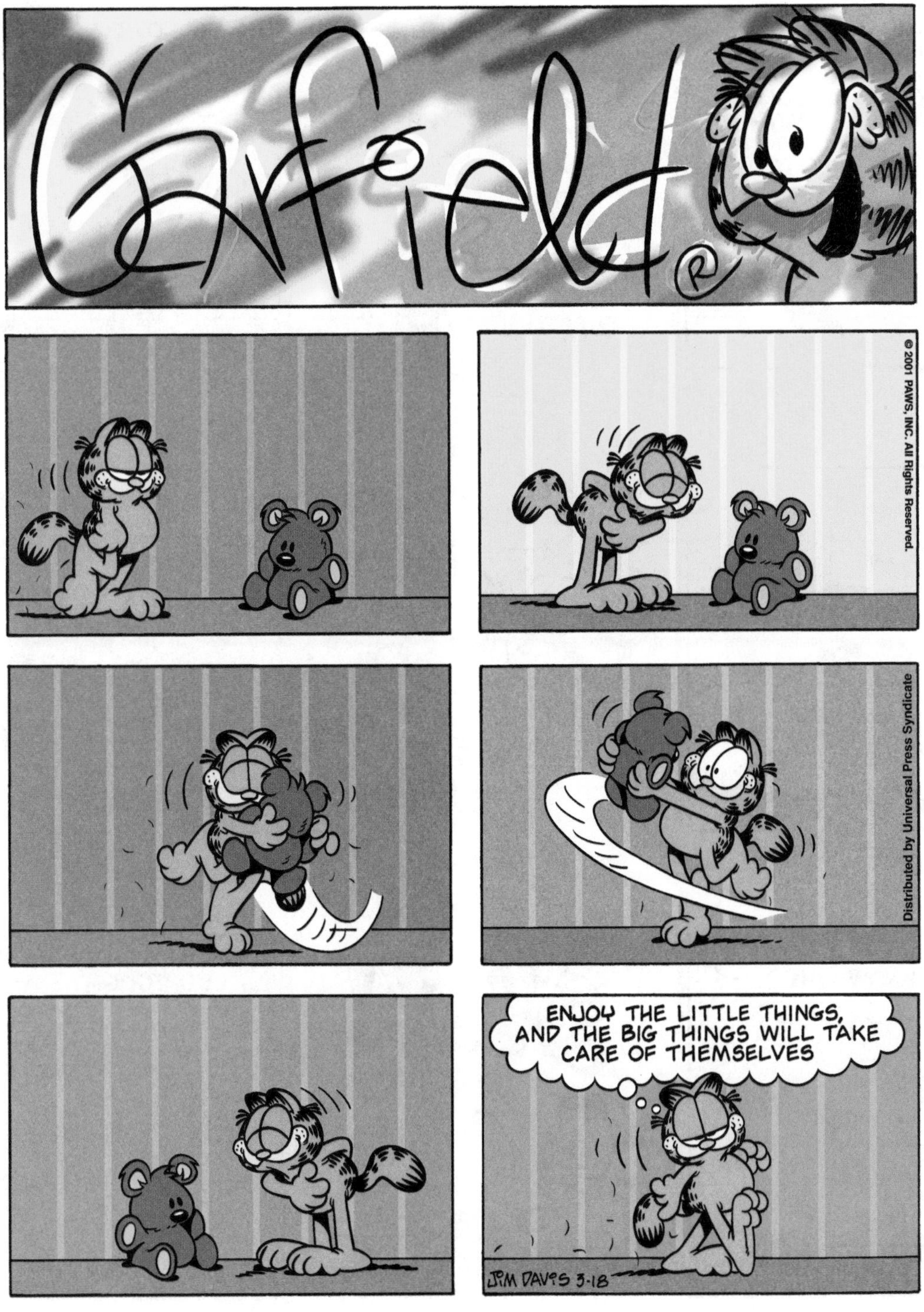
Garfield®
© 2001 PAWS, INC. All Rights Reserved.
Distributed by Universal Press Syndicate
ENJOY THE LITTLE THINGS, AND THE BIG THINGS WILL TAKE CARE OF THEMSELVES
JIM DAVIS 3-18

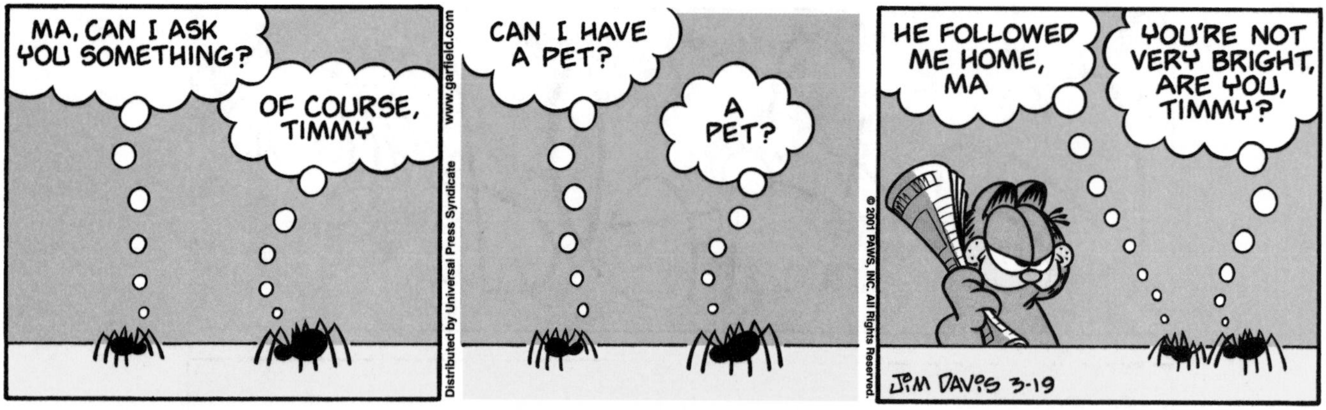
MA, CAN I ASK YOU SOMETHING?
OF COURSE, TIMMY
Distributed by Universal Press Syndicate www.garfield.com
CAN I HAVE A PET?
A PET?
© 2001 PAWS, INC. All Rights Reserved.
HE FOLLOWED ME HOME, MA
YOU'RE NOT VERY BRIGHT, ARE YOU, TIMMY?
JIM DAVIS 3-19

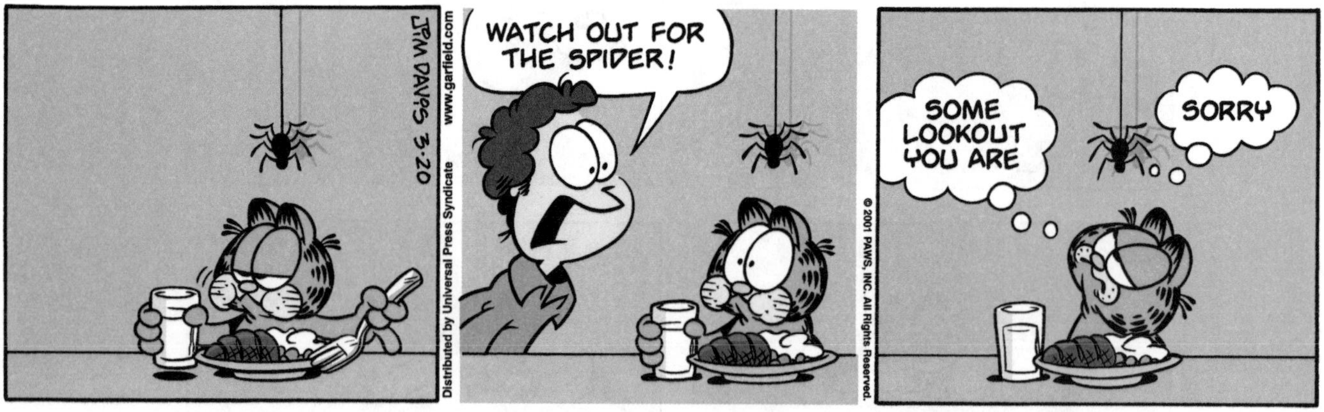
JIM DAVIS 3-20
Distributed by Universal Press Syndicate www.garfield.com
WATCH OUT FOR THE SPIDER!
© 2001 PAWS, INC. All Rights Reserved.
SOME LOOKOUT YOU ARE
SORRY

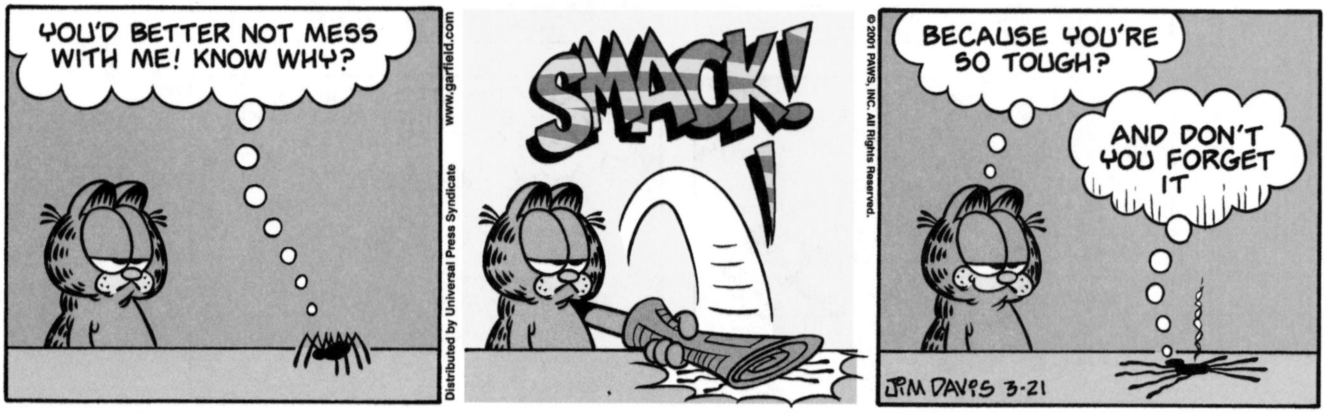
YOU'D BETTER NOT MESS WITH ME! KNOW WHY?
Distributed by Universal Press Syndicate www.garfield.com
SMACK!
© 2001 PAWS, INC. All Rights Reserved.
BECAUSE YOU'RE SO TOUGH?
AND DON'T YOU FORGET IT
JIM DAVIS 3-21

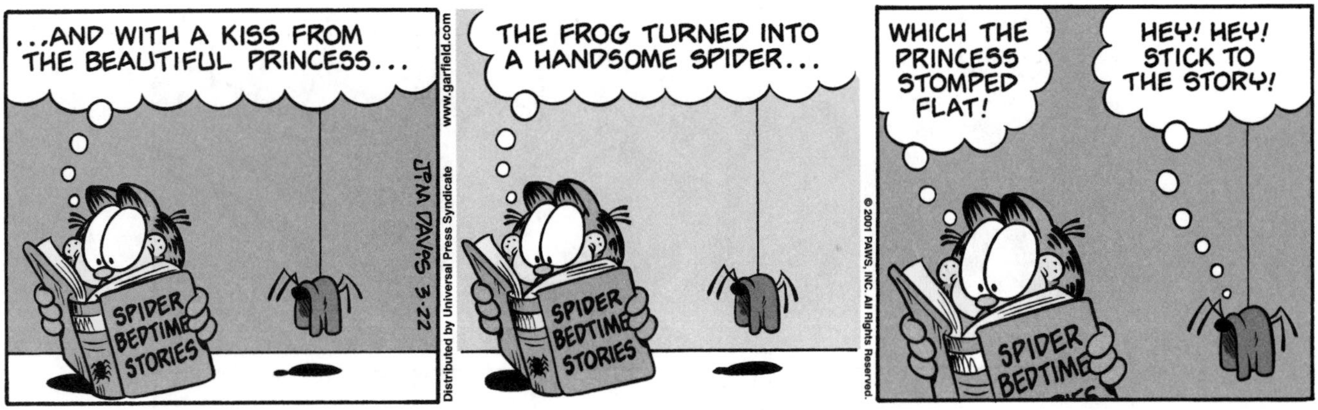
...AND WITH A KISS FROM THE BEAUTIFUL PRINCESS...
SPIDER BEDTIME STORIES
JIM DAVIS 3-22
www.garfield.com
Distributed by Universal Press Syndicate
THE FROG TURNED INTO A HANDSOME SPIDER...
© 2001 PAWS, INC. All Rights Reserved.
WHICH THE PRINCESS STOMPED FLAT!
HEY! HEY! STICK TO THE STORY!

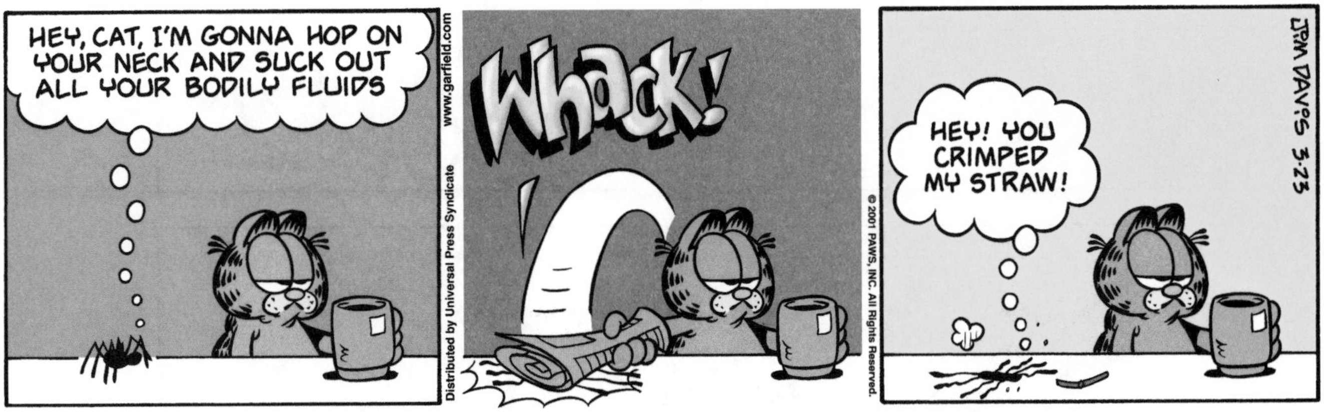
HEY, CAT, I'M GONNA HOP ON YOUR NECK AND SUCK OUT ALL YOUR BODILY FLUIDS
www.garfield.com
Distributed by Universal Press Syndicate
WHACK!
© 2001 PAWS, INC. All Rights Reserved.
HEY! YOU CRIMPED MY STRAW!
JIM DAVIS 3-23

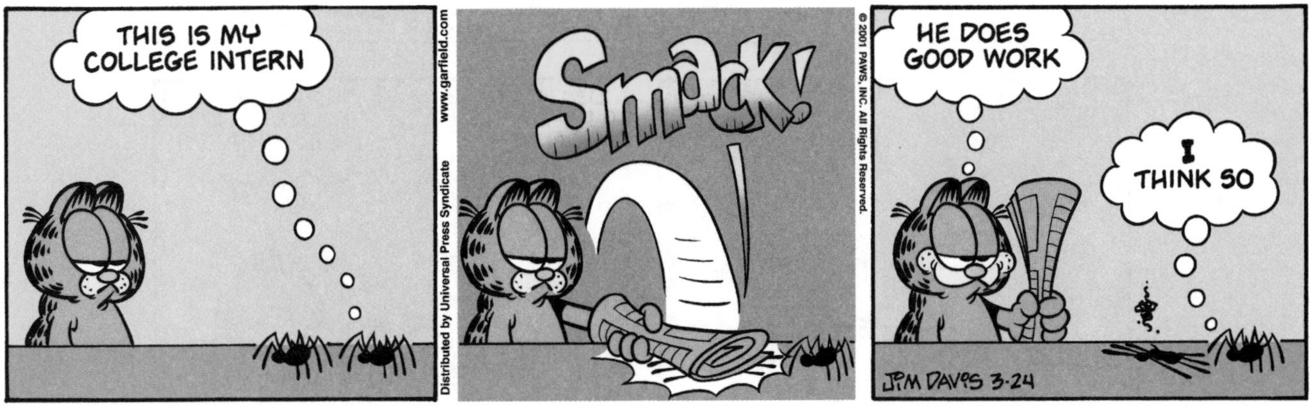
THIS IS MY COLLEGE INTERN
www.garfield.com
Distributed by Universal Press Syndicate
SMACK!
© 2001 PAWS, INC. All Rights Reserved.
HE DOES GOOD WORK
I THINK SO
JIM DAVIS 3-24

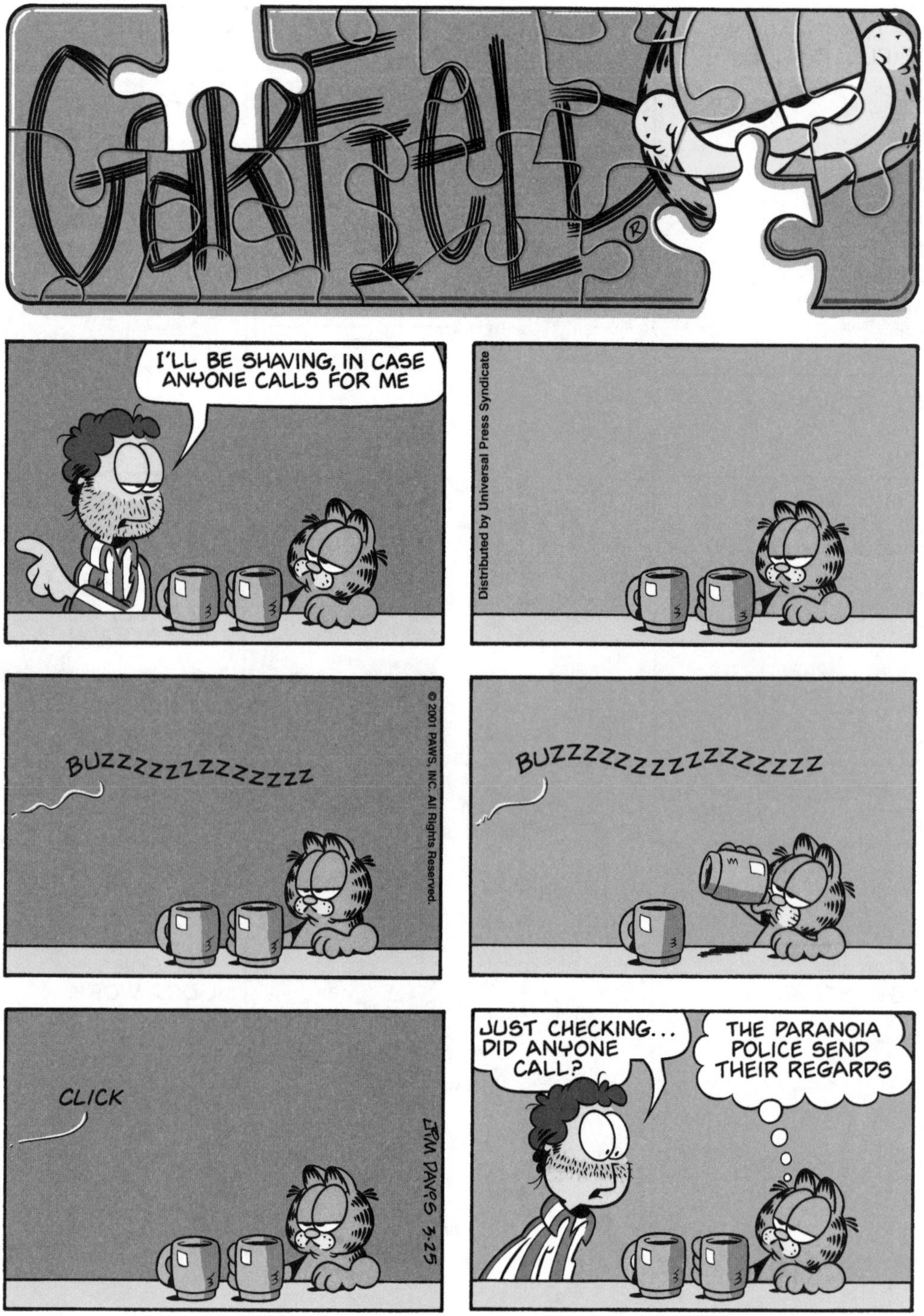
GARFIELD®
I'LL BE SHAVING, IN CASE ANYONE CALLS FOR ME
Distributed by Universal Press Syndicate
© 2001 PAWS, INC. All Rights Reserved.
BUZZZZZZZZZZZZZ
BUZZZZZZZZZZZZZZZZ
CLICK
JIM DAVIS 3-25
JUST CHECKING... DID ANYONE CALL?
THE PARANOIA POLICE SEND THEIR REGARDS

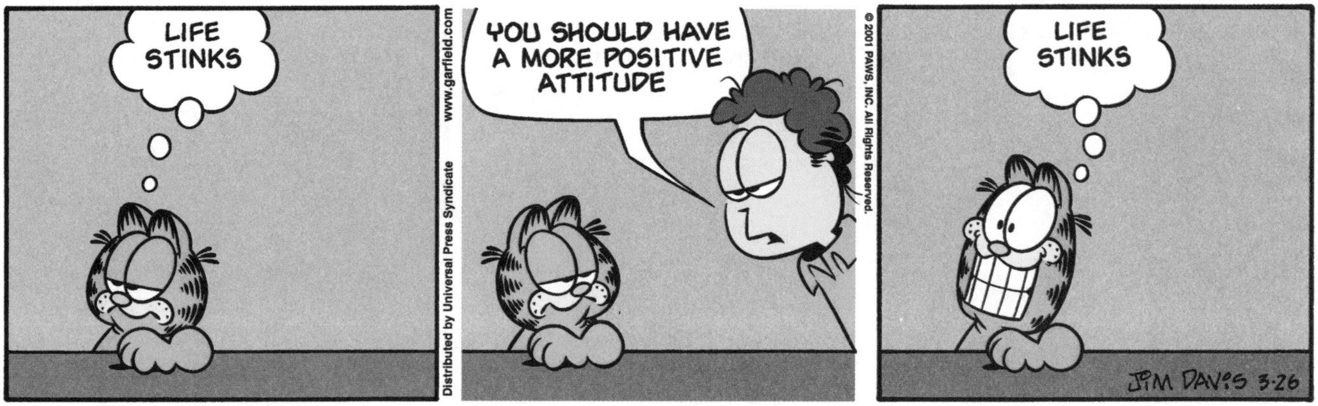
LIFE STINKS
www.garfield.com
Distributed by Universal Press Syndicate
YOU SHOULD HAVE A MORE POSITIVE ATTITUDE
© 2001 PAWS, INC. All Rights Reserved.
LIFE STINKS
JIM DAVIS 3-26

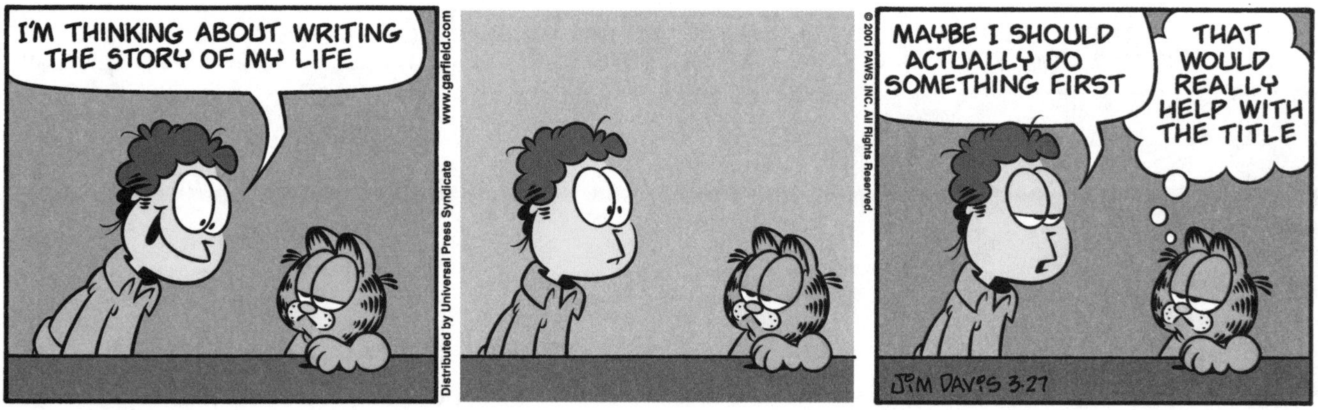
I'M THINKING ABOUT WRITING THE STORY OF MY LIFE
www.garfield.com
Distributed by Universal Press Syndicate
© 2001 PAWS, INC. All Rights Reserved.
MAYBE I SHOULD ACTUALLY DO SOMETHING FIRST
THAT WOULD REALLY HELP WITH THE TITLE
JIM DAVIS 3-27

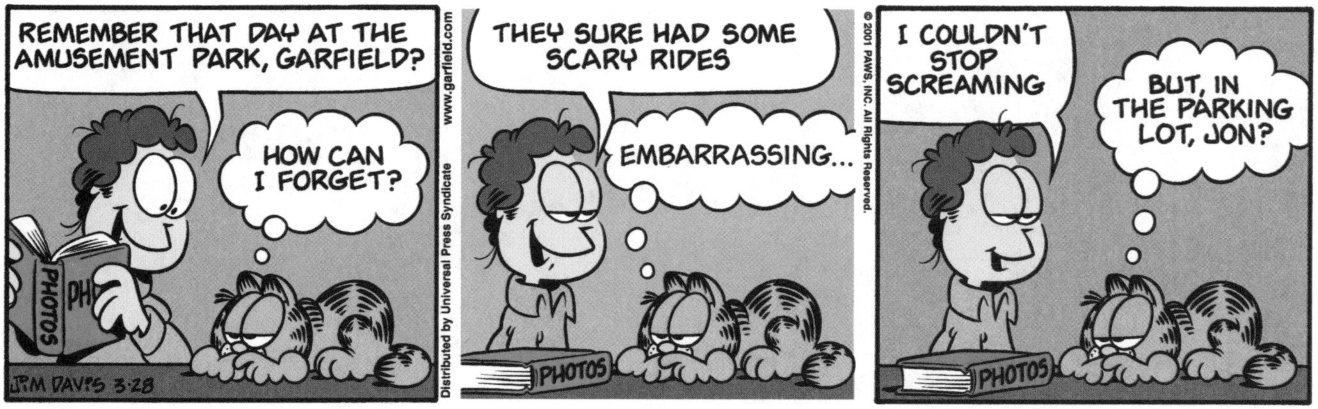
REMEMBER THAT DAY AT THE AMUSEMENT PARK, GARFIELD?
HOW CAN I FORGET?
PHOTOS
JIM DAVIS 3-28
www.garfield.com
Distributed by Universal Press Syndicate
THEY SURE HAD SOME SCARY RIDES
EMBARRASSING...
PHOTOS
© 2001 PAWS, INC. All Rights Reserved.
I COULDN'T STOP SCREAMING
BUT, IN THE PARKING LOT, JON?
PHOTOS

WHEN COMMUNICATING WITH PETS...
JIM DAVIS 3-29
www.garfield.com
Distributed by Universal Press Syndicate
PETS
KEEP COMMANDS SIMPLE AND TO THE POINT
PETS
© 2001 PAWS, INC. All Rights Reserved.
LOSE... SOME... WEIGHT
GET... A... LIFE
PETS

MAYBE I'LL GET TOGETHER WITH FRIENDS TONIGHT
www.garfield.com
Distributed by Universal Press Syndicate
WE'LL LAUGH AND ENGAGE IN STIMULATING CONVERSATION...
© 2001 PAWS, INC. All Rights Reserved.
OR MAYBE I'LL STAY HOME AND FLOSS
REALITY SETS IN
JIM DAVIS 3-30

DO YOU KNOW WHAT'S WRONG WITH CATS?
www.garfield.com
Distributed by Universal Press Syndicate
THEY...
CLICK
JIM DAVIS 3-31
© 2001 PAWS, INC. All Rights Reserved.
HEY!
YOU WATCH TOO MUCH TELEVISION

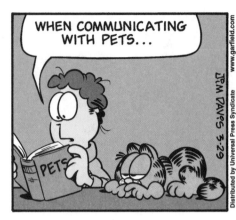

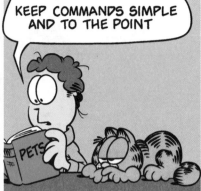

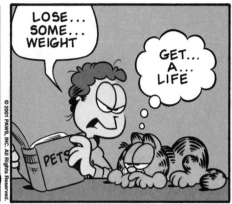

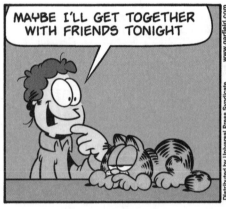

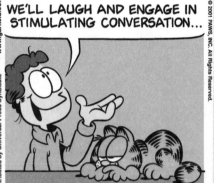

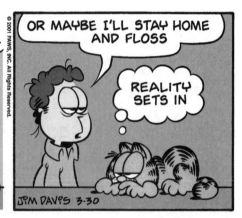

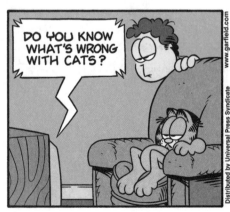

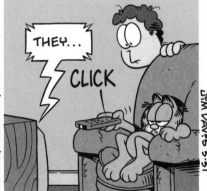

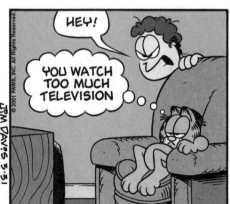

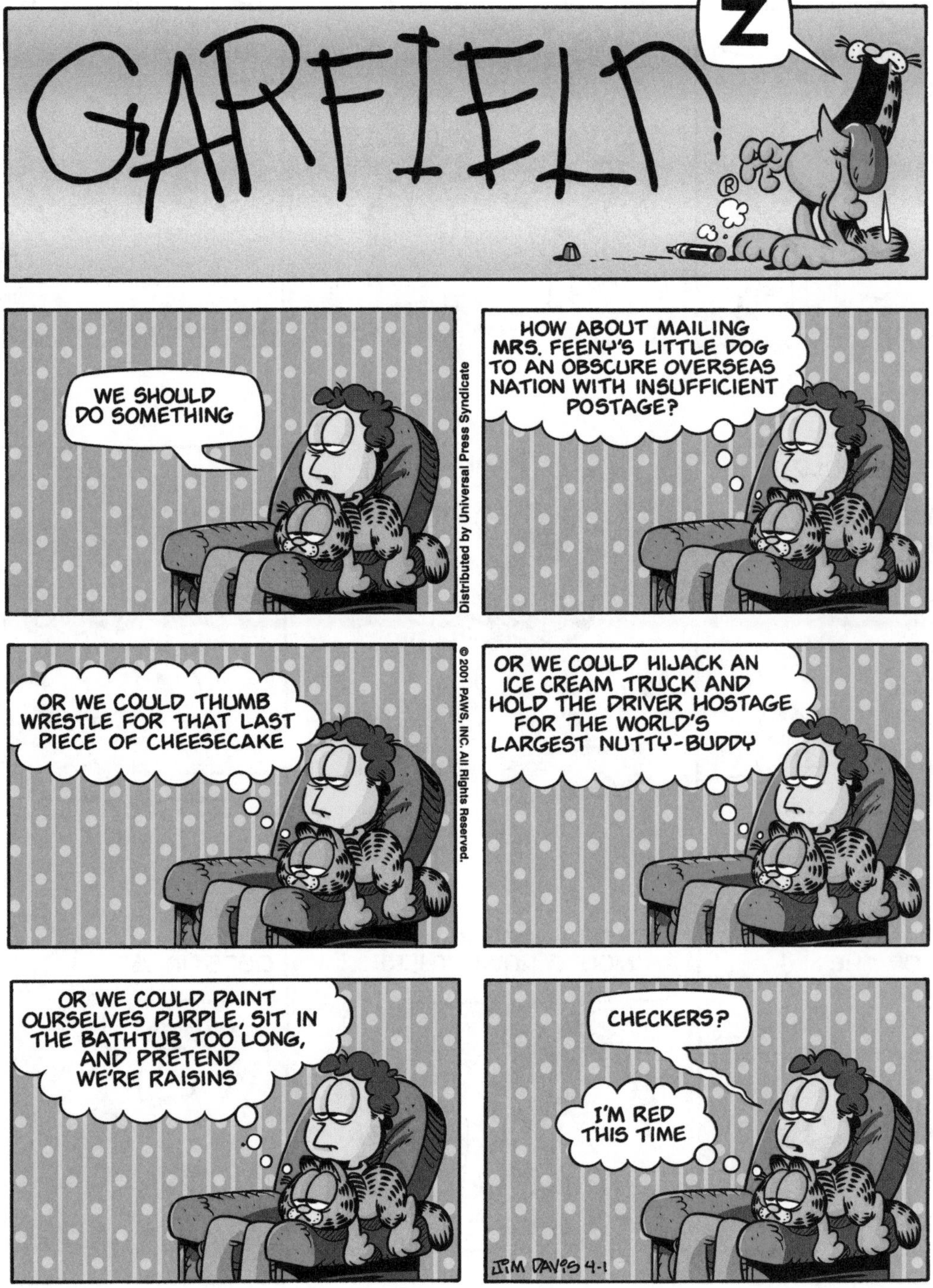
GARFIELD
Z
WE SHOULD DO SOMETHING
HOW ABOUT MAILING MRS. FEENY'S LITTLE DOG TO AN OBSCURE OVERSEAS NATION WITH INSUFFICIENT POSTAGE?
OR WE COULD THUMB WRESTLE FOR THAT LAST PIECE OF CHEESECAKE
OR WE COULD HIJACK AN ICE CREAM TRUCK AND HOLD THE DRIVER HOSTAGE FOR THE WORLD'S LARGEST NUTTY-BUDDY
OR WE COULD PAINT OURSELVES PURPLE, SIT IN THE BATHTUB TOO LONG, AND PRETEND WE'RE RAISINS
CHECKERS?
I'M RED THIS TIME
JIM DAVIS 4-1

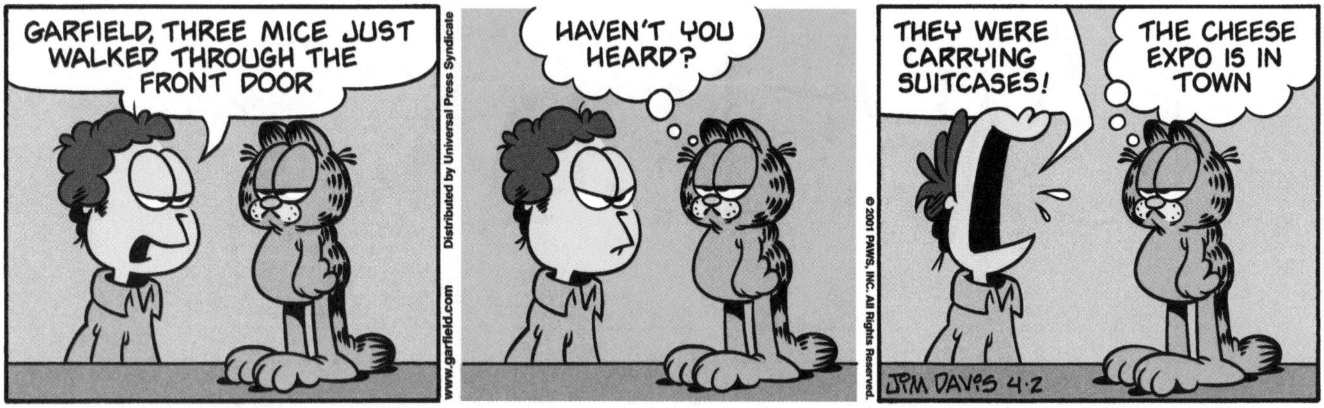
GARFIELD, THREE MICE JUST WALKED THROUGH THE FRONT DOOR
HAVEN'T YOU HEARD?
THEY WERE CARRYING SUITCASES!
THE CHEESE EXPO IS IN TOWN
JIM DAVIS 4-2
www.garfield.com Distributed by Universal Press Syndicate
© 2001 PAWS, INC. All Rights Reserved.

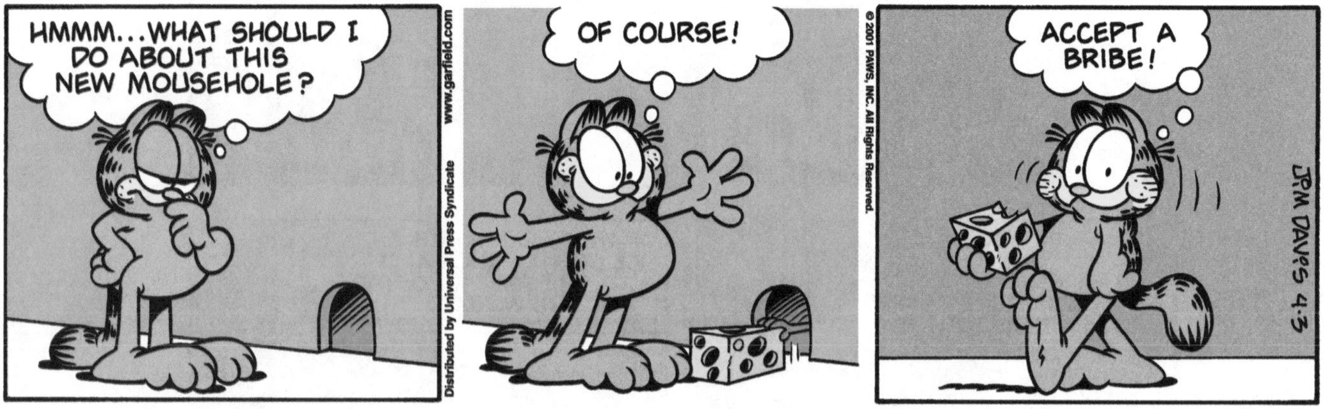
HMMM...WHAT SHOULD I DO ABOUT THIS NEW MOUSEHOLE?
OF COURSE!
ACCEPT A BRIBE!
JIM DAVIS 4-3
Distributed by Universal Press Syndicate www.garfield.com
© 2001 PAWS, INC. All Rights Reserved.

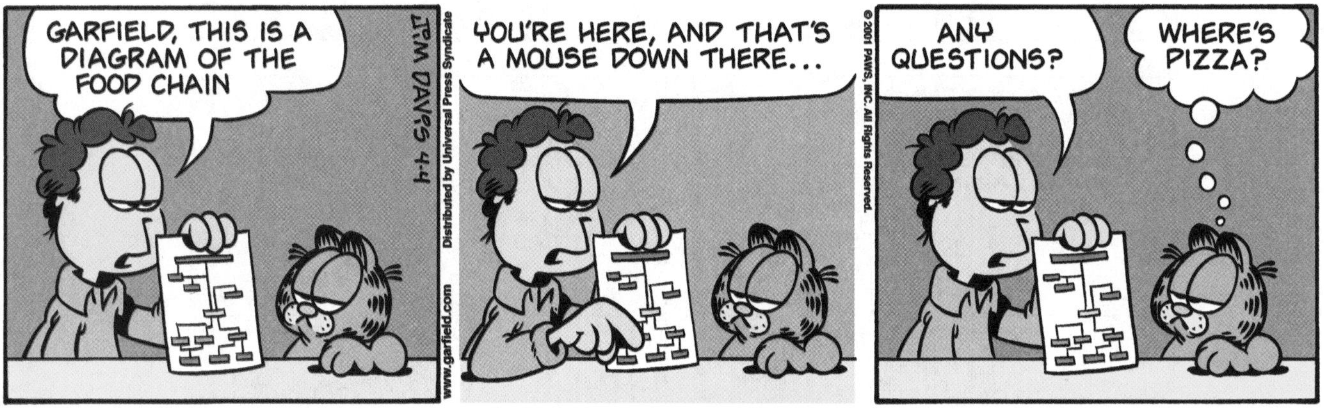
GARFIELD, THIS IS A DIAGRAM OF THE FOOD CHAIN
JIM DAVIS 4-4
YOU'RE HERE, AND THAT'S A MOUSE DOWN THERE...
ANY QUESTIONS?
WHERE'S PIZZA?
www.garfield.com Distributed by Universal Press Syndicate
© 2001 PAWS, INC. All Rights Reserved.

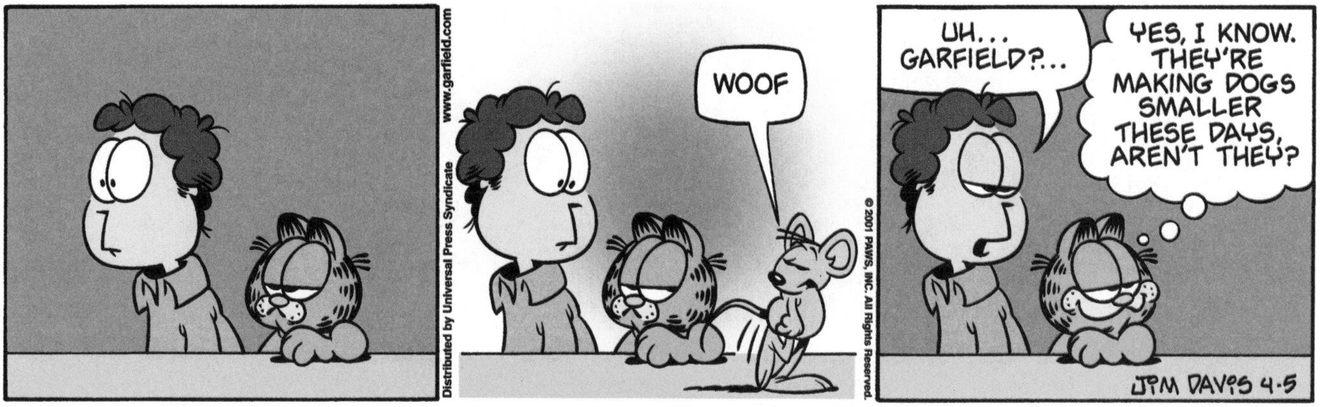
WOOF
UH... GARFIELD?...
YES, I KNOW. THEY'RE MAKING DOGS SMALLER THESE DAYS, AREN'T THEY?
JIM DAVIS 4-5
www.garfield.com
Distributed by Universal Press Syndicate
© 2001 PAWS, INC. All Rights Reserved.

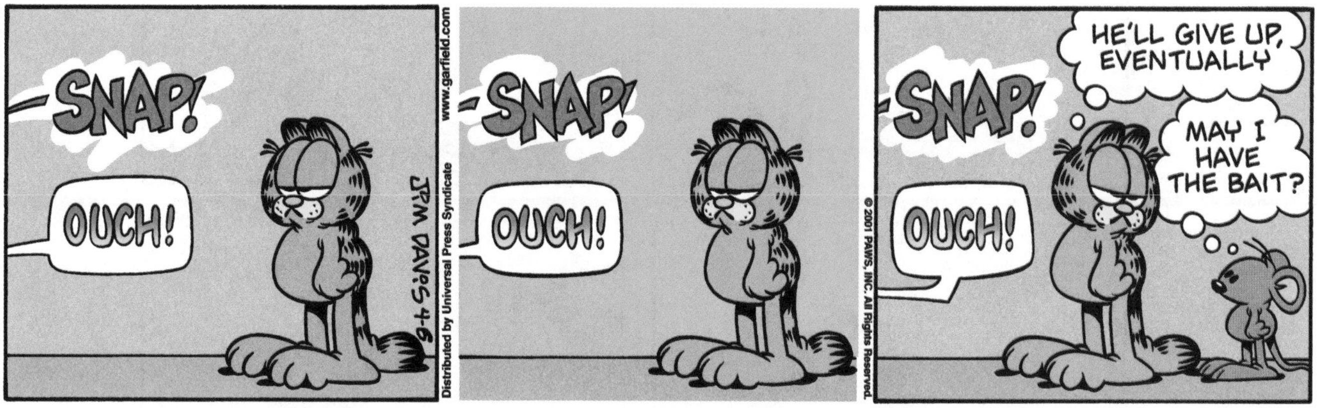
SNAP!
OUCH!
JIM DAVIS 4-6
SNAP!
OUCH!
SNAP!
OUCH!
HE'LL GIVE UP, EVENTUALLY
MAY I HAVE THE BAIT?
www.garfield.com
Distributed by Universal Press Syndicate
© 2001 PAWS, INC. All Rights Reserved.

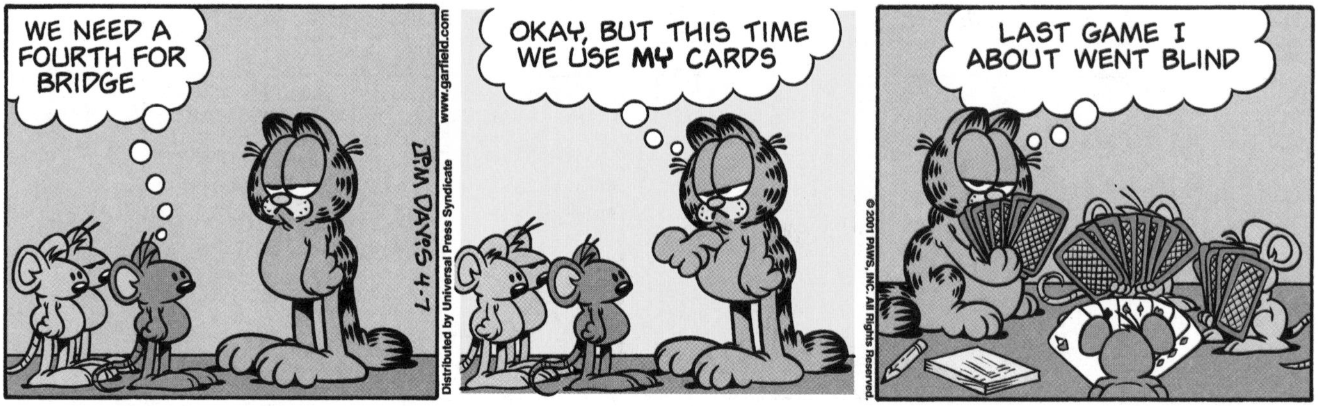
WE NEED A FOURTH FOR BRIDGE
JIM DAVIS 4-7
OKAY, BUT THIS TIME WE USE MY CARDS
LAST GAME I ABOUT WENT BLIND
www.garfield.com
Distributed by Universal Press Syndicate
© 2001 PAWS, INC. All Rights Reserved.

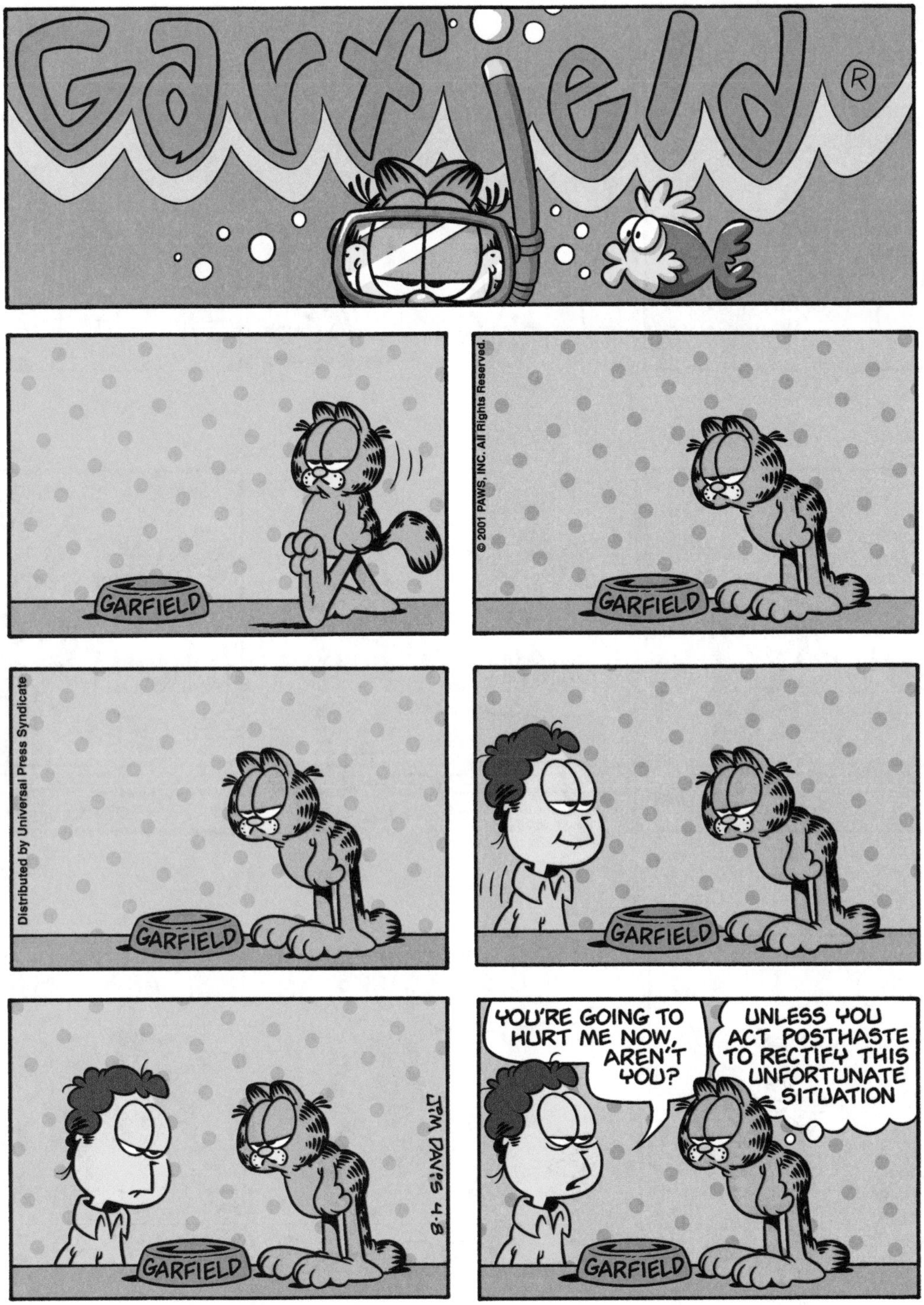

Garfield®
GARFIELD
© 2001 PAWS, INC. All Rights Reserved.
GARFIELD
Distributed by Universal Press Syndicate
GARFIELD
GARFIELD
JIM DAVIS 4-8
GARFIELD
YOU'RE GOING TO HURT ME NOW, AREN'T YOU?
UNLESS YOU ACT POSTHASTE TO RECTIFY THIS UNFORTUNATE SITUATION
GARFIELD

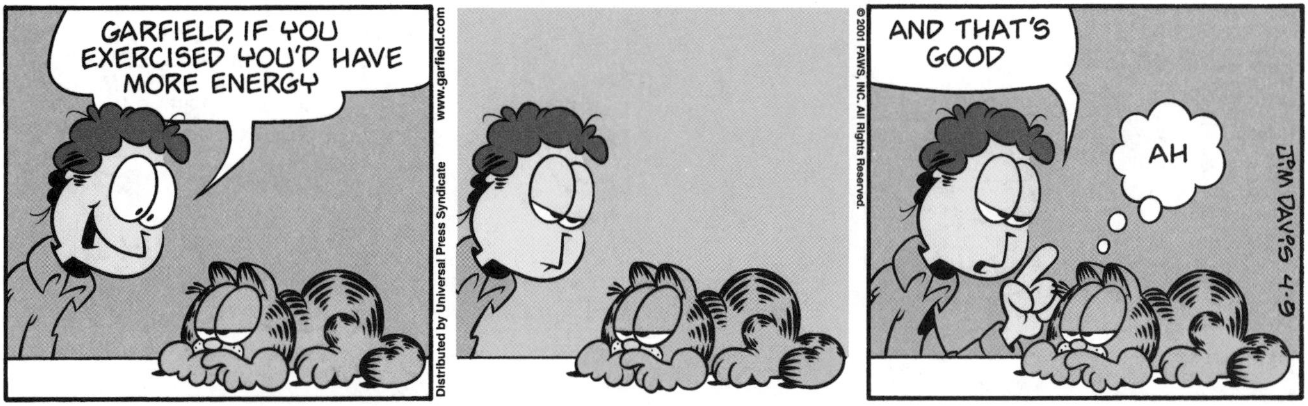
GARFIELD, IF YOU EXERCISED YOU'D HAVE MORE ENERGY
Distributed by Universal Press Syndicate www.garfield.com
© 2001 PAWS, INC. All Rights Reserved.
AND THAT'S GOOD
AH
JPM DAVIS 4-9

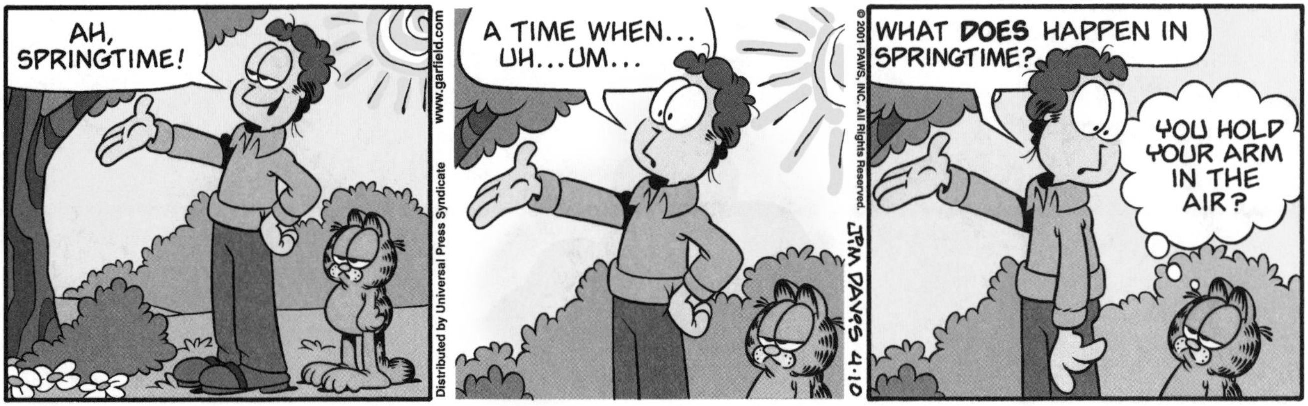
AH, SPRINGTIME!
Distributed by Universal Press Syndicate www.garfield.com
A TIME WHEN... UH...UM...
JPM DAVIS 4-10
© 2001 PAWS, INC. All Rights Reserved.
WHAT **DOES** HAPPEN IN SPRINGTIME?
YOU HOLD YOUR ARM IN THE AIR?

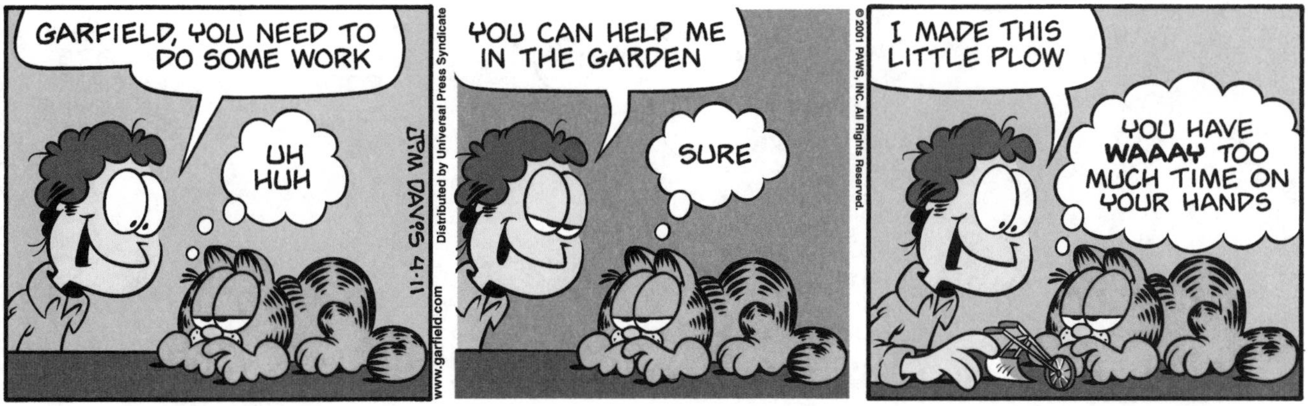
GARFIELD, YOU NEED TO DO SOME WORK
UH HUH
JPM DAVIS 4-11
Distributed by Universal Press Syndicate www.garfield.com
YOU CAN HELP ME IN THE GARDEN
SURE
© 2001 PAWS, INC. All Rights Reserved.
I MADE THIS LITTLE PLOW
YOU HAVE **WAAAY** TOO MUCH TIME ON YOUR HANDS

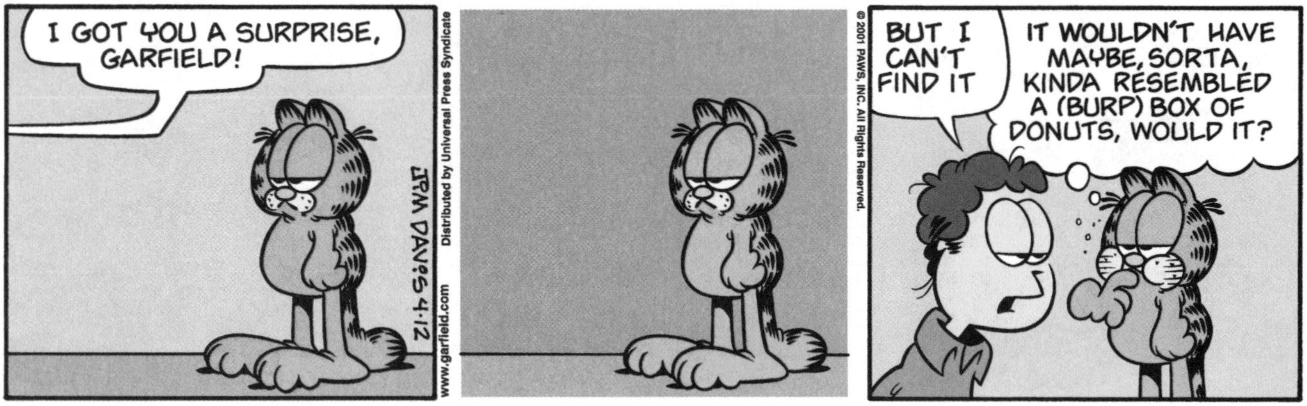
I GOT YOU A SURPRISE, GARFIELD!
JIM DAVIS 4-12
www.garfield.com Distributed by Universal Press Syndicate
© 2001 PAWS, INC. All Rights Reserved.
BUT I CAN'T FIND IT
IT WOULDN'T HAVE MAYBE, SORTA, KINDA RESEMBLED A (BURP) BOX OF DONUTS, WOULD IT?

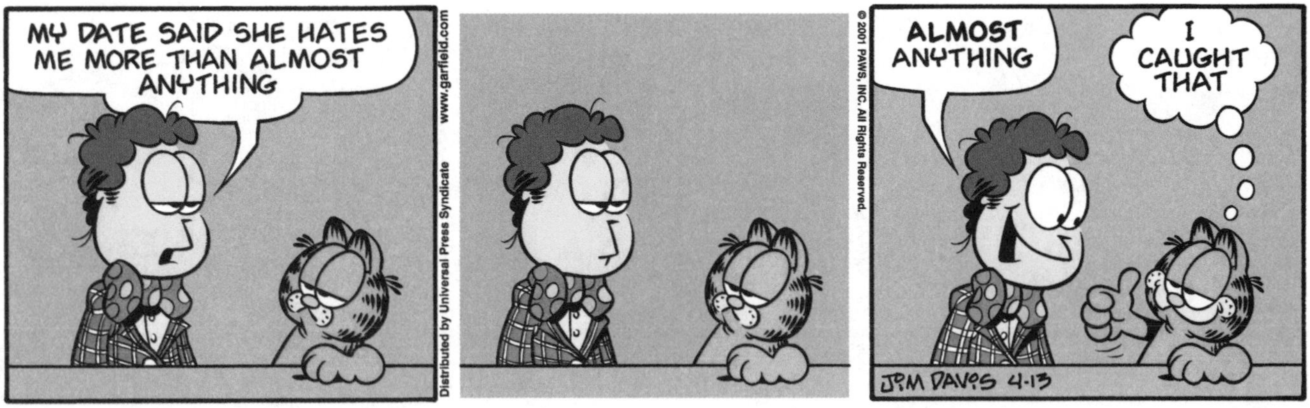
MY DATE SAID SHE HATES ME MORE THAN ALMOST ANYTHING
Distributed by Universal Press Syndicate www.garfield.com
© 2001 PAWS, INC. All Rights Reserved.
ALMOST ANYTHING
I CAUGHT THAT
JIM DAVIS 4-13

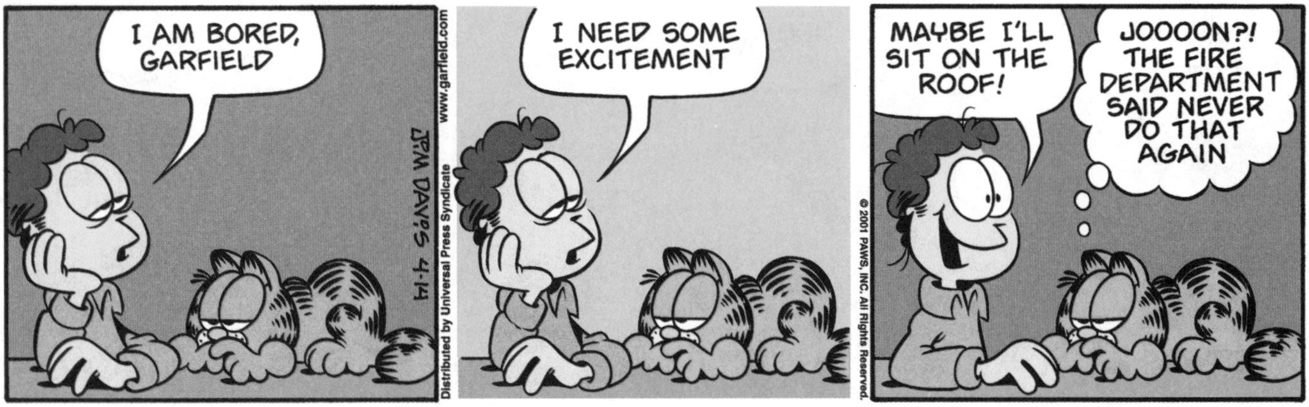
I AM BORED, GARFIELD
JIM DAVIS 4-14
Distributed by Universal Press Syndicate www.garfield.com
I NEED SOME EXCITEMENT
© 2001 PAWS, INC. All Rights Reserved.
MAYBE I'LL SIT ON THE ROOF!
JOOOON?! THE FIRE DEPARTMENT SAID NEVER DO THAT AGAIN

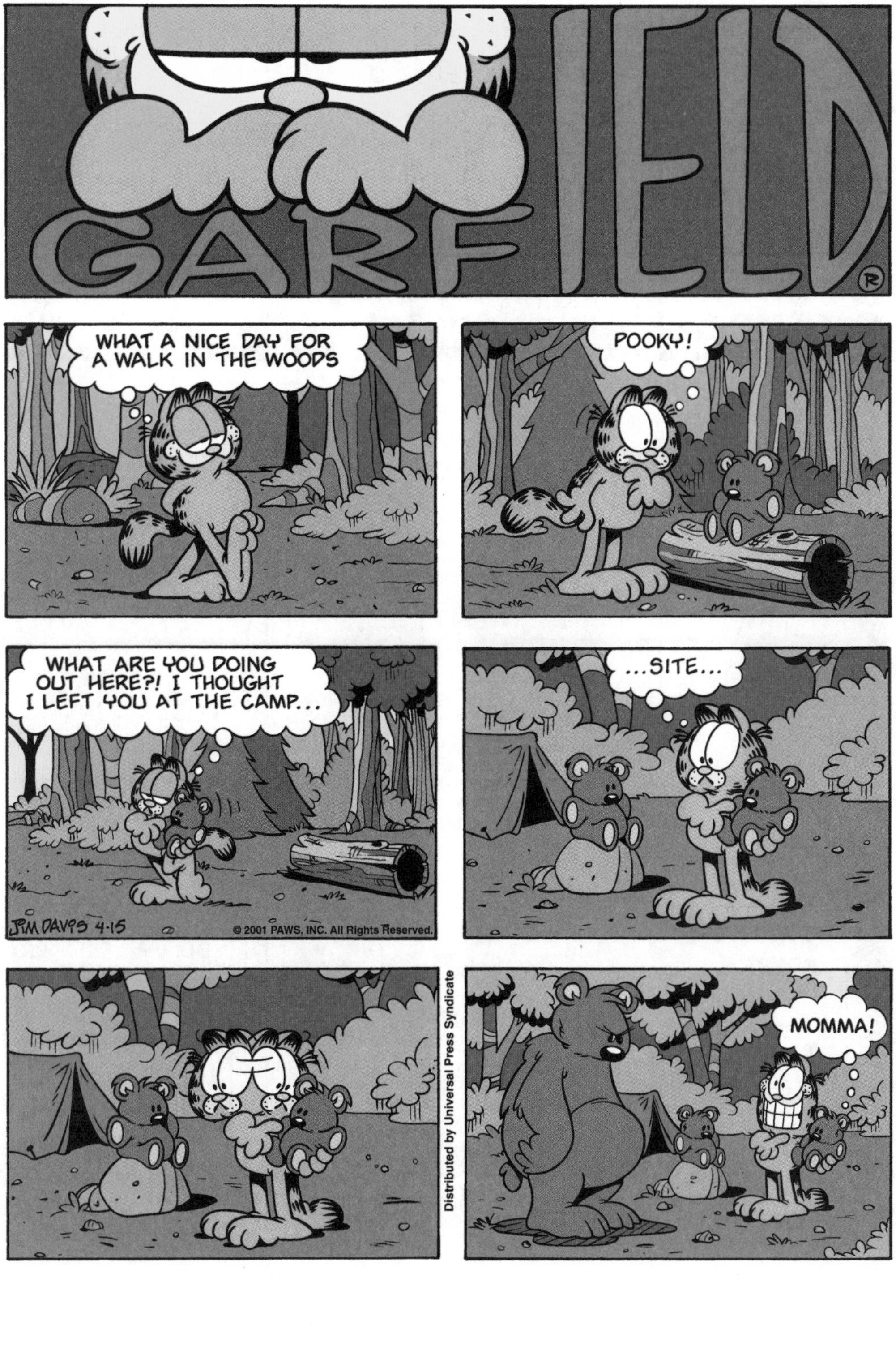
GARFIELD
WHAT A NICE DAY FOR A WALK IN THE WOODS
POOKY!
WHAT ARE YOU DOING OUT HERE?! I THOUGHT I LEFT YOU AT THE CAMP...
...SITE...
MOMMA!
JIM DAVIS 4·15
© 2001 PAWS, INC. All Rights Reserved.
Distributed by Universal Press Syndicate

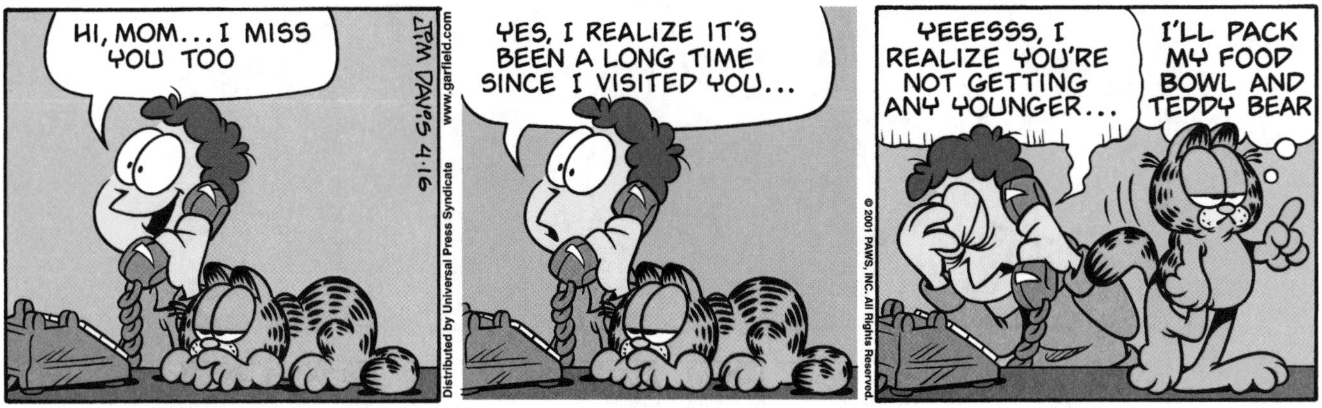
HI, MOM... I MISS YOU TOO
JIM DAVIS 4·16
www.garfield.com
Distributed by Universal Press Syndicate
YES, I REALIZE IT'S BEEN A LONG TIME SINCE I VISITED YOU...
© 2001 PAWS, INC. All Rights Reserved.
YEEESSS, I REALIZE YOU'RE NOT GETTING ANY YOUNGER...
I'LL PACK MY FOOD BOWL AND TEDDY BEAR

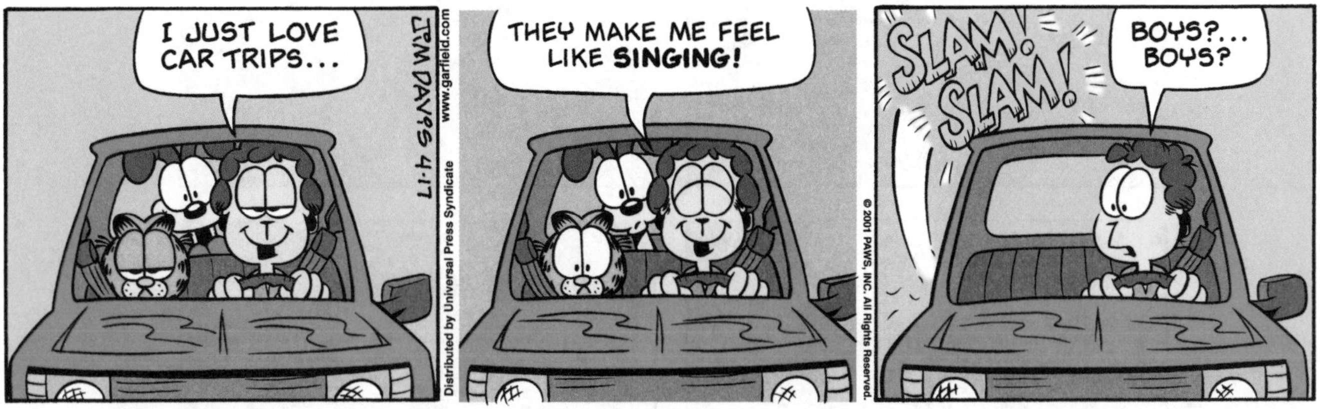
I JUST LOVE CAR TRIPS...
JIM DAVIS 4·17
www.garfield.com
Distributed by Universal Press Syndicate
THEY MAKE ME FEEL LIKE **SINGING!**
© 2001 PAWS, INC. All Rights Reserved.
SLAM! SLAM!
BOYS?... BOYS?

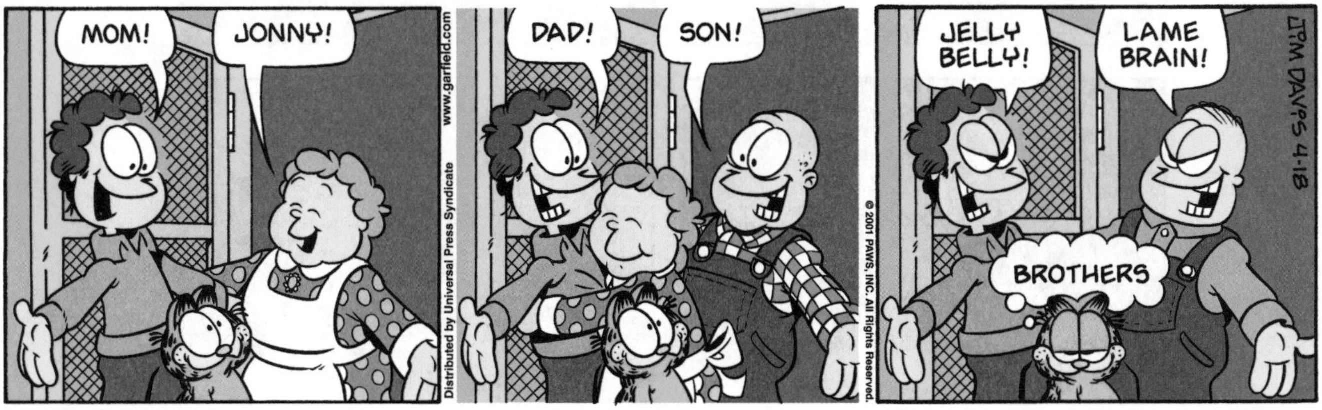
MOM!
JONNY!
www.garfield.com
Distributed by Universal Press Syndicate
DAD!
SON!
© 2001 PAWS, INC. All Rights Reserved.
JELLY BELLY!
LAME BRAIN!
JIM DAVIS 4·18
BROTHERS

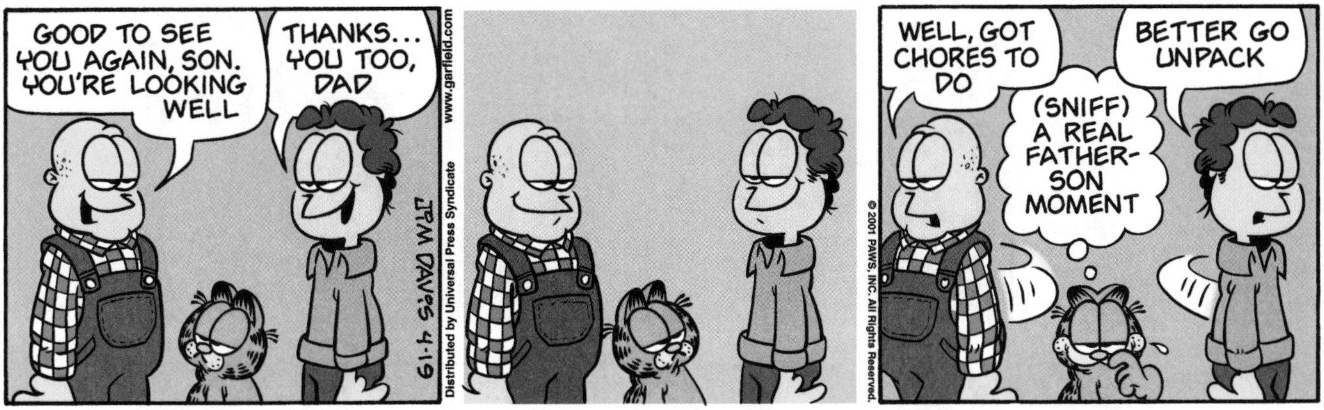
GOOD TO SEE YOU AGAIN, SON. YOU'RE LOOKING WELL
THANKS... YOU TOO, DAD
JPM DAVPS 4·19
www.garfield.com
Distributed by Universal Press Syndicate
WELL, GOT CHORES TO DO
(SNIFF) A REAL FATHER-SON MOMENT
BETTER GO UNPACK
© 2001 PAWS, INC. All Rights Reserved.

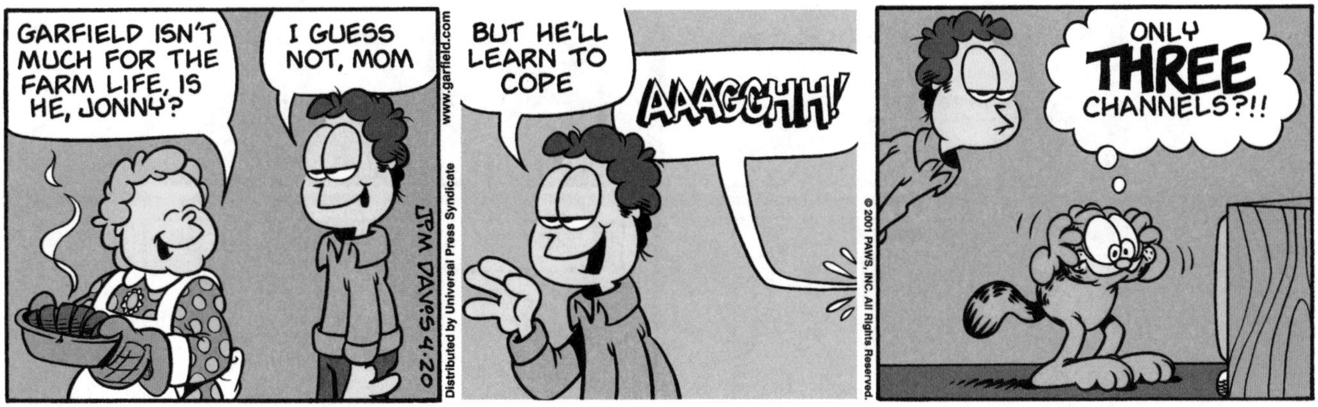
GARFIELD ISN'T MUCH FOR THE FARM LIFE, IS HE, JONNY?
I GUESS NOT, MOM
JPM DAVPS 4·20
www.garfield.com
Distributed by Universal Press Syndicate
BUT HE'LL LEARN TO COPE
AAAGGHH!
ONLY THREE CHANNELS?!!
© 2001 PAWS, INC. All Rights Reserved.

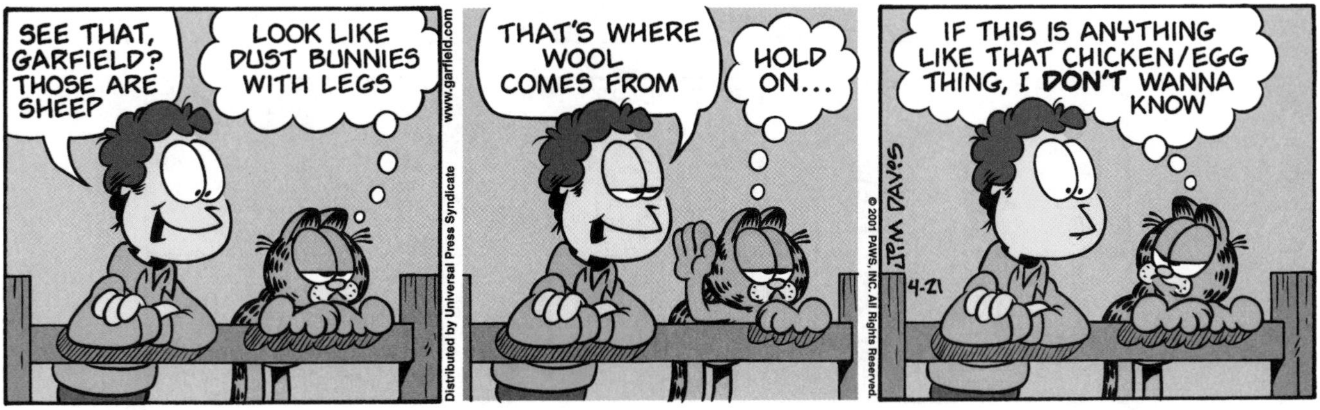
SEE THAT, GARFIELD? THOSE ARE SHEEP
LOOK LIKE DUST BUNNIES WITH LEGS
www.garfield.com
Distributed by Universal Press Syndicate
THAT'S WHERE WOOL COMES FROM
HOLD ON...
JPM DAVPS 4-21
© 2001 PAWS, INC. All Rights Reserved.
IF THIS IS ANYTHING LIKE THAT CHICKEN/EGG THING, I DON'T WANNA KNOW

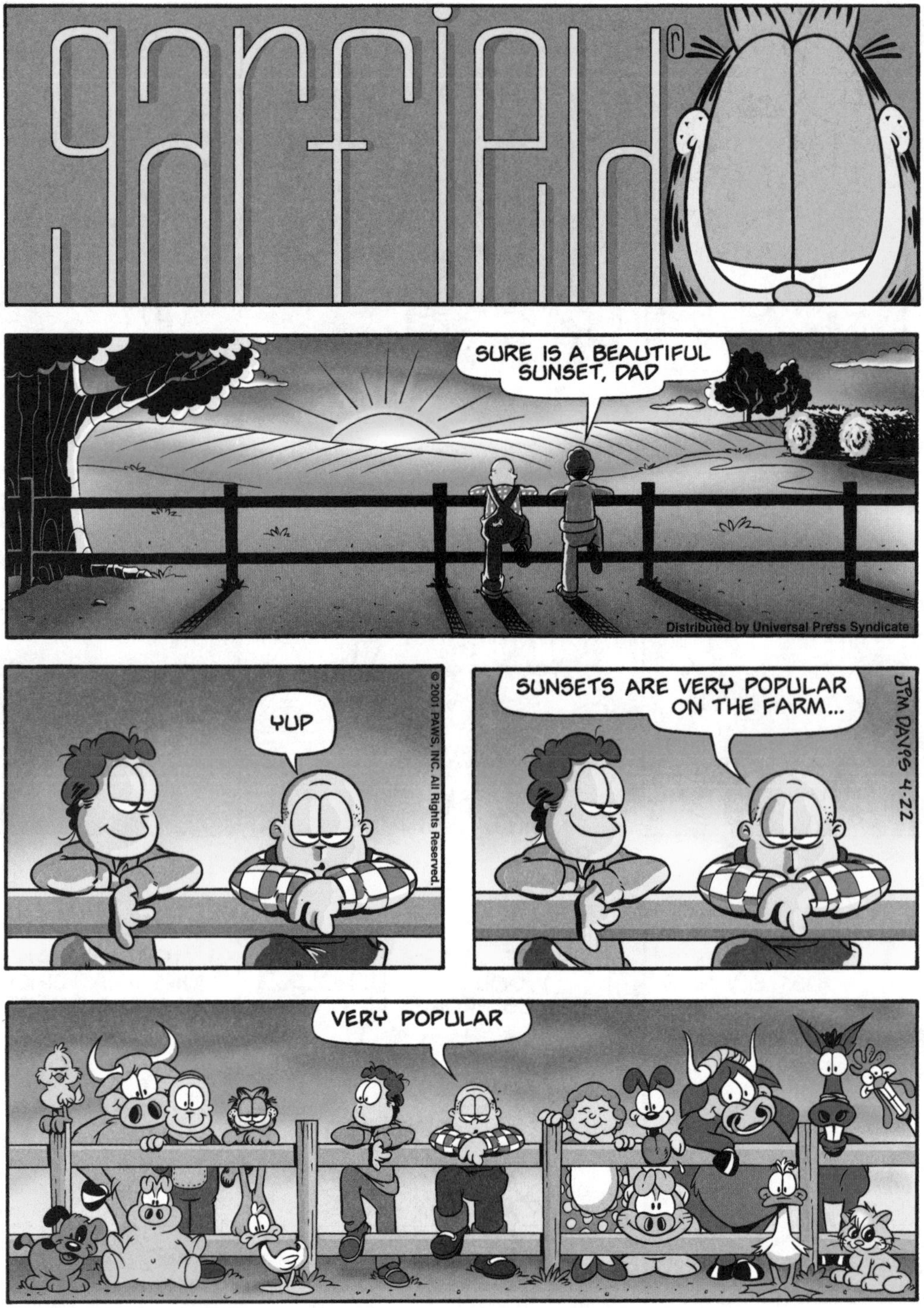
garfield
SURE IS A BEAUTIFUL SUNSET, DAD
Distributed by Universal Press Syndicate
YUP
© 2001 PAWS, INC. All Rights Reserved.
SUNSETS ARE VERY POPULAR ON THE FARM...
JIM DAVIS 4-22
VERY POPULAR

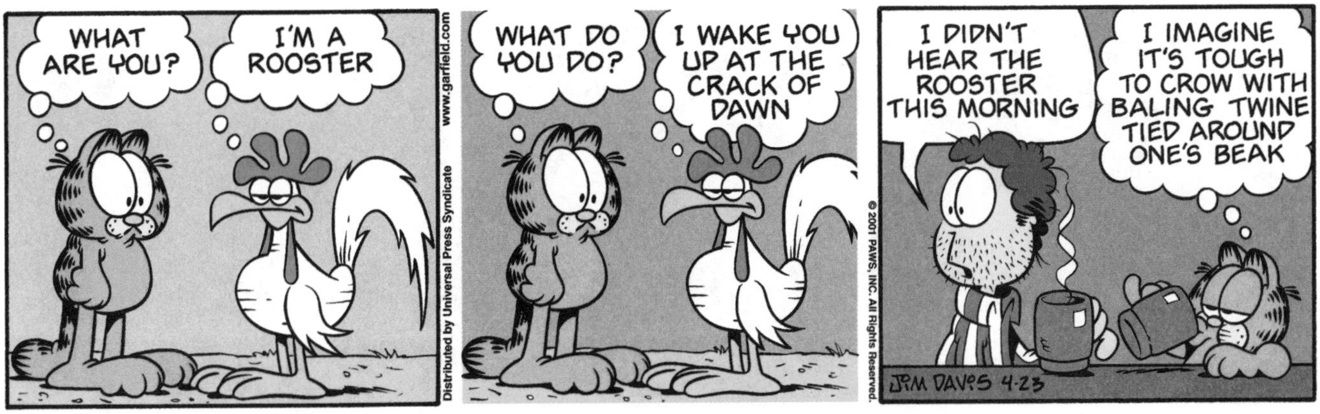
WHAT ARE YOU?
I'M A ROOSTER
WHAT DO YOU DO?
I WAKE YOU UP AT THE CRACK OF DAWN
I DIDN'T HEAR THE ROOSTER THIS MORNING
I IMAGINE IT'S TOUGH TO CROW WITH BALING TWINE TIED AROUND ONE'S BEAK
JIM DAVIS 4-23
www.garfield.com
Distributed by Universal Press Syndicate
© 2001 PAWS, INC. All Rights Reserved.

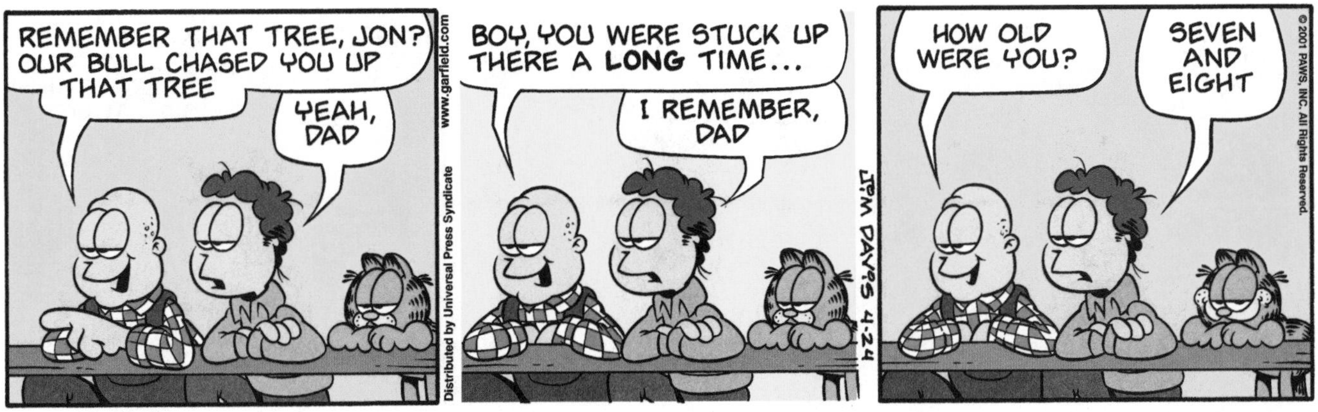
REMEMBER THAT TREE, JON? OUR BULL CHASED YOU UP THAT TREE
YEAH, DAD
BOY, YOU WERE STUCK UP THERE A **LONG** TIME...
I REMEMBER, DAD
HOW OLD WERE YOU?
SEVEN AND EIGHT
JIM DAVIS 4-24
www.garfield.com
Distributed by Universal Press Syndicate
© 2001 PAWS, INC. All Rights Reserved.

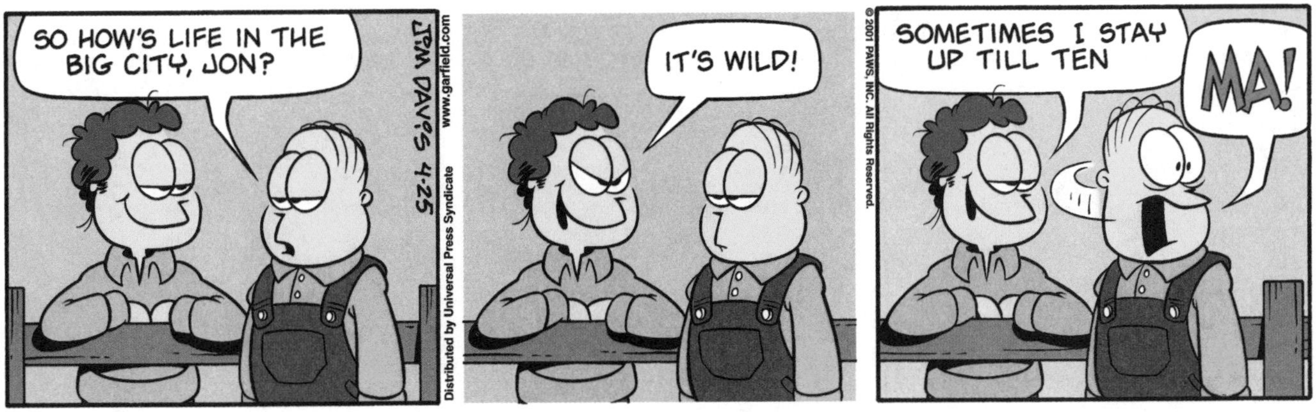
SO HOW'S LIFE IN THE BIG CITY, JON?
IT'S WILD!
SOMETIMES I STAY UP TILL TEN
MA!
JIM DAVIS 4-25
www.garfield.com
Distributed by Universal Press Syndicate
© 2001 PAWS, INC. All Rights Reserved.

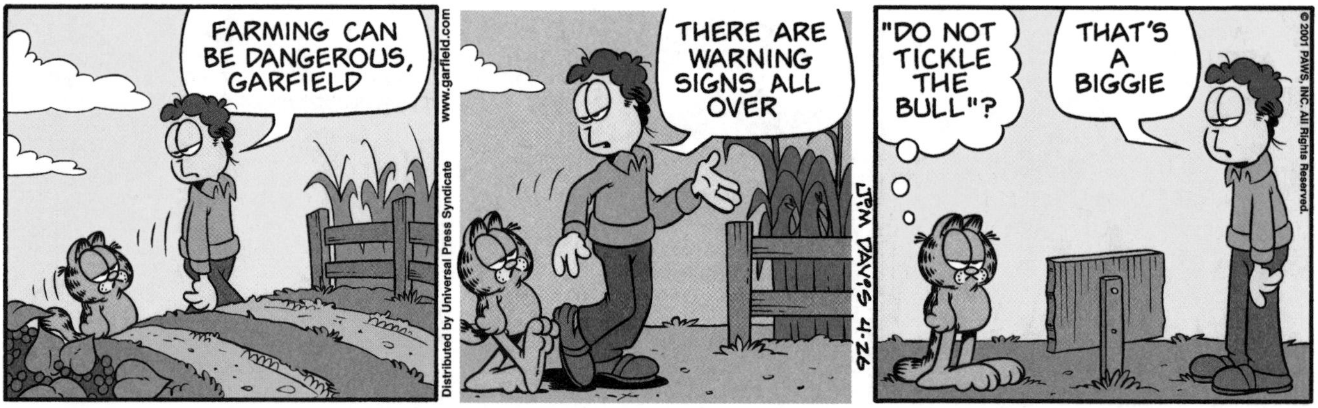
FARMING CAN BE DANGEROUS, GARFIELD
www.garfield.com
Distributed by Universal Press Syndicate
THERE ARE WARNING SIGNS ALL OVER
JIM DAVIS 4-26
"DO NOT TICKLE THE BULL"?
THAT'S A BIGGIE
© 2001 PAWS, INC. All Rights Reserved.

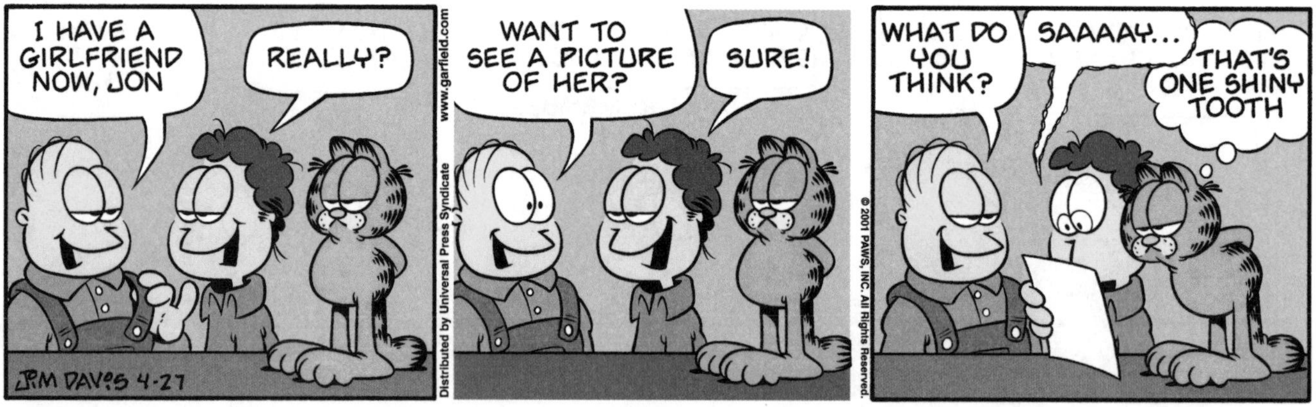
I HAVE A GIRLFRIEND NOW, JON
REALLY?
JIM DAVIS 4-27
www.garfield.com
Distributed by Universal Press Syndicate
WANT TO SEE A PICTURE OF HER?
SURE!
© 2001 PAWS, INC. All Rights Reserved.
WHAT DO YOU THINK?
SAAAAY...
THAT'S ONE SHINY TOOTH

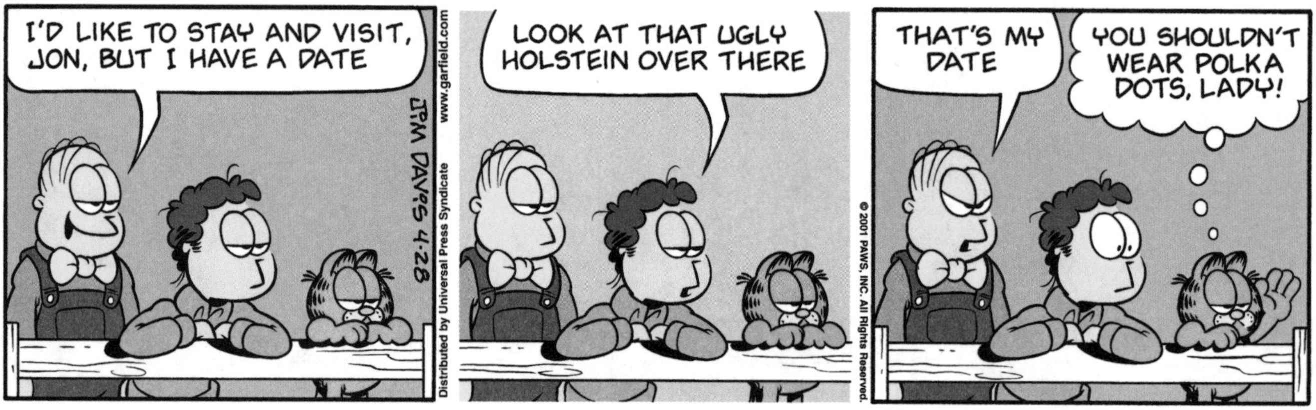
I'D LIKE TO STAY AND VISIT, JON, BUT I HAVE A DATE
www.garfield.com
Distributed by Universal Press Syndicate
JIM DAVIS 4-28
LOOK AT THAT UGLY HOLSTEIN OVER THERE
© 2001 PAWS, INC. All Rights Reserved.
THAT'S MY DATE
YOU SHOULDN'T WEAR POLKA DOTS, LADY!

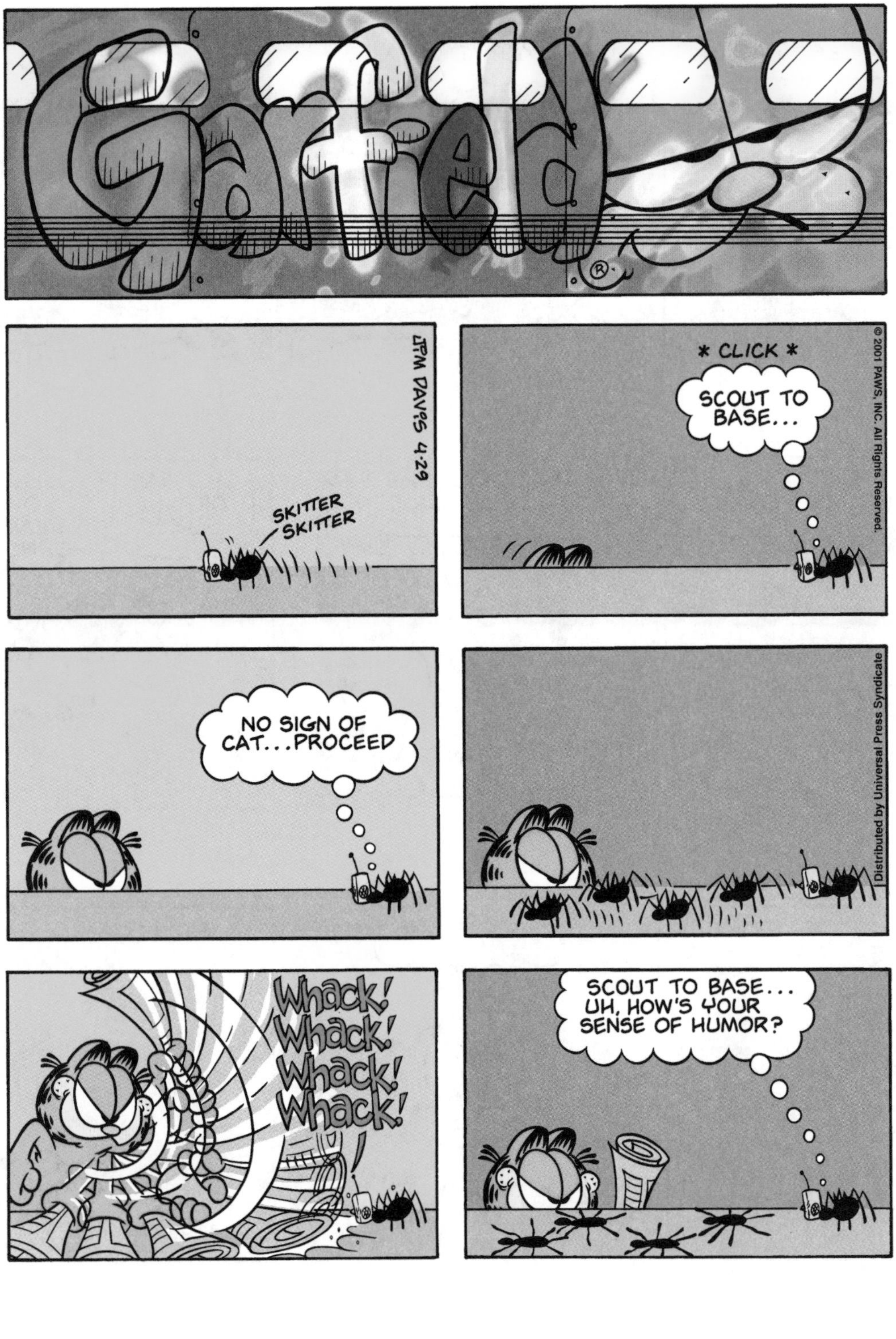
Garfield®
JPM DAVIS 4-29
SKITTER SKITTER
* CLICK *
SCOUT TO BASE...
© 2001 PAWS, INC. All Rights Reserved.
NO SIGN OF CAT...PROCEED
Distributed by Universal Press Syndicate
Whack! Whack! Whack! Whack!
SCOUT TO BASE... UH, HOW'S YOUR SENSE OF HUMOR?

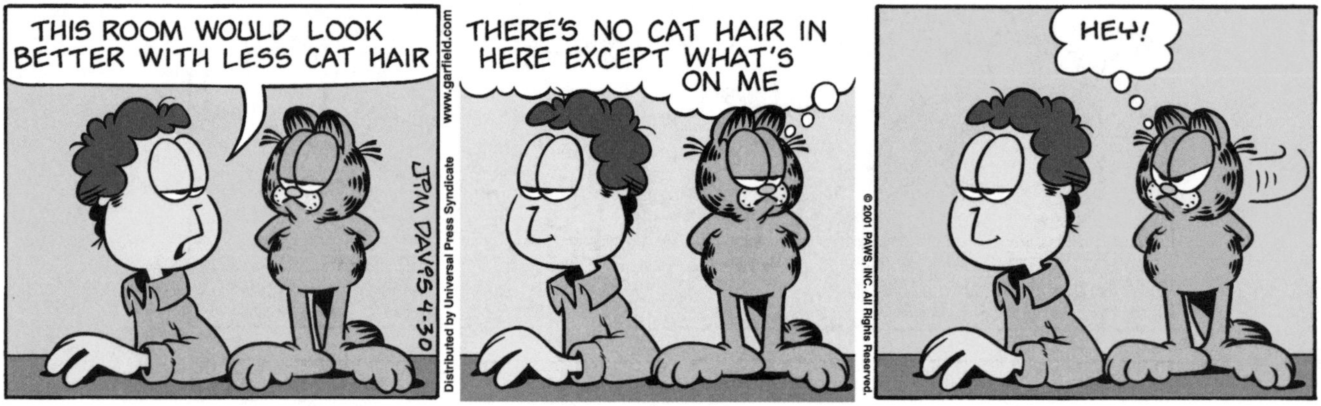
THIS ROOM WOULD LOOK BETTER WITH LESS CAT HAIR
JIM DAVIS 4-30
www.garfield.com
Distributed by Universal Press Syndicate
THERE'S NO CAT HAIR IN HERE EXCEPT WHAT'S ON ME
© 2001 PAWS, INC. All Rights Reserved.
HEY!

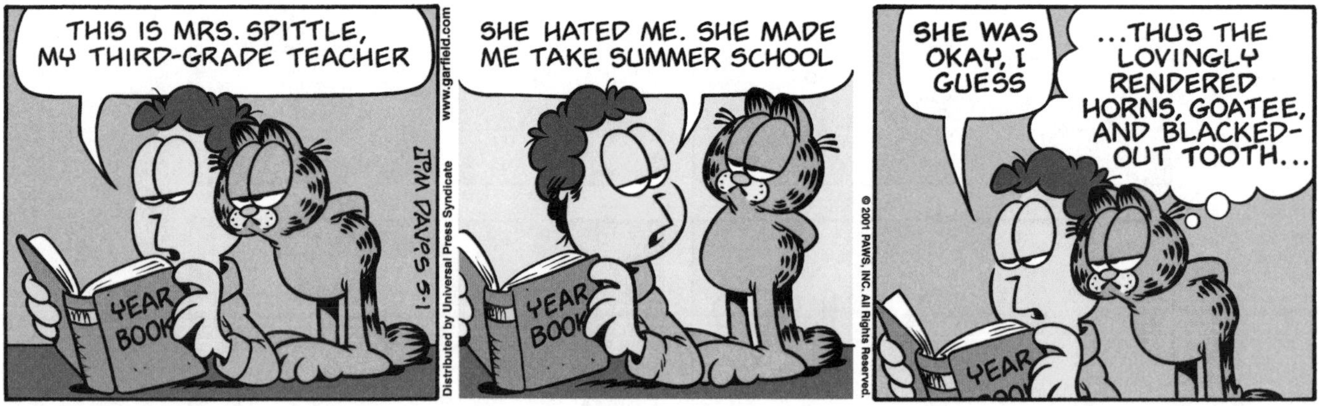
THIS IS MRS. SPITTLE, MY THIRD-GRADE TEACHER
YEAR BOOK
JIM DAVIS 5-1
www.garfield.com
Distributed by Universal Press Syndicate
SHE HATED ME. SHE MADE ME TAKE SUMMER SCHOOL
YEAR BOOK
© 2001 PAWS, INC. All Rights Reserved.
SHE WAS OKAY, I GUESS
...THUS THE LOVINGLY RENDERED HORNS, GOATEE, AND BLACKED-OUT TOOTH...

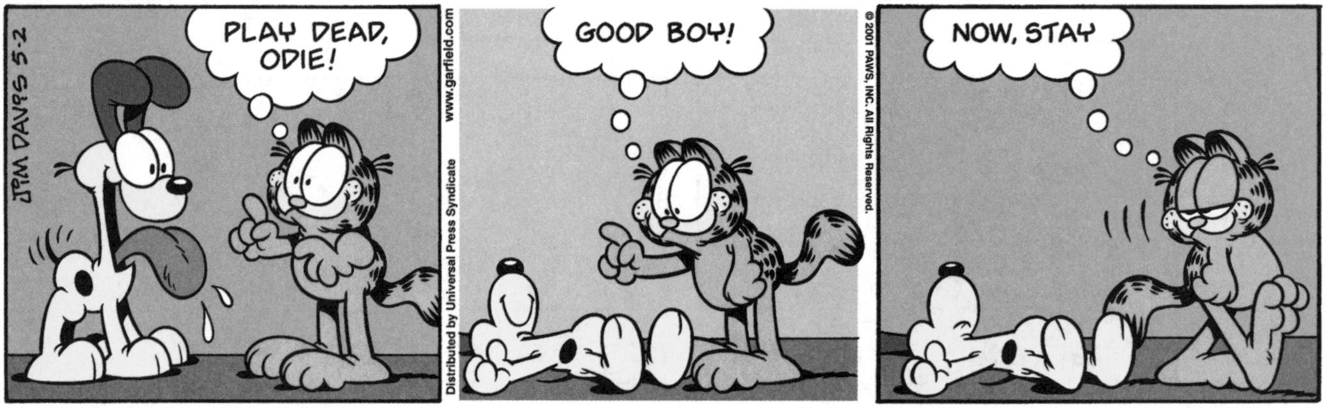
JIM DAVIS 5-2
PLAY DEAD, ODIE!
www.garfield.com
Distributed by Universal Press Syndicate
GOOD BOY!
© 2001 PAWS, INC. All Rights Reserved.
NOW, STAY

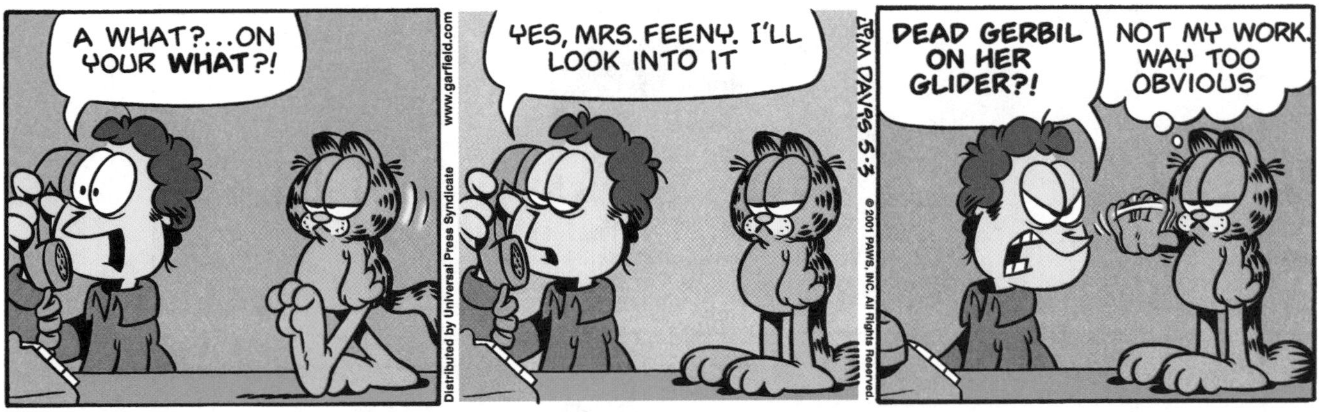
A WHAT?...ON YOUR WHAT?!
www.garfield.com
Distributed by Universal Press Syndicate
YES, MRS. FEENY. I'LL LOOK INTO IT
JIM DAVIS 5-3
© 2001 PAWS, INC. All Rights Reserved.
DEAD GERBIL ON HER GLIDER?!
NOT MY WORK. WAY TOO OBVIOUS

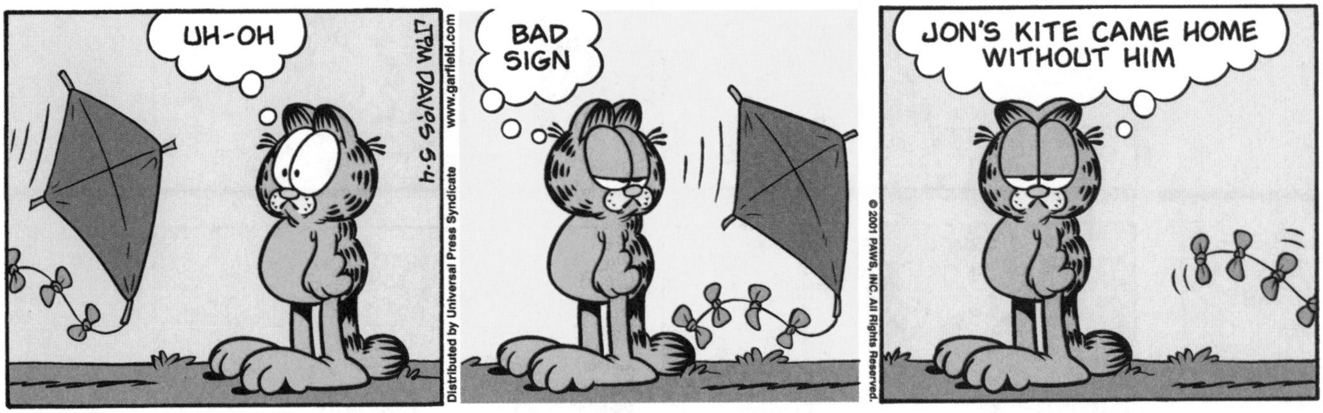
UH-OH
JIM DAVIS 5-4
www.garfield.com
Distributed by Universal Press Syndicate
BAD SIGN
© 2001 PAWS, INC. All Rights Reserved.
JON'S KITE CAME HOME WITHOUT HIM

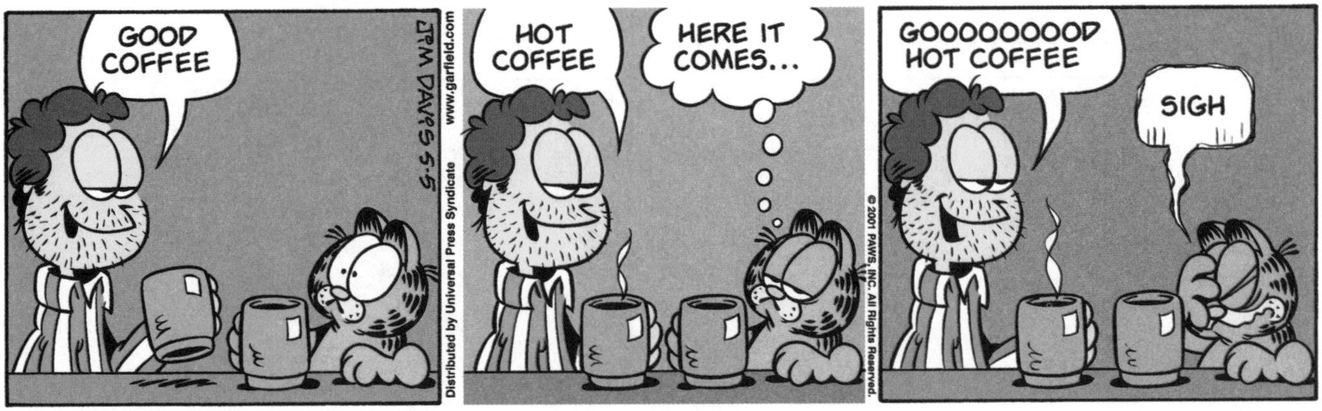
GOOD COFFEE
JIM DAVIS 5-5
www.garfield.com
Distributed by Universal Press Syndicate
HOT COFFEE
HERE IT COMES...
© 2001 PAWS, INC. All Rights Reserved.
GOOOOOOOOD HOT COFFEE
SIGH

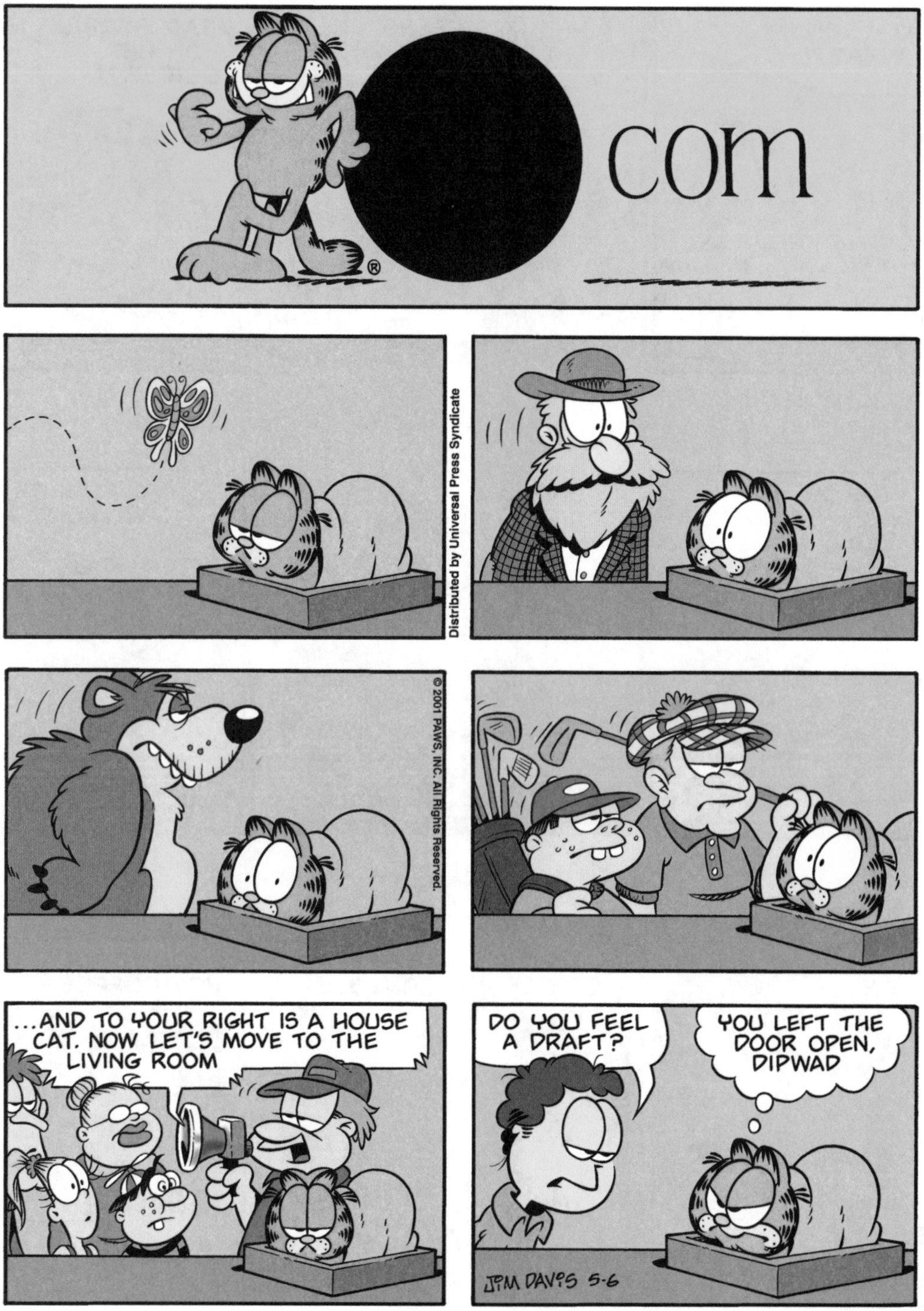
com
Distributed by Universal Press Syndicate
© 2001 PAWS, INC. All Rights Reserved.
...AND TO YOUR RIGHT IS A HOUSE CAT. NOW LET'S MOVE TO THE LIVING ROOM
DO YOU FEEL A DRAFT?
YOU LEFT THE DOOR OPEN, DIPWAD
JIM DAVIS 5-6

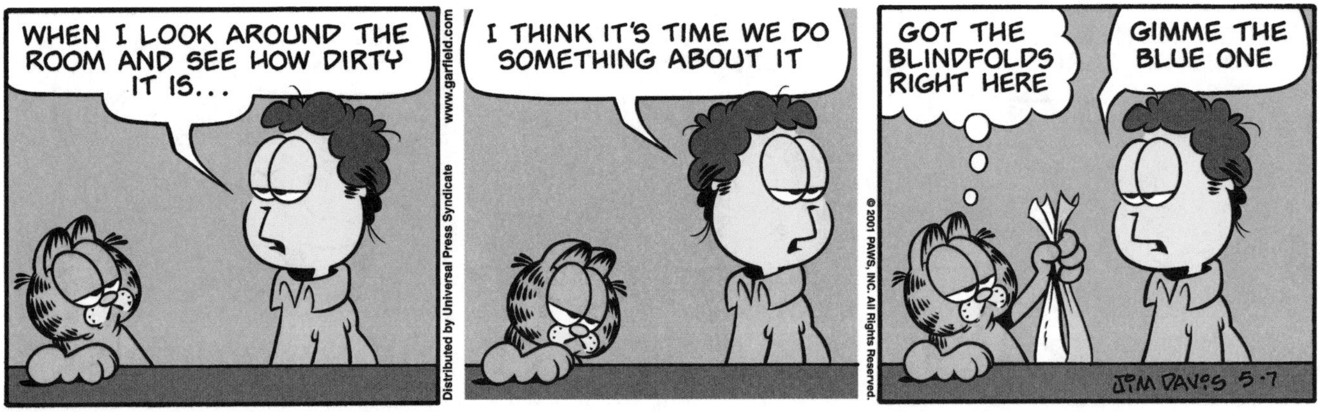
WHEN I LOOK AROUND THE ROOM AND SEE HOW DIRTY IT IS...
I THINK IT'S TIME WE DO SOMETHING ABOUT IT
GOT THE BLINDFOLDS RIGHT HERE
GIMME THE BLUE ONE
JIM DAVIS 5-7

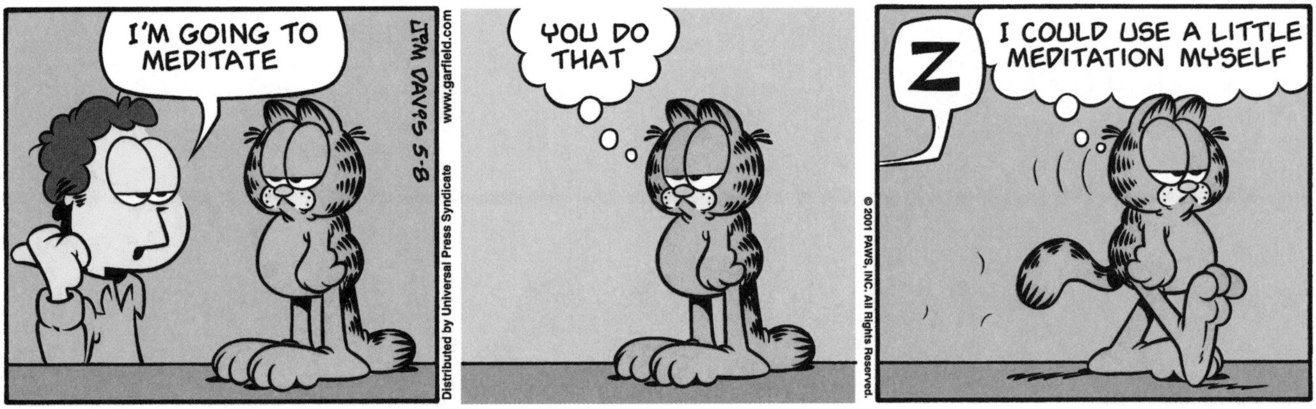
I'M GOING TO MEDITATE
JIM DAVIS 5-8
YOU DO THAT
Z
I COULD USE A LITTLE MEDITATION MYSELF

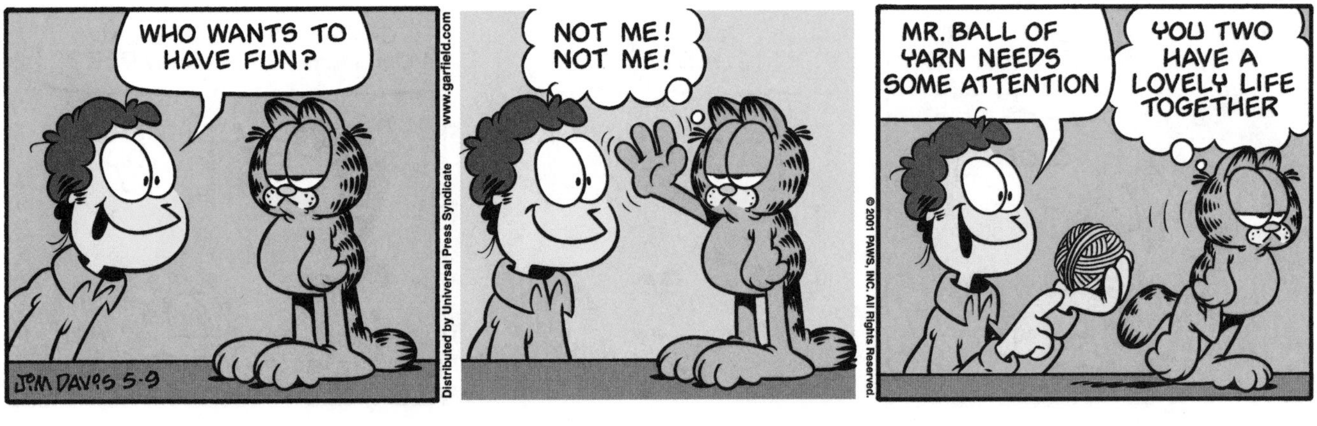
WHO WANTS TO HAVE FUN?
JIM DAVIS 5-9
NOT ME! NOT ME!
MR. BALL OF YARN NEEDS SOME ATTENTION
YOU TWO HAVE A LOVELY LIFE TOGETHER

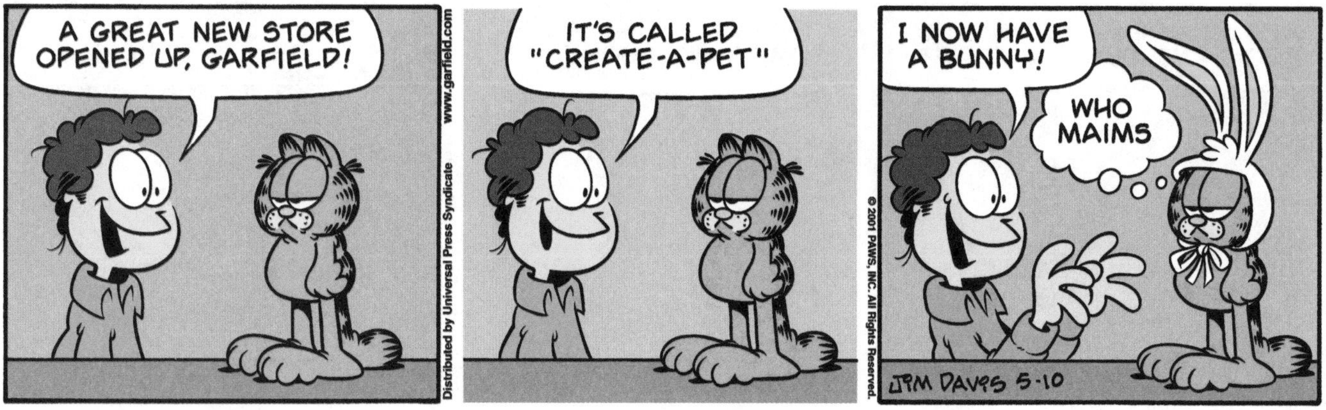
A GREAT NEW STORE OPENED UP, GARFIELD!
IT'S CALLED "CREATE-A-PET"
I NOW HAVE A BUNNY!
WHO MAIMS
JIM DAVIS 5-10
Distributed by Universal Press Syndicate www.garfield.com
© 2001 PAWS, INC. All Rights Reserved.

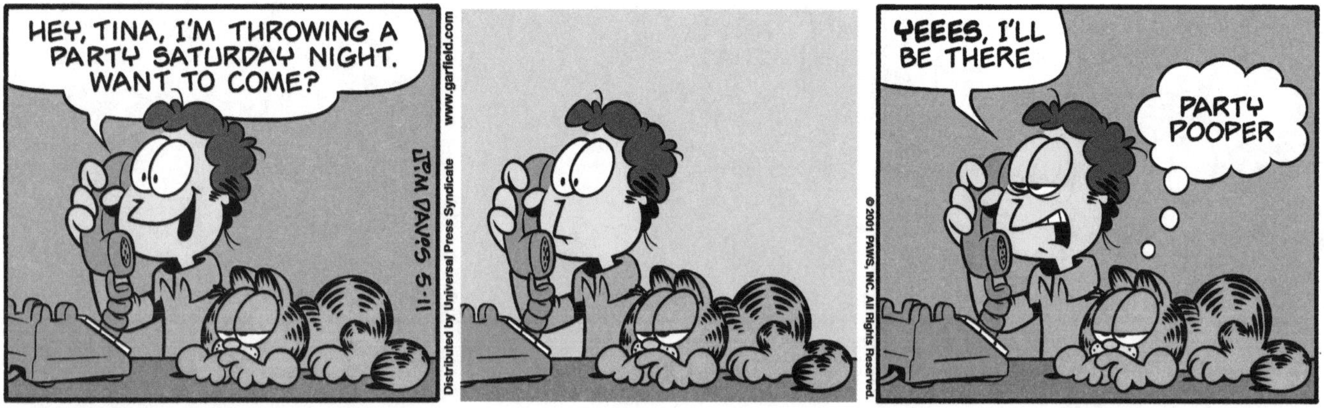
HEY, TINA, I'M THROWING A PARTY SATURDAY NIGHT. WANT TO COME?
JIM DAVIS 5-11
YEEES, I'LL BE THERE
PARTY POOPER
Distributed by Universal Press Syndicate www.garfield.com
© 2001 PAWS, INC. All Rights Reserved.

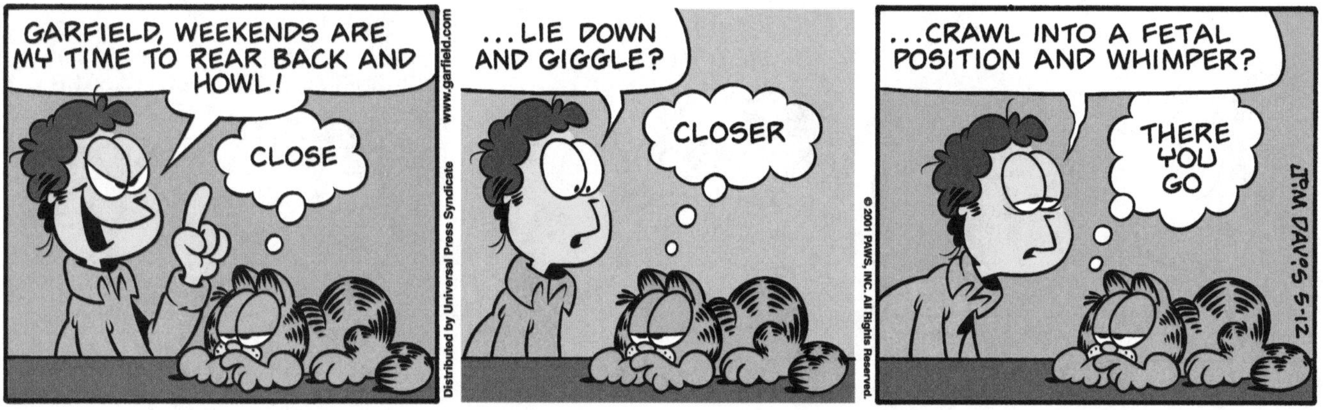
GARFIELD, WEEKENDS ARE MY TIME TO REAR BACK AND HOWL!
CLOSE
...LIE DOWN AND GIGGLE?
CLOSER
...CRAWL INTO A FETAL POSITION AND WHIMPER?
THERE YOU GO
JIM DAVIS 5-12
Distributed by Universal Press Syndicate www.garfield.com
© 2001 PAWS, INC. All Rights Reserved.

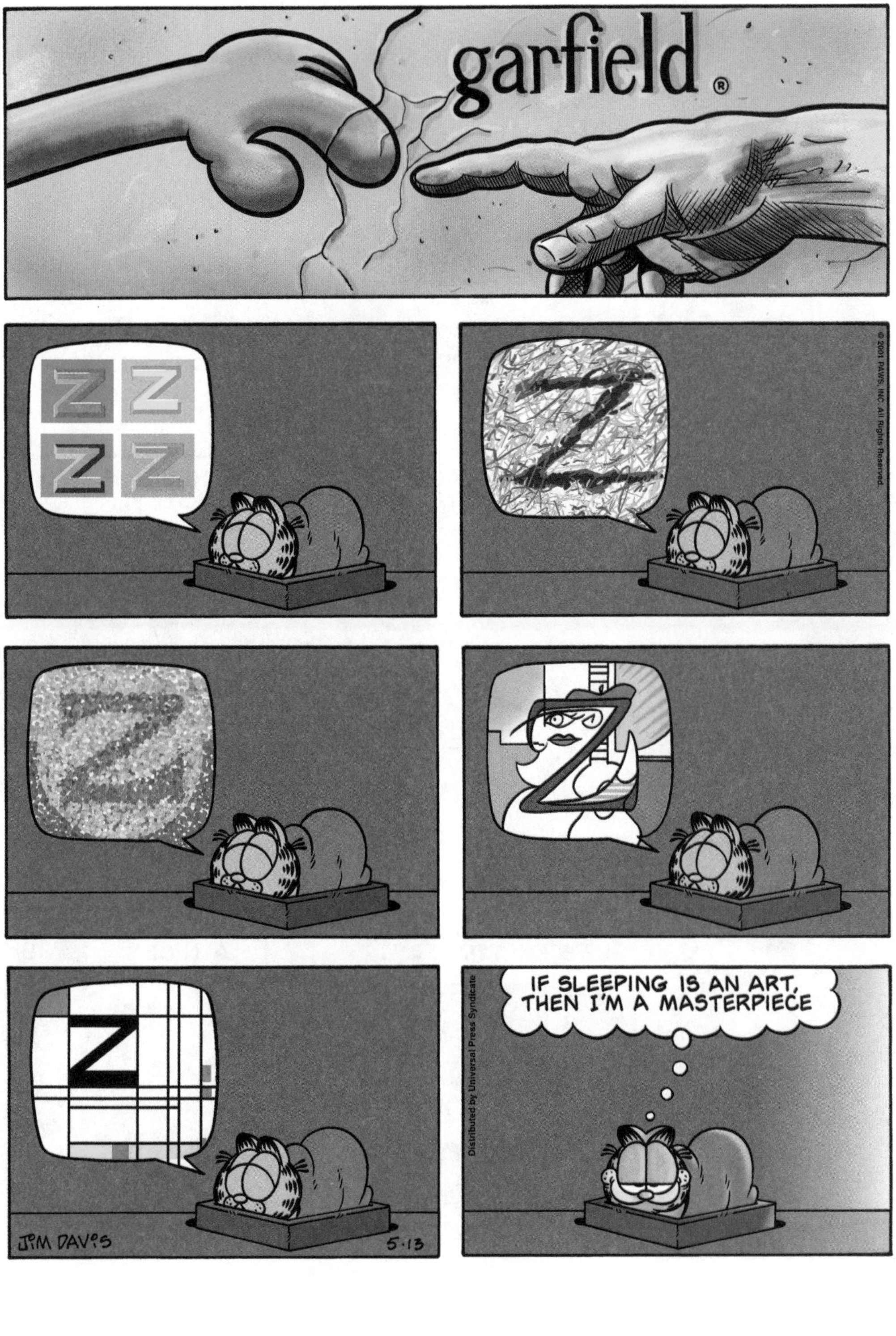
garfield
Z Z
Z Z
Z
Z
Z
Z
JIM DAVIS
5·13
IF SLEEPING IS AN ART, THEN I'M A MASTERPIECE
© 2001 PAWS, INC. All Rights Reserved.
Distributed by Universal Press Syndicate

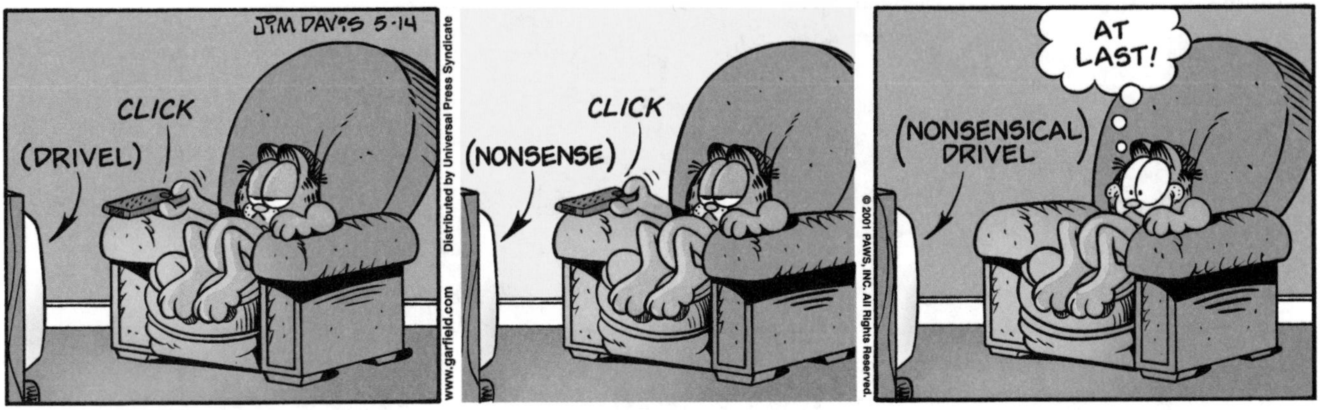
JIM DAVIS 5-14
(DRIVEL)
CLICK
(NONSENSE)
CLICK
(NONSENSICAL DRIVEL)
AT LAST!
www.garfield.com Distributed by Universal Press Syndicate
© 2001 PAWS, INC. All Rights Reserved.

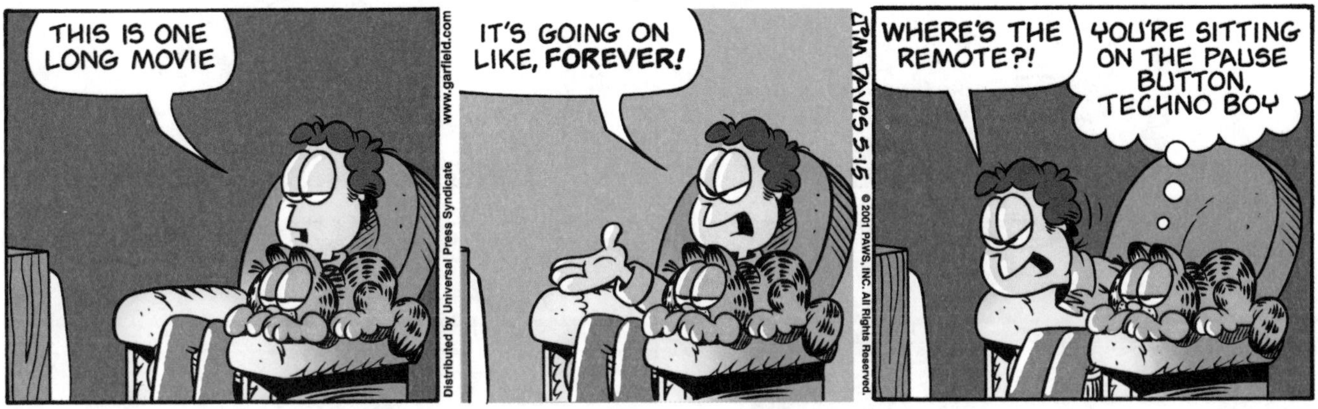
THIS IS ONE LONG MOVIE
IT'S GOING ON LIKE, **FOREVER!**
JIM DAVIS 5-15
WHERE'S THE REMOTE?!
YOU'RE SITTING ON THE PAUSE BUTTON, TECHNO BOY
Distributed by Universal Press Syndicate www.garfield.com
© 2001 PAWS, INC. All Rights Reserved.

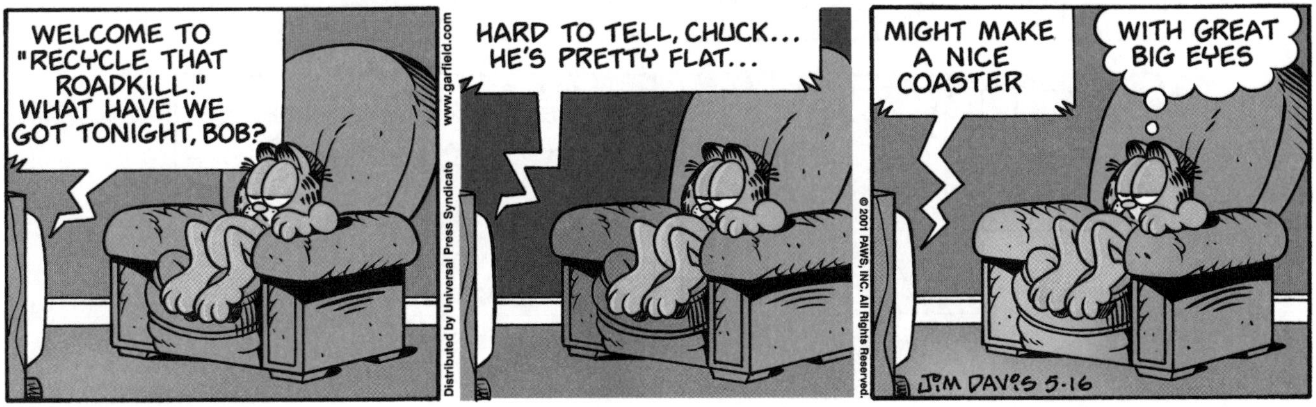
WELCOME TO "RECYCLE THAT ROADKILL." WHAT HAVE WE GOT TONIGHT, BOB?
HARD TO TELL, CHUCK... HE'S PRETTY FLAT...
MIGHT MAKE A NICE COASTER
WITH GREAT BIG EYES
JIM DAVIS 5-16
Distributed by Universal Press Syndicate www.garfield.com
© 2001 PAWS, INC. All Rights Reserved.

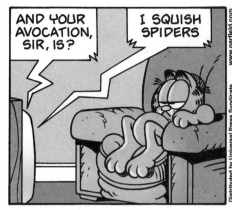

AND YOUR AVOCATION, SIR, IS?
I SQUISH SPIDERS
www.garfield.com
Distributed by Universal Press Syndicate
CARE TO DEMONSTRATE?
CERTAINLY
© 2001 PAWS, INC. All Rights Reserved.
SQUISH!
LOUSY FORM
NO FOLLOW-THROUGH AT ALL
JIM DAVIS 5-17

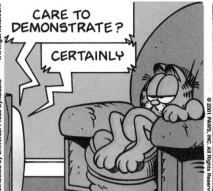

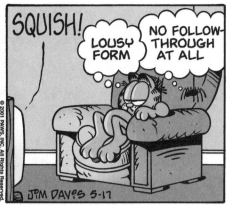

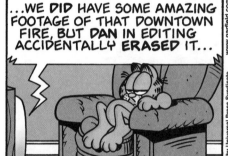

...WE **DID** HAVE SOME AMAZING FOOTAGE OF THAT DOWNTOWN FIRE, BUT **DAN** IN EDITING ACCIDENTALLY **ERASED** IT...
JIM DAVIS 5-18
www.garfield.com
Distributed by Universal Press Syndicate
SO, INSTEAD OF EXCITING FIRE FOOTAGE, WE PRESENT **DAN** IN HIS UNDERSHIRT AND BOXER SHORTS PLAYING A COMB WITH TISSUE PAPER:
© 2001 PAWS, INC. All Rights Reserved.
FFFT
FFFT
FFFT
I'D TAKE THIS OVER A FIRE ANY OLD DAY

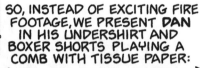

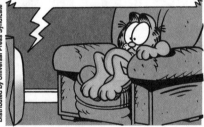

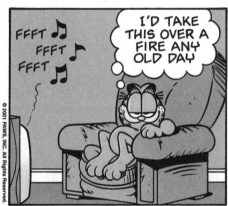

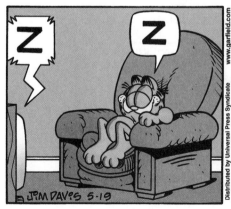

Z
Z
JIM DAVIS 5-19
www.garfield.com
Distributed by Universal Press Syndicate
Z
Z
© 2001 PAWS, INC. All Rights Reserved.
THIS HAS BEEN "NAP ALONG WITH FLUFFY"
YAWN

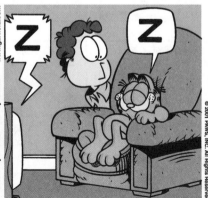

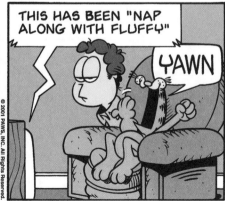

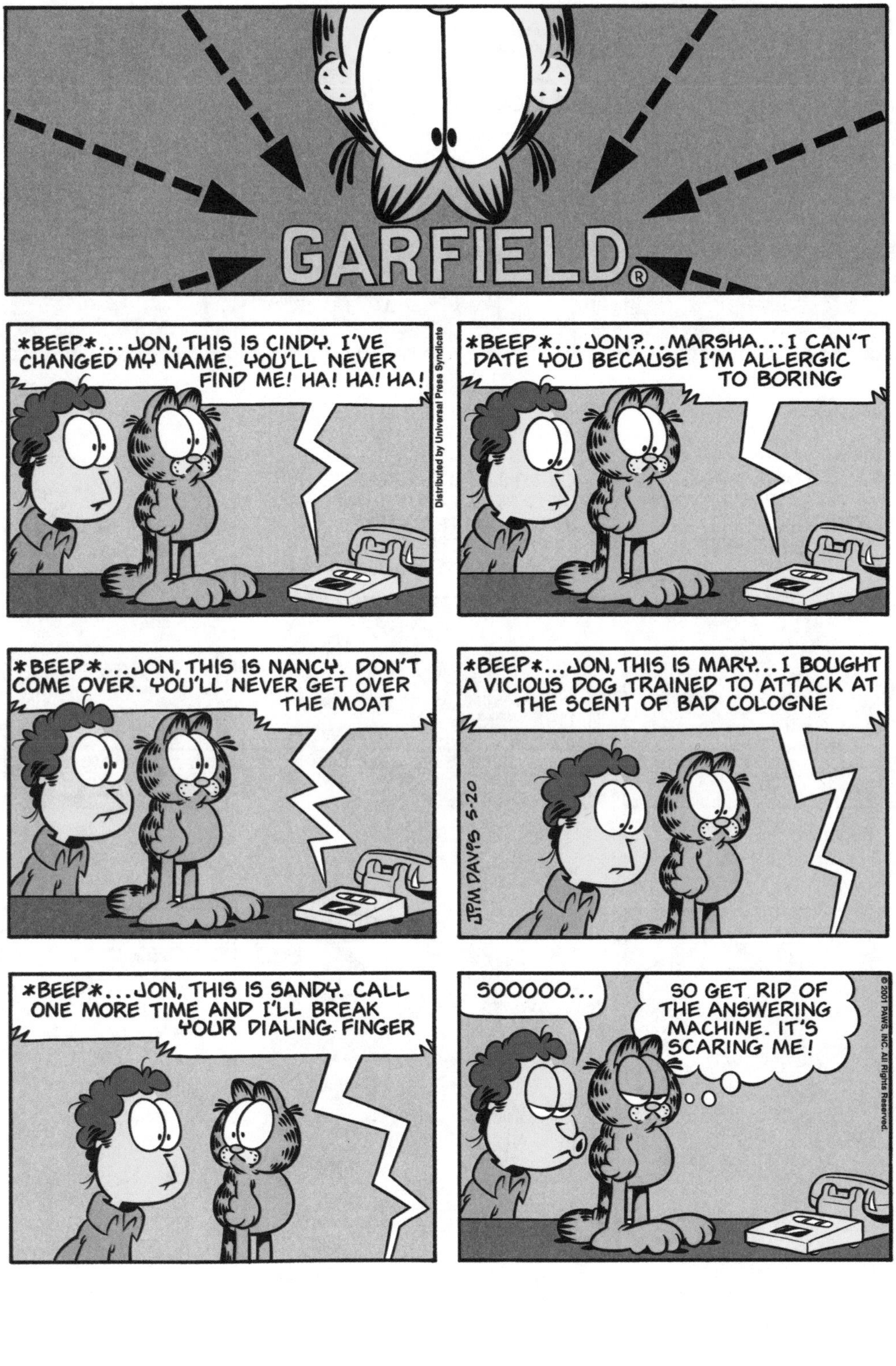
GARFIELD®
BEEP... JON, THIS IS CINDY. I'VE CHANGED MY NAME. YOU'LL NEVER FIND ME! HA! HA! HA!
Distributed by Universal Press Syndicate
BEEP... JON?... MARSHA... I CAN'T DATE YOU BECAUSE I'M ALLERGIC TO BORING
BEEP... JON, THIS IS NANCY. DON'T COME OVER. YOU'LL NEVER GET OVER THE MOAT
BEEP... JON, THIS IS MARY... I BOUGHT A VICIOUS DOG TRAINED TO ATTACK AT THE SCENT OF BAD COLOGNE
JPM DAVPS 5-20
BEEP... JON, THIS IS SANDY. CALL ONE MORE TIME AND I'LL BREAK YOUR DIALING FINGER
SOOOOO...
SO GET RID OF THE ANSWERING MACHINE. IT'S SCARING ME!
© 2001 PAWS, INC. All Rights Reserved.

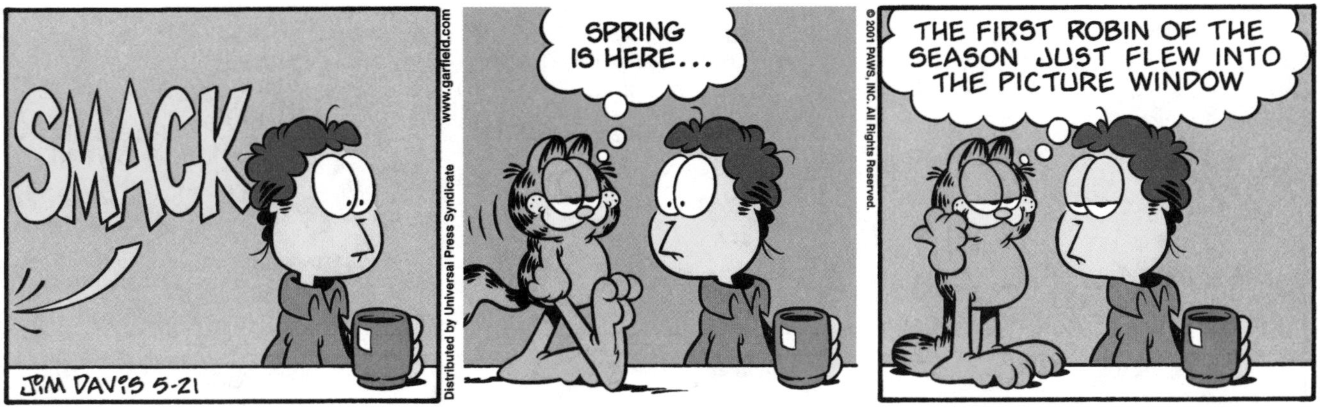
SMACK
JIM DAVIS 5-21
www.garfield.com
Distributed by Universal Press Syndicate
SPRING IS HERE...
© 2001 PAWS, INC. All Rights Reserved.
THE FIRST ROBIN OF THE SEASON JUST FLEW INTO THE PICTURE WINDOW

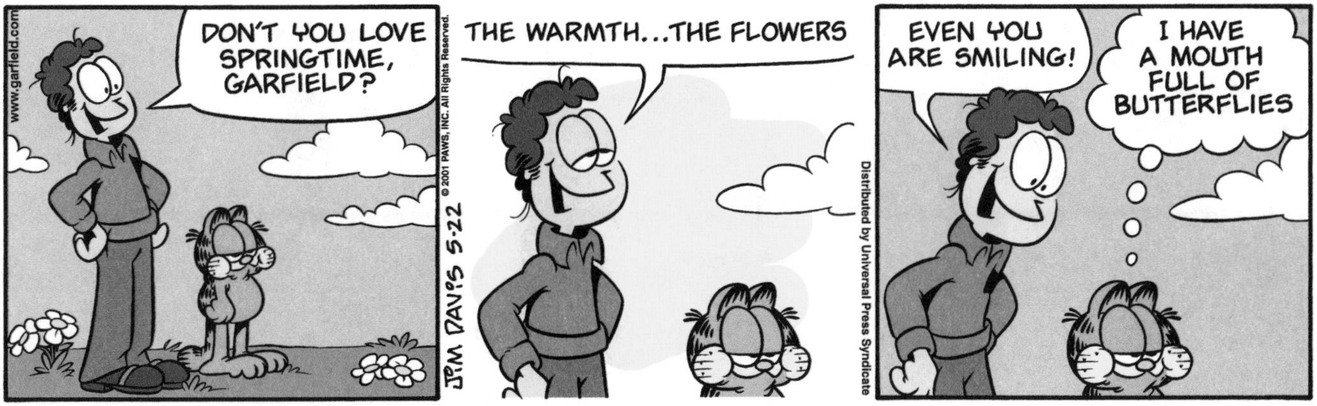
www.garfield.com
DON'T YOU LOVE SPRINGTIME, GARFIELD?
© 2001 PAWS, INC. All Rights Reserved.
JIM DAVIS 5-22
THE WARMTH...THE FLOWERS
Distributed by Universal Press Syndicate
EVEN YOU ARE SMILING!
I HAVE A MOUTH FULL OF BUTTERFLIES

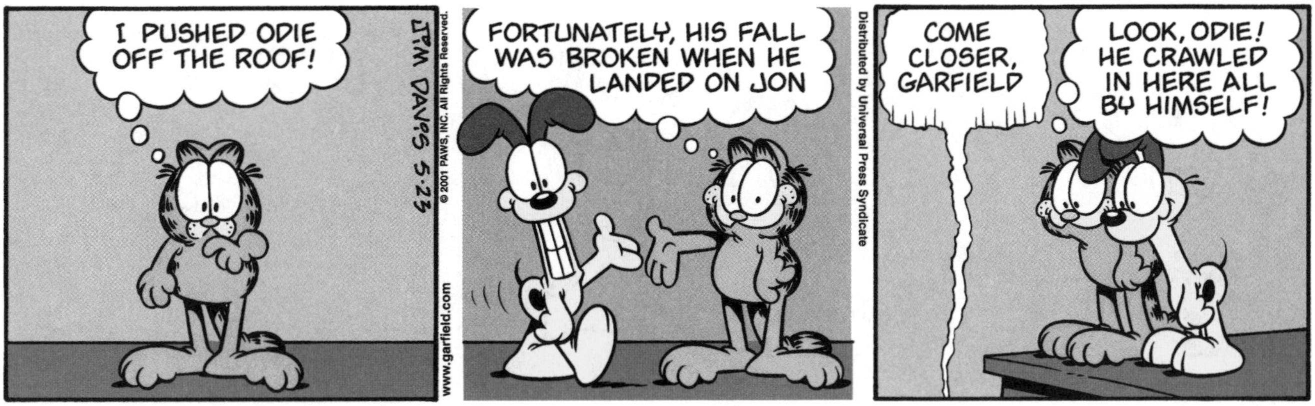
I PUSHED ODIE OFF THE ROOF!
JIM DAVIS 5-23
© 2001 PAWS, INC. All Rights Reserved.
www.garfield.com
FORTUNATELY, HIS FALL WAS BROKEN WHEN HE LANDED ON JON
Distributed by Universal Press Syndicate
COME CLOSER, GARFIELD
LOOK, ODIE! HE CRAWLED IN HERE ALL BY HIMSELF!

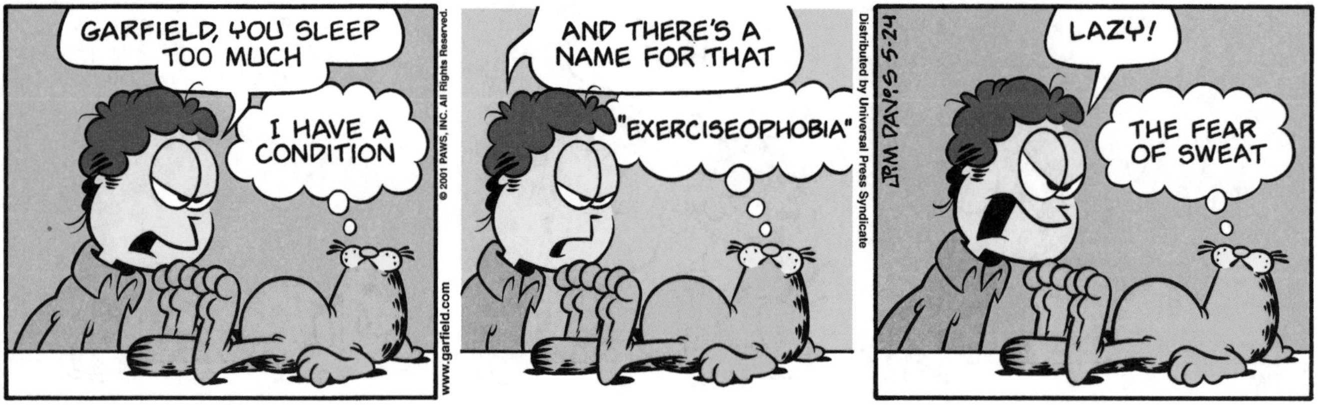
GARFIELD, YOU SLEEP TOO MUCH
I HAVE A CONDITION
AND THERE'S A NAME FOR THAT
"EXERCISEOPHOBIA"
LAZY!
THE FEAR OF SWEAT
JIM DAVIS 5-24
© 2001 PAWS, INC. All Rights Reserved.
www.garfield.com
Distributed by Universal Press Syndicate

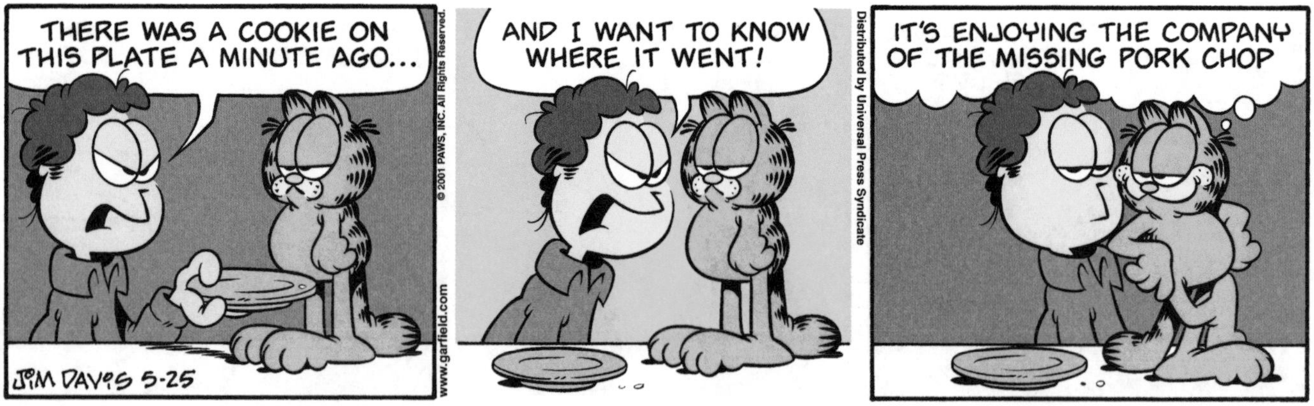
THERE WAS A COOKIE ON THIS PLATE A MINUTE AGO...
AND I WANT TO KNOW WHERE IT WENT!
IT'S ENJOYING THE COMPANY OF THE MISSING PORK CHOP
JIM DAVIS 5-25
© 2001 PAWS, INC. All Rights Reserved.
www.garfield.com
Distributed by Universal Press Syndicate

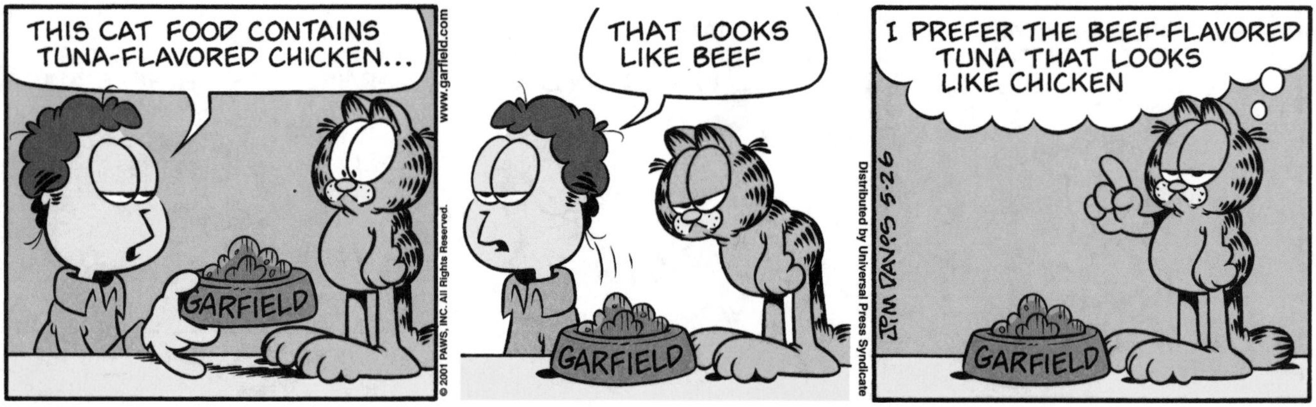
THIS CAT FOOD CONTAINS TUNA-FLAVORED CHICKEN...
GARFIELD
THAT LOOKS LIKE BEEF
GARFIELD
I PREFER THE BEEF-FLAVORED TUNA THAT LOOKS LIKE CHICKEN
GARFIELD
JIM DAVIS 5-26
© 2001 PAWS, INC. All Rights Reserved.
www.garfield.com
Distributed by Universal Press Syndicate

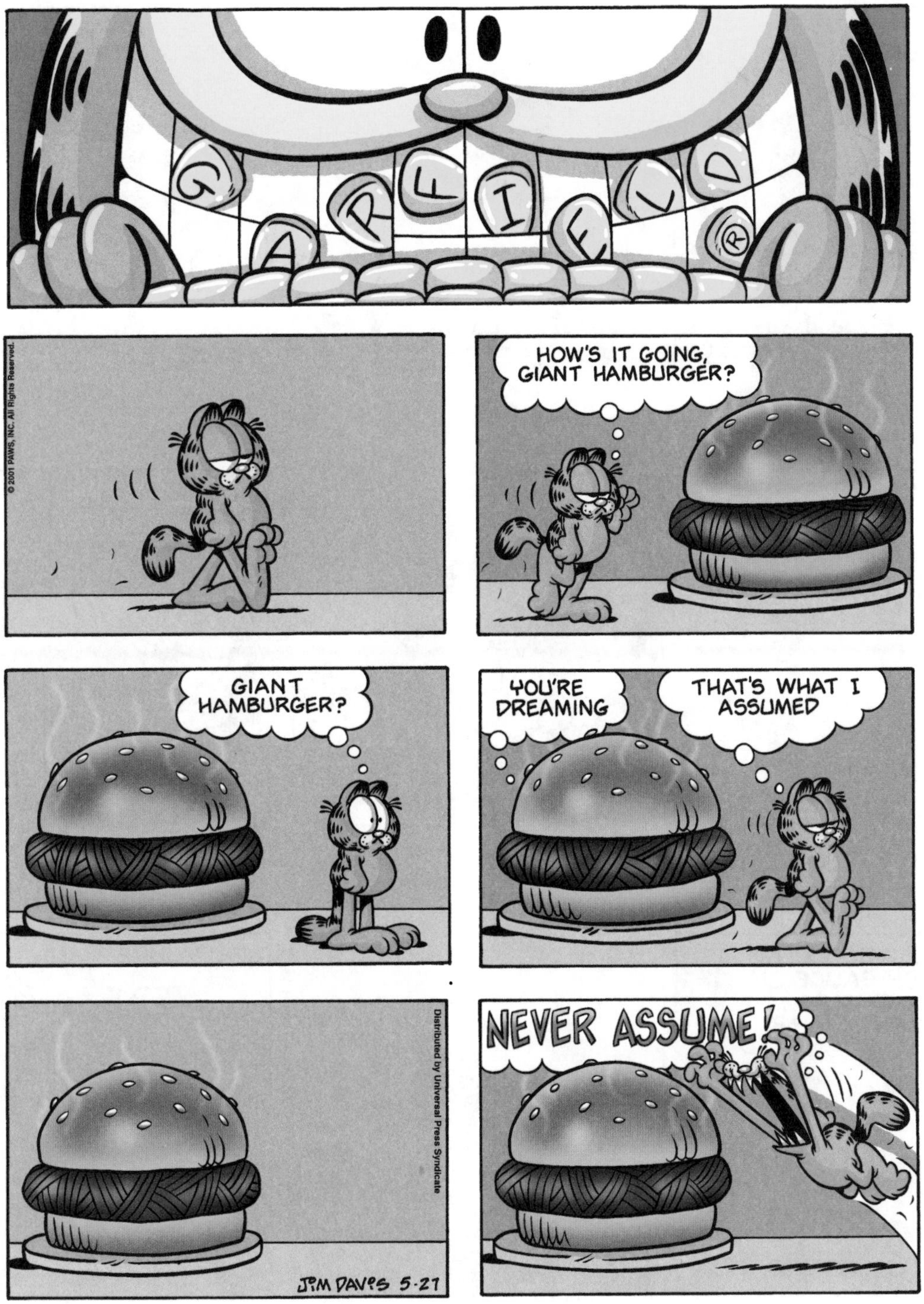
GARFIELD®
© 2001 PAWS, INC. All Rights Reserved.
HOW'S IT GOING, GIANT HAMBURGER?
GIANT HAMBURGER?
YOU'RE DREAMING
THAT'S WHAT I ASSUMED
Distributed by Universal Press Syndicate
JIM DAVIS 5-27
NEVER ASSUME!

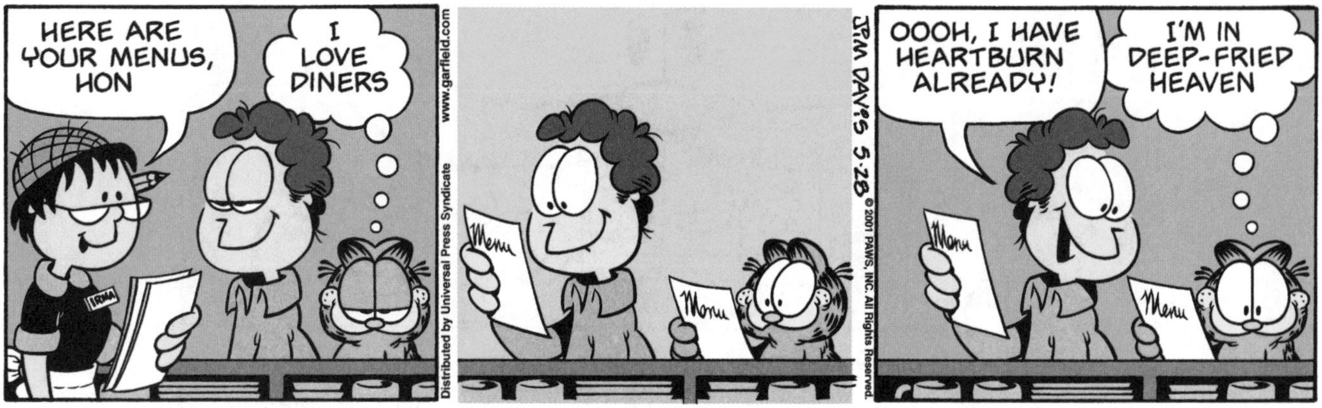
HERE ARE YOUR MENUS, HON
I LOVE DINERS
www.garfield.com Distributed by Universal Press Syndicate
JIM DAVIS 5-28 © 2001 PAWS, INC. All Rights Reserved.
OOOH, I HAVE HEARTBURN ALREADY!
I'M IN DEEP-FRIED HEAVEN

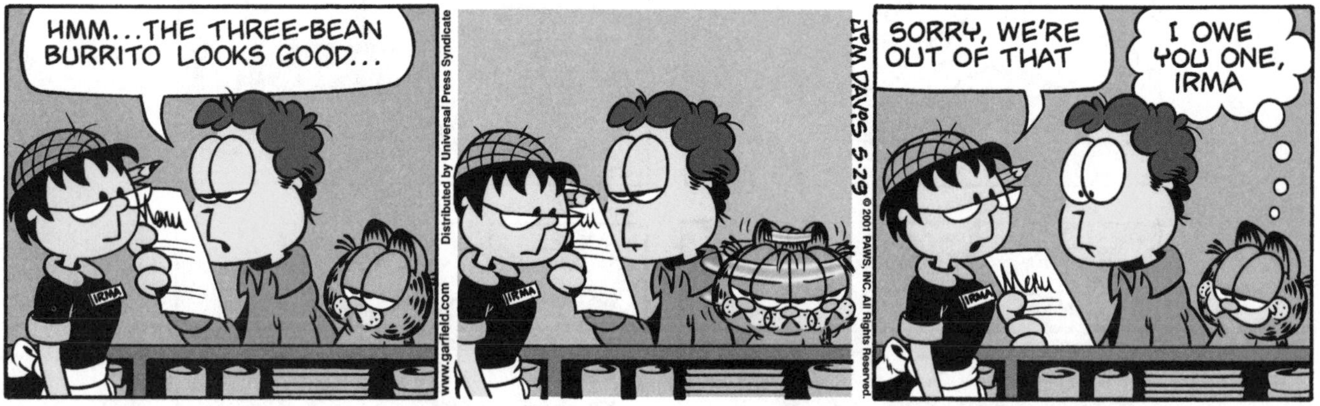
HMM...THE THREE-BEAN BURRITO LOOKS GOOD...
Distributed by Universal Press Syndicate www.garfield.com
JIM DAVIS 5-29 © 2001 PAWS, INC. All Rights Reserved.
SORRY, WE'RE OUT OF THAT
I OWE YOU ONE, IRMA

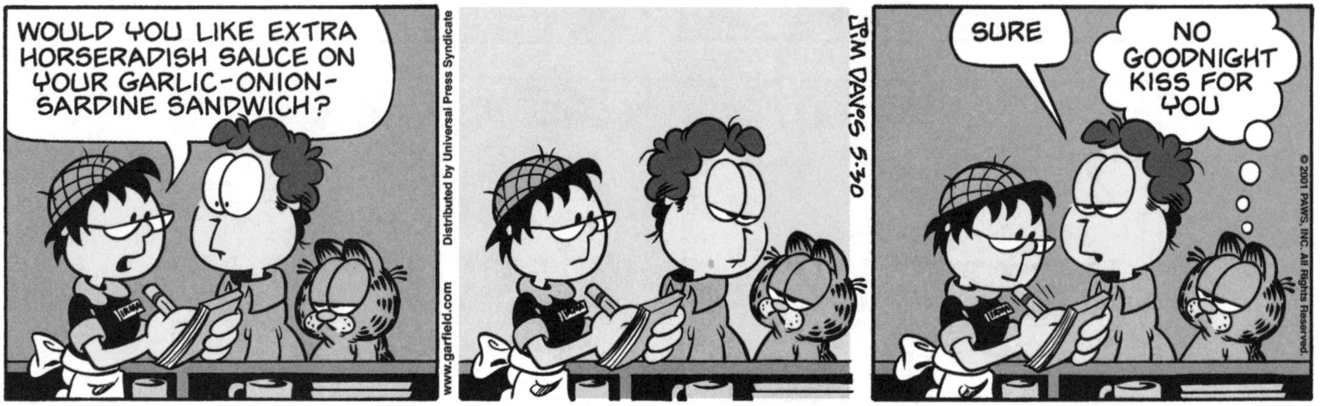
WOULD YOU LIKE EXTRA HORSERADISH SAUCE ON YOUR GARLIC-ONION-SARDINE SANDWICH?
Distributed by Universal Press Syndicate www.garfield.com
JIM DAVIS 5-30
SURE
NO GOODNIGHT KISS FOR YOU
© 2001 PAWS, INC. All Rights Reserved.

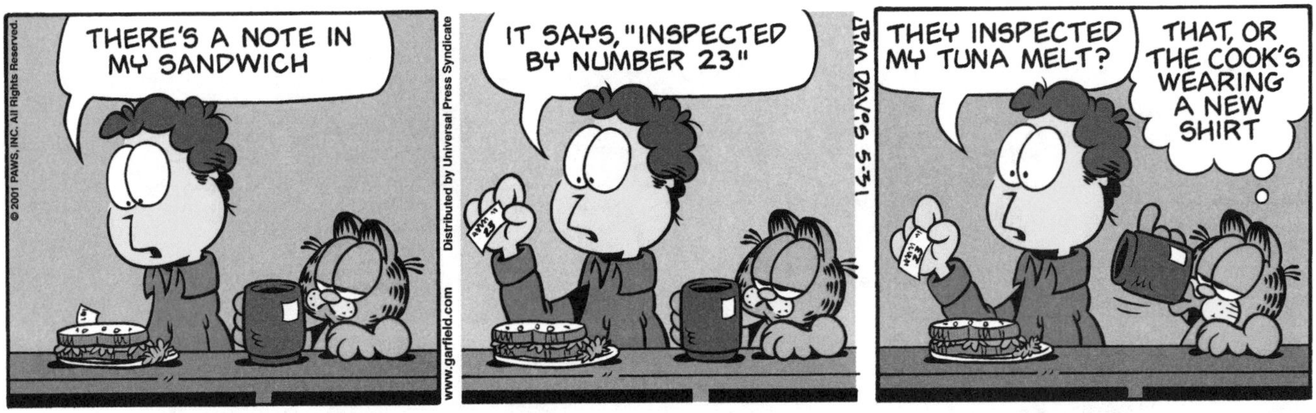
THERE'S A NOTE IN MY SANDWICH
IT SAYS, "INSPECTED BY NUMBER 23"
THEY INSPECTED MY TUNA MELT?
THAT, OR THE COOK'S WEARING A NEW SHIRT
© 2001 PAWS, INC. All Rights Reserved.
www.garfield.com Distributed by Universal Press Syndicate
JPM DAVPS 5-31

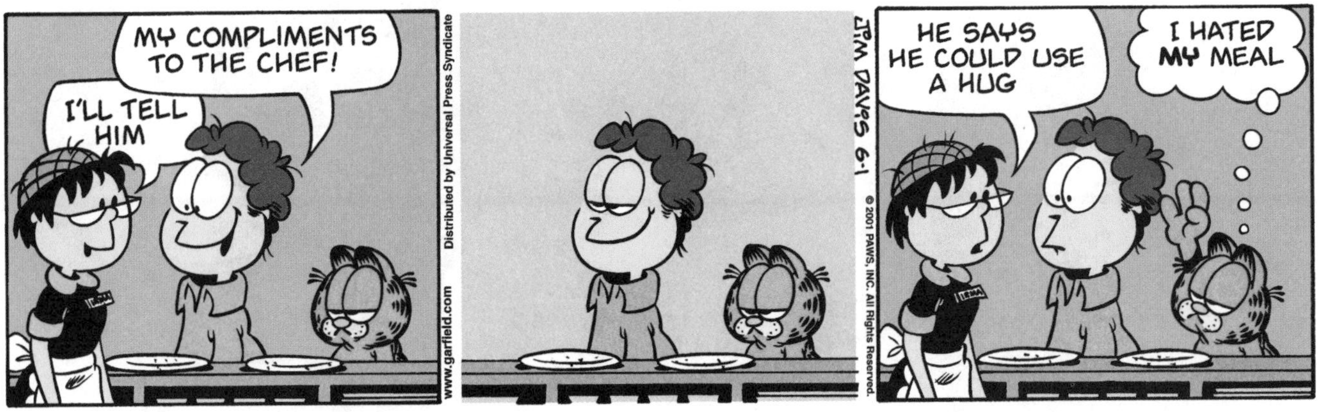
MY COMPLIMENTS TO THE CHEF!
I'LL TELL HIM
HE SAYS HE COULD USE A HUG
I HATED **MY** MEAL
www.garfield.com Distributed by Universal Press Syndicate
© 2001 PAWS, INC. All Rights Reserved.
JPM DAVPS 6-1

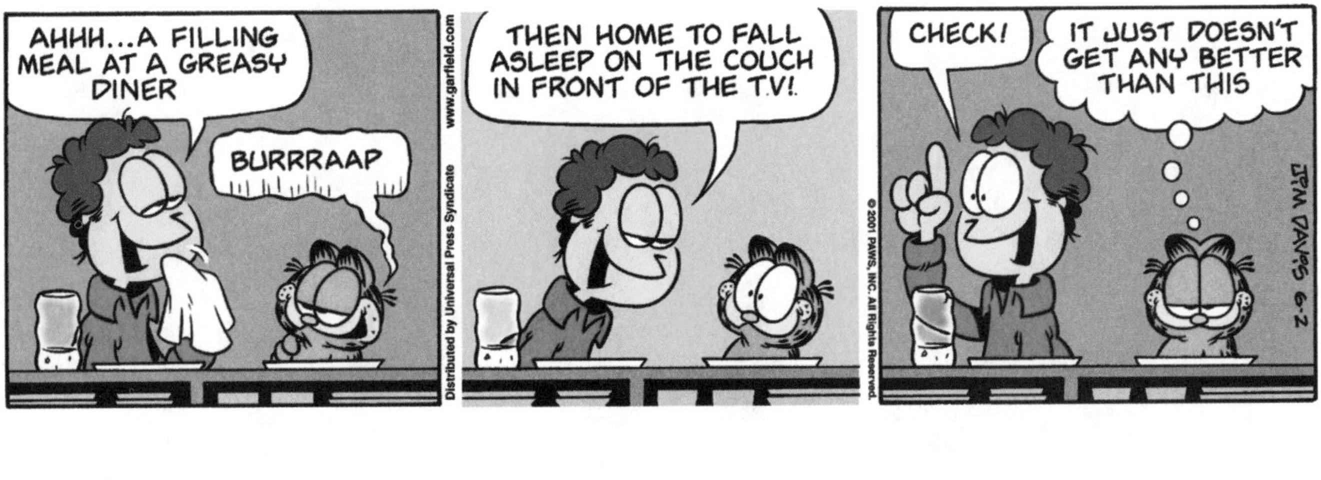
AHHH...A FILLING MEAL AT A GREASY DINER
BURRRAAP
THEN HOME TO FALL ASLEEP ON THE COUCH IN FRONT OF THE T.V!.
CHECK!
IT JUST DOESN'T GET ANY BETTER THAN THIS
Distributed by Universal Press Syndicate www.garfield.com
© 2001 PAWS, INC. All Rights Reserved.
JPM DAVPS 6-2

YOU KNOW YOU'RE A NERD WHEN...

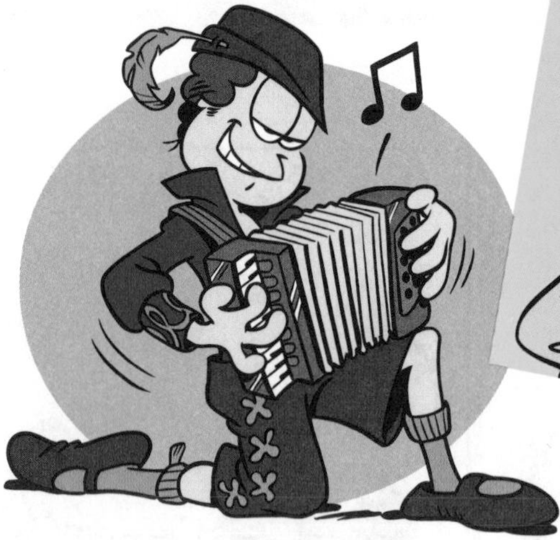

You think playing the accordion makes you look "hot"

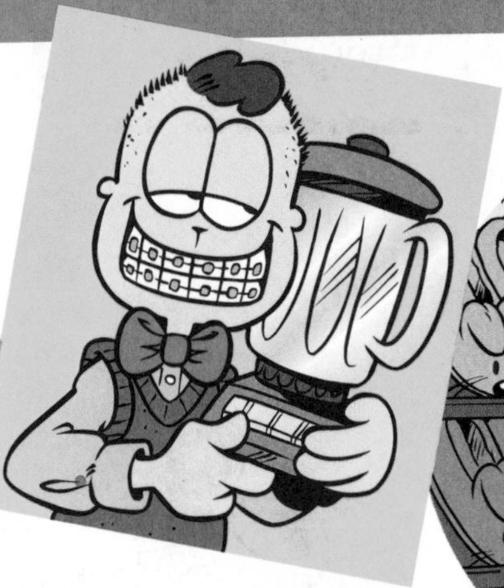

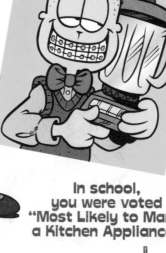

In school, you were voted "Most Likely to Marry a Kitchen Appliance"

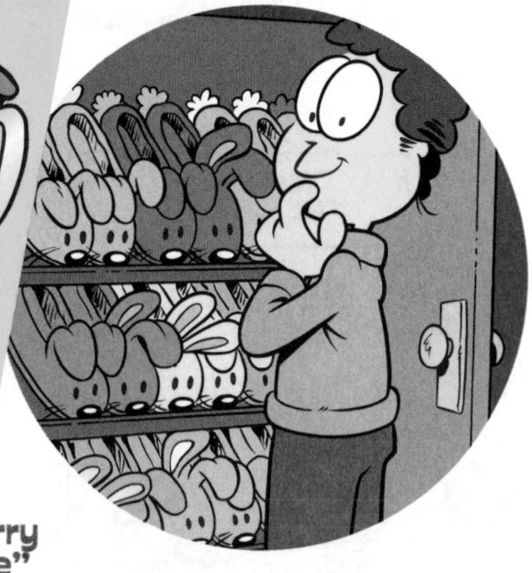

You own an extensive collection of bunny slippers

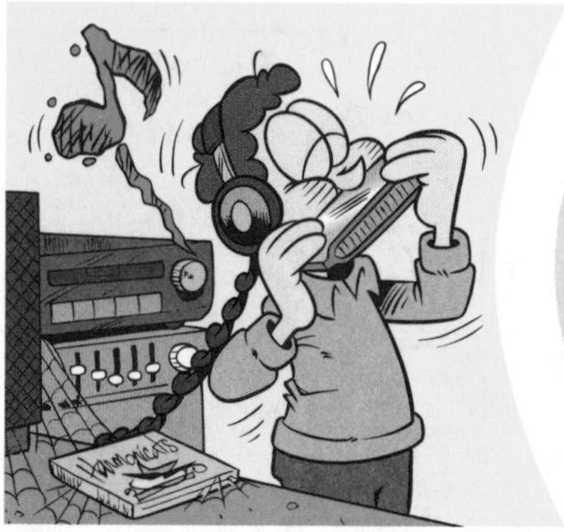
Harmonicats

The last CD you bought was "Best of the Harmonicats"

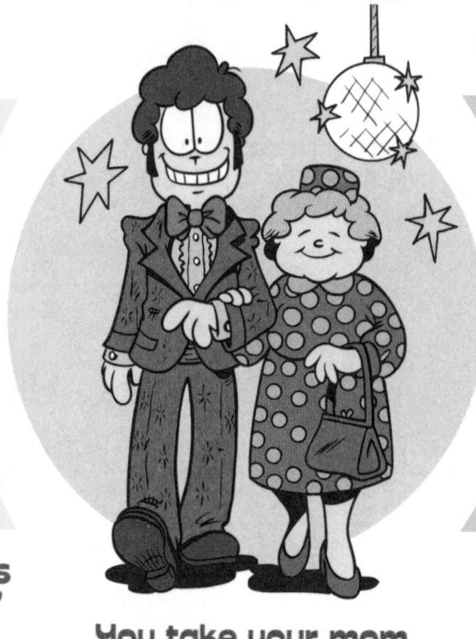

You take your mom to the prom

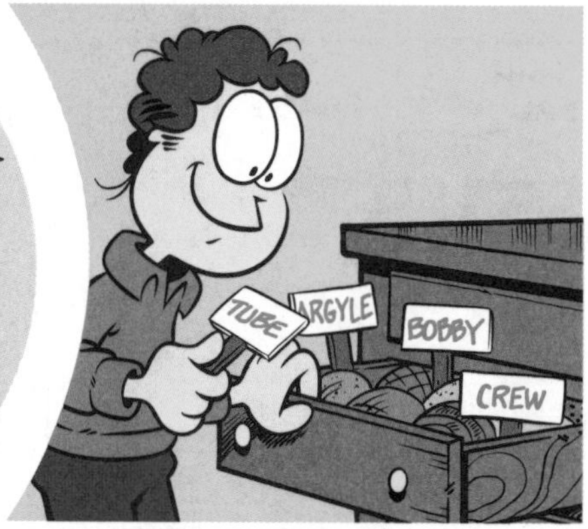
TUBE
ARGYLE
BOBBY
CREW

You alphabetize your sock drawer

STRIPS, SPECIALS, OR BESTSELLING BOOKS...
GARFIELD'S ON EVERYONE'S MENU

Don't miss even one episode in the Tubby Tabby's hilarious series!

GARFIELD AT LARGE **New larger, full-color format!**
....(#1) 0-345-44382-9
GARFIELD GAINS WEIGHT **New larger, full-color format!**
....(#2) 0-345-44975-4
GARFIELD BIGGER THAN LIFE **New larger, full-color format!**
....(#3) 0-345-45027-2
GARFIELD WEIGHS IN **New larger, full-color format!**
....(#4) 0-345-45205-4
GARFIELD TAKES THE CAKE ....(#5) 0-345-44978-9
GARFIELD EATS HIS HEART OUT ....(#6) 0-345-32018-2
GARFIELD SITS AROUND THE HOUSE ...(#7) 0-345-32011-5
GARFIELD TIPS THE SCALES ....(#8) 0-345-33580-5
GARFIELD LOSES HIS FEET ....(#9) 0-345-31805-6
GARFIELD MAKES IT BIG ....(#10) 0-345-31928-1
GARFIELD ROLLS ON ....(#11) 0-345-32634-2
GARFIELD OUT TO LUNCH....................(#12) 0-345-33118-4
GARFIELD FOOD FOR THOUGHT..........(#13) 0-345-34129-5
GARFIELD SWALLOWS HIS PRIDE........(#14) 0-345-34725-0
GARFIELD WORLDWIDE.........................(#15) 0-345-35158-4
GARFIELD ROUNDS OUT ....(#16) 0-345-35388-9
GARFIELD CHEWS THE FAT ....(#17) 0-345-35956-9
GARFIELD GOES TO WAIST...................(#18) 0-345-36430-9
GARFIELD HANGS OUT ....(#19) 0-345-36835-5
GARFIELD TAKES UP SPACE.................(#20) 0-345-37029-5
GARFIELD SAYS A MOUTHFUL..............(#21) 0-345-37368-5
GARFIELD BY THE POUND ....(#22) 0-345-37579-3
GARFIELD KEEPS HIS CHINS UP ....(#23) 0-345-37959-4
GARFIELD TAKES HIS LICKS ....(#24) 0-345-38170-X
GARFIELD HITS THE BIG TIME..............(#25) 0-345-38332-X

GARFIELD PULLS HIS WEIGHT ....(#26) 0-345-38666-3
GARFIELD DISHES IT OUT ....(#27) 0-345-39287-6
GARFIELD LIFE IN THE FAT LANE ....(#28) 0-345-39776-2
GARFIELD TONS OF FUN.......................(#29) 0-345-40386-X
GARFIELD BIGGER AND BETTER..........(#30) 0-345-40770-9
GARFIELD HAMS IT UP.........................(#31) 0-345-41241-9
GARFIELD THINKS BIG ....(#32) 0-345-41671-6
GARFIELD THROWS HIS WEIGHT AROUND
....(#33) 0-345-42749-1
GARFIELD LIFE TO THE FULLEST.........(#34) 0-345-43239-8
GARFIELD FEEDS THE KITTY ....(#35) 0-345-43673-3
GARFIELD HOGS THE SPOTLIGHT ....(#36) 0-345-43922-8
GARFIELD BEEFS UP.............................(#37) 0-345-44109-5
GARFIELD GETS COOKIN'.....................(#38) 0-345-44582-1
GARFIELD EATS CROW.........................(#39) 0-345-45201-1

GARFIELD AT HIS SUNDAY BEST!

GARFIELD TREASURY 0-345-32106-5
THE SECOND GARFIELD TREASURY.............0-345-33276-8
THE THIRD GARFIELD TREASURY 0-345-32635-0
THE FOURTH GARFIELD TREASURY 0-345-34726-9
THE FIFTH GARFIELD TREASURY 0-345-36268-3
THE SIXTH GARFIELD TREASURY 0-345-37367-7
THE SEVENTH GARFIELD TREASURY...........0-345-38427-X
THE EIGHTH GARFIELD TREASURY 0-345-39778-9
THE NINTH GARFIELD TREASURY 0-345-41670-8
THE TENTH GARFIELD TREASURY 0-345-43674-1

AND DON'T MISS...

GARFIELD AT 25: IN DOG YEARS I'D BE DEAD
....0-345-45530-4

GARFIELD **25** YEARS!
1978   2003